Sustainable Investing in Practice

Sustainable Investing in Practice

ESG challenges and opportunities

Simon Smiles and James Purcell

Publisher's note

Every possible effort has been made to ensure that the information contained in this book is accurate at the time of going to press, and the publishers and authors cannot accept responsibility for any errors or omissions, however caused. No responsibility for loss or damage occasioned to any person acting, or refraining from action, as a result of the material in this publication can be accepted by the editor, the publisher or the author.

First published in Great Britain and the United States in 2023 by Kogan Page Limited

2nd Floor, 45 Gee Street
London
EC1V 3RS
United Kingdom
www.koganpage.com

8 W 38th Street, Suite 902
New York, NY 10018
USA

4737/23 Ansari Road
Daryaganj
New Delhi 110002
India

Kogan Page books are printed on paper from sustainable forests.

ISBNs

Hardback 978 1 3986 0792 7
Paperback 978 1 3986 0790 3
Ebook 978 1 3986 0791 0

British Library Cataloguing-in-Publication Data

A CIP record for this book is available from the British Library.

Library of Congress Control Number

2022048480

Typeset by Hong Kong FIVE Workshop, Hong Kong
Print production managed by Jellyfish
Printed and bound by CPI Group (UK) Ltd, Croydon CR0 4YY

For Miah, Isabelle, Scarlett and Aaron

CONTENTS

ABOUT THE AUTHORS

James Purcell is the Group Head of Sustainable Frameworks at Credit Suisse. He and his team coordinate the firm's approach to sustainable investing and lending. Previously, James was the Group Head of Sustainable, Thematic and Impact Investing at Quintet Private Bank, a privately held bank operating out of 50 cities across Europe. Earlier in his career he was a managing director at UBS, where he spent more than a decade in roles based in London, Hong Kong, and Zurich. James graduated from the University of Oxford with a BA (honours) in Modern History and graduated from the University of Chicago Booth School of Business with an MBA (high honours). He holds the CFA qualification.

Simon Smiles retired from UBS in 2020 after spending more than 15 years there, most recently as a group managing director and the Chief Investment Officer for Ultra High Net Worth Clients, where he established and ran the wealth management sustainable and impact investing teams. An IIF Future Leader, WEF Young Global Leader and member of the Milken Institute's Young Leaders Circle, he appeared regularly in global financial media speaking about sustain-ability and investments. Before moving to Zurich, Simon worked in Sydney and Hong Kong and earned a PhD in economics from the Australian National University, as well as first class honours in both economics and finance from the University of Sydney.

PREFACE

Handing in a final manuscript to one's publisher is a moment of mixed feelings for any author. Relief and euphoria quickly give way to mild panic and pangs of regret. Is our argumentation logical and succinct? Did we choose the right examples? Will anyone 'get' our attempts at humour or references to Beyoncé?

Completing this book was particularly conflicting as I finished it without my friend, mentor and co-author Simon Smiles. Simon was undoubtedly the brightest individual I have ever had the good fortune to know. Highly innovative and full of productive energy, he had an uncanny ability to see lateral connections, implications and opportunities that mere mortals like I would overlook. Speaking with Simon could be frustrating at times because he would understand my ideas, digest them, find the error in them and formulate a better solution within seconds of me finishing an oration. He was truly brilliant. There is simply no other way to say it.

For much of our careers Simon and I worked side by side. We would ferociously debate ideas and disagree as often as we agreed. Not once, however, did either of us take the other's opposite viewpoint as a personal affront. Soon we'd be laughing and sharing an 'office beer' (or a gin and tonic) – much to the unease of conservative colleagues. I like to think that we chose to work together for so long because we knew that, through our differences and debate, we made each other better.

In the context of this project, the chapters that we co-wrote together are immeasurably better than the original notes. Simon worked his usual magic, a handful of his pen strokes turning disjointed fragments into a logical and powerful thesis. As I completed the manuscript alone and added the necessary argumentation, I wished I had been able to seek his advice and improve the text further. I hope that his voice and thoughts still shine through with their original force. I like to think that, in delivering this book, Simon and I as co-authors have – one last time – made each other better.

Simon, thank you for everything.

James

ACKNOWLEDGEMENTS

We express thanks to Thomas Gundy whose superb editing ensured that our written words were more coherent than our original thoughts. We are grateful to Latifah Salaudeen for her diligent assistance in checking and compiling references. We applaud the team at our publisher Kogan Page – in particular, Amy Minshull, Anne-Marie Heeney, Bruna Sperotto, Isabelle Cheng, Rebecca Norman and Ryan Norman – and the many friends who reviewed chapters and gave honest feedback.

Finally, we are immensely grateful to the incredible industry experts who contributed their exclusive interviews: David H Petreaus, Gillian Tett, Paul Polman, Catherine Howarth, Richard Curtis, Rick Lacaille and Robert G Eccles. We know that many readers will endure our laborious prose solely so that they may have the opportunity to read our experts' insights.

Introduction

Imagine walking into a huge grocery store. It looks like other modern grocery stores you've shopped in but you soon realize that its aisles are improperly marked and its product packaging is either unhelpful or misleading. The salt is labelled as sugar, the sugar is labelled as flour and the flour has no label at all. You stroll the gleaming canyons of canned goods, which do not distinguish between the soups, the San Marzano tomatoes and the cling peaches. The breakfast cereals are just blank boxes that say 'cereal'.

Confused, you notice a clerk stocking the shelves and ask for help. She is happy to assist you, but she speaks a language you don't recognize. It resembles English but the terminology she uses leaves you even more perplexed.

Chances are, blinking under the artificial lighting in a state of bewilderment, you'd turn around and exit the store without making a purchase.

For many years the sustainable investing industry has resembled such a baffling supermarket, plagued by a lack of common standards, data and even vocabulary.

In 2022, it is (grudgingly) accepted that two of the leading industry observers disagree on the size of the sustainable investment market by a whopping 1400 per cent, i.e., a cool $30 trillion (GSIA, 2021; Morningstar, 2022). It is the norm that 15 companies in the fast-moving consumer goods (FMCG) sector report 22 different, non-comparable employee gender classifications (World Economic Forum, 2019). And market participants and government regulators churn out hundreds of pages of white papers that cite, explore and (re)define upwards of 100 industry terms, most of which serve as partial synonyms of one another (IIF, 2019).

Against this backdrop we, as long-term practitioners of sustainable investing, seek to cut through the complexity and confusion and present straightforward information in handy book form that focuses on the practical challenges and opportunities that we see in our favourite financial discipline. Welcome to: *Sustainable Investing in Practice: ESG challenges and opportunities.*

Let's get you settled in...

We aim to make the sustainable approach to investing relevant for a broad range of people. Our goal is to appeal to students, financial professionals and those immersed in the sustainability ecosystem – from regulators to development practitioners to activists – as well as anyone else with an abiding interest in this important and timely topic. We hope we've found the right balance between accessibility and depth, though we are cognisant of the impossibility of pleasing all stakeholders all of the time.

We've dedicated significant portions of our careers to conceptualizing sustainable solutions and helping to channel billions of dollars of capital into these investments. However, we are also pragmatists. We are well aware that global temperatures continue to rise, that many millions of people around the world still live in poverty and that a range of social justice causes remain sadly unfulfilled. These challenging realities still exist despite a rapid increase in sustainable investing's popularity and an explosion of sustainable-themed government and corporate policy, commitments and marketing communications.

This book pursues a middle path, rare as that may be in the politically polarized climate of the 2020s! We don't evangelize for our industry and claim it has solved (or will solve) the world's problems. Nor is this a whistle-blowing account of former true believers who have since turned to the dark side.

Like many things in life, sustainability issues are rarely binary. There are shades of green. And rational individuals can and do disagree about concepts and solutions. As the book's title suggests, the subsequent pages tackle the challenges that sustainable investment currently faces and the opportunities that could lead to materially better outcomes for people and the planet. We hope that our experience in running commercially successful sustainable investing operations, as well as our prior navigation of an array of complex incentives and trade-offs, helps illuminate these challenges and opportunities in a way that you find interesting, thought-provoking and ultimately action-inspiring.

Getting the most out of this book

To get the most out of this book there are three things you, the reader, need to know and consider.

The first is that there are many people smarter than us. We've been fortunate enough to meet a number of them in our careers and we've invited seven of the best and brightest to contribute interviews to this book. You'll find one interview in each chapter (excluding the Conclusion). Naturally, as authors we may not agree with every idea they voice and, of course, their involvement does not imply that they endorse the positions we articulate in the book. As sustainability advocates, we value diversity of thought: each of our seven experts has taken highly interesting paths to become involved in sustainability. The roster includes: a military general, a journalist, a Fortune Global 500 CEO, a charity CEO, a filmmaker, an investor and a professor. We hope you enjoy reading their contributions as much as we enjoyed collecting them.

The second point is that sustainable investing can at times prove inaccessible, opaque and downright confusing. Many of those 100-plus terms that serve as partial synonyms get whittled down into irritating acronyms (IIF, 2019). We've frequently been told that to invest sustainably requires 'learning a new language'. Forcing people to become bilingual so they can enter the world of sustainability is (in the view of two Anglo-Saxon expats living in Switzerland) extremely counterproductive.

We've therefore avoided adding our own bespoke terminology to the jargon jungle. Instead we liberally deploy pop culture references and analogies to everyday life. If you are a fan of *Star Trek*, *McDonald's* or the sitcom *Friends* you are in luck. Similarly, if you bought this book to hear the occasional tale of James' attempts to body build, buy a new suit, or manage his relationship with his mother, you are also in for a treat. For those versed in the sustainability zeitgeist who find these periodic asides annoying or irrelevant we (half-heartedly) apologize and repeat the words of one of our contributors Robert G Eccles: 'There never is an optimal solution because people have very different views of what is optimal' (Eccles, 2022).

The third thing – and this one is very important – this book is just a book. We've spent many years working as sustainable investors and have tried to be, in keeping with the practice of mainstream non-fiction, as thorough in our research and referencing as possible. However, many topics we address are worthy of hundreds of pages in their own right, but for practical reasons we have distilled, summarized and in many cases simplified them.

A recurring feature of the text is a Q&A format. To make the reader's life more pleasant we start these Q&A sections with a brief – sometimes one-word – summary. In 'Chapter 3 – Sustainable public equity markets', for example, we pose the hot-button question: 'Does exclusion [the act of selling or refusing to buy the shares of 'unsavoury' companies] help people and the planet?' And we succinctly answer 'No'.

Such is the diversity of viewpoints held across the sustainable (and political) spectrum that we fully expect our forthright answers to both delight and upset our readership. If you do disagree, please do not burn the book (it creates unnecessary carbon emissions) nor, as one of our contributors Gillian Tett wisely puts it in her interview, 'slip into cynicism and seek a "gotcha" moment for its own sake'. We prefer that our words are not taken out of context and used to incite an internet riot.

How we got here

Before we undertake a whistle stop tour of the contents of the book, we'd like to briefly reflect on the environment in which we wrote it. We live in remarkable – in some ways the best and worst of – times, and our humble writings owe the same debt, good and bad, to their context as does Charles Dickens' deathless prose.

The year 2021 ended, financially, on a triumphant note. The global variant of the most widely followed sustainable public equity index celebrated its sixth consecutive year of outperforming its mainstream equivalent (MSCI, 2022). Assets managed by sustainable investors swelled: Goldman Sachs reported that sustainable funds received one of every four dollars of new investor capital (Goldman Sachs, n.d.). These dynamics were accompanied by a political sea change in the world's largest economy as US President Joe Biden acquainted himself with his new oval-shaped office. All this, briefly, made sustainability and sustainable investing appear invincible.

That said, beneath the surface counter-currents were forming. BlackRock (the world's largest asset manager) (Thinking Ahead Institute, 2021) had to deal with its former CIO of Sustainable Investing sensationally claiming in March 2021 that 'Wall Street is greenwashing the financial world' (Fancy, 2021). German asset manager DWS also encountered difficulties. A whistle-blowing action from its former chief sustainability officer cast doubt on the degree to which environmental, social and governance (ESG) metrics were integrated into its investment strategies. This complaint triggered a US Securities Exchange Commission (SEC) investigation and then, in May 2022, a dramatic raid by German police on the firm's Frankfurt headquarters (Langley and Miller, 2022).

However, it took the 'animal spirits' of changing market sentiment to truly turn the tide against sustainable investing. In the first six months of 2022, the aforementioned MSCI global sustainable public equity index underperformed by almost 3 per cent as surging oil prices and rising interest rates pummelled many sustainable assets (MSCI, 2022). A firestorm also erupted in May 2022, when HSBC

Asset Management's head of responsible investment gave a provocative speech. It included statements such as 'climate change is not a financial risk we need to worry about' and 'who cares if Miami is six metres underwater', which triggered polarized responses. The HSBC manager was lauded by the *Wall Street Journal* (2022) while being vehemently criticized by others and promptly suspended by his firm (Makortoff, 2022).

The combined fallout from these events created a domino effect. The former head of sustainability at the Calpers pension fund, a known sustainable investing advocate, told a New York conference, 'I think it's time for RIP ESG' (Tett, 2022), while *Barron's* declared that 'sustainable investing failed its first big test' and that 'a reckoning is coming' (Foster, 2022). The *Financial Times* solemnly noted that sustainable investing had been 'exposed in a world of changing priorities' (Tett, 2022).

Around the world, regulators also leapt into action. In addition to the aforementioned difficulties at DWS, BNY Mellon agreed to pay a fine for 'material misstatements and omissions' on a number of fund documents. US investment banking giant Goldman Sachs was also placed under investigation by the US Securities Exchange Commission for potential misalignments between marketing materials and investment practices (Quinson, 2022). On the other side of the pond the European Union pressed ahead with a raft of complex sustainable investing legislation, much of it focused on 'tackling greenwashing and promoting transparency' (ESMA, 2022).

Against this uncertain and polarized backdrop we hope that this book, a pragmatic contribution containing suggestions for constructive change, finds receptive ears. We don't believe that indiscriminately berating sustainable investors will help solve the pressing issues facing people and the planet. Nor do we think that by engaging in ivory tower pontification about the nuances of taxonomies and definitions we will catalyse voters, investors and CEOs into becoming an army of change agents. We find that, in most situations, business and personal alike, listening, being open minded and seeking to align stakeholder incentives offer a more probable path to achieving one's objectives. We wrote this book in that spirit.

The whistle stop tour

How this book is structured

Many of our readers are incredibly busy. Countless demands press on a professional's time while our student readers somehow have to fit multiple rounds of beer pong into their schedules. With this in mind we've prepared this short whistle stop tour that aims to summarize the remaining 300 pages.

The book follows a deliberate sequence. It is also written in such a manner that readers can skip to a later chapter if they prefer and encounter only the occasional reference to a previously mentioned concept or argument.

For the most part, the chapters follow a standard framework.

- We start with a brief introduction that covers the chapter's main points. Three sections follow, each containing three subsections.
- The first two sections blend history, explanation and a discussion of the topic's challenges. Each subsection starts with a personal or pop culture reference to wade into the relevant concept. For the investment chapters (3 to 7), each section ends with a trio of pithy questions and answers.
- You'll find what we consider the highlights of the book – our industry interviews – sandwiched between the second and third section of each chapter. These dialogues have influenced our thinking and the solutions we propose. So it is appropriate that the insights shared precede the final 'opportunities' section.
- The third section of each chapter discusses 'The potential opportunities and how we might get there'. It contains three pragmatic ideas to help improve the industry and create positive benefits for people and the planet.

Chapter 1 – What is sustainable investing?

This chapter might appear to target the uninitiated. But that is not the case because the titular question is not a rhetorical but a critical one that, remarkably, the industry has yet to fully, satisfyingly answer.

Worryingly, more than 100 different terms are used as either partial or full synonyms for sustainable investing, their many nuances of interest only to the hard-core fringe of the sustainability movement (IIF, 2019). While a degree of ambiguity prevails throughout financial markets, sustainable investing stands alone as a discipline characterized and defined by it.

We explore the different things sustainable investing can mean. The short answer is 'almost anything'. This unfortunate fact is perhaps best evidenced by two major firms that track the sustainable investing ecosystem differing in their estimates of the industry's sustainable assets by a cool $30 trillion (GSIA, 2021; Morningstar, 2022). The reader learns about the negative consequences that derive from definition disagreement. A significant result is that investment managers are incentivized to inflate their assets-under-management figures and that standards setters too are encouraged to create liberal frameworks so they too can represent the largest pools of assets possible.

In an overview of the ways sustainable investors select sustainable instruments we focus on two fundamental methods. The first emphasizes what companies *do* – the products and services they create – and the second how they *act* – their behaviour toward their employees, their social and environmental policies, etc. The investment outputs differ substantially depending on which method is used.

The net result of emphasizing one or the other method is, unsurprisingly, that no two sustainable investors are alike. This lack of agreement can produce 'overconfidence bias', taking a blinkered view that one's own approach to sustainable investing is optimal. 'Horizontal hostility' can arise as investors and other stakeholders in the sustainable investing ecosystem end up criticizing one another's chosen approach or beliefs. This infighting is baffling at best and at worst an active turnoff for would-be sustainable investors and the public.

An exclusive interview with Gillian Tett follows. A successful British author and journalist, Gillian currently chairs the editorial board and serves as editor-at-large, US, of the *Financial Times*. Her journalistic career has given her a ring-side seat for the changes sustainable investing has undergone. She is thus the perfect commentator to aid our debate on 'What is Sustainable Investing?'

The final section puts us to the test. We present the potential opportunities and how we might get there. We won't discuss these opportunities in this brief introduction and, instead, as with all subsequent chapter summaries, will save them for the chapter itself. A summary of them is also found in the Conclusion.

Chapter 2 – Sustainable data and ESG ratings

At first glance the topic seems straightforward. Don't investors simply collect the relevant sustainability data and score a corporate's sustainability accordingly? The devil of course is in the details and this chapter's first two sections highlight the demonic difficulties of trying to put what sounds simple and straightforward into practice.

The reader learns how sustainable data originates, is measured and is disclosed. We look at the obstacles that arise when originating the data, which is frequently self-disclosed by corporations without third-party audit or assurance.

The issue of measurement itself brings more difficulties. Companies often measure what is immaterial to the future of their business. And the useful things they do measure are often reported in non-standardized units or with a unique scope. Comparing the data published by one company with that of another becomes problematic for investors. And this disclosure creates hurdles of its own, involving a surfeit of standards that compete for corporate and investor attention.

A discussion of how sustainable data is used ensues. Often, it is aggregated into environmental, social and governance (ESG) ratings. In 'How sustainable data is aggregated to form ESG ratings' we begin by considering the inputs – the methodologies that combine the reported numbers into ESG ratings – before moving on to the outputs and how and why ratings and scores diverge among providers. We close this section by considering whether the sustainable data ecosystem and ESG ratings create real-world impact and catalyse positive change for people and the planet.

An exclusive interview with Professor Robert G Eccles precedes the final section. Robert, as the founding chairman of the Sustainability Accounting Standards Board (SASB) and co-founder of the International Integrated Reporting Council (IIRC), has an unrivalled knowledge of sustainability data and ratings.

In the final section, we peer once more into the crystal ball to consider the potential opportunities and how we might get there.

Chapter 3 – Sustainable public equity markets

This first of three chapters focuses on practically applying sustainable investing within an asset class deals with the most common instruments found in sustainable portfolios – public equities. It is also the first chapter to include our quick-fire Q&A format that addresses hot button issues such as popularity, performance and real-world impact. And it breaks our beloved 'rule of three' by having four sections because the three broad techniques applied by sustainable investors – exclusion, integration and engagement – can't be shoehorned into two categories.

How exclusion processes operate reviews sustainable investing's historical focus on 'exclusion' – the practice of removing companies, sectors or economic activities from an investment universe or portfolio based on an investor's preferences, moral or social values, and/or risk tolerance. We assess the strategy's estimated size in terms of assets, the operational hurdles facing investors and the cultural differences that can lead investors to exclude activities that differ markedly from one another.

Our initial Q&A section asks and answers:

- Does the practice of exclusion add to investment performance? (Answer: No.)
- Does it detract from investment performance? (Answer: It can.)
- Does it help people and the planet? (Answer: No.)

Exclusion interprets sustainability in a negative way – by proscribing certain practices – and later gave way to 'integration'. A more positive concept, it seeks to demonstrate what sustainability can do for portfolios by including sustainability information in the investment decision-making process.

In 'How integration processes operate' we assess the strategy's estimated size in terms of assets and address whether its 'mainstreaming' has blurred the lines about it to the point that the term no longer refers to a discrete approach. A short discussion on the incentives that can entice firms to overstate the extent of their integration processes leads to our Q&A.

We consider the two types of integration in theory and in practice to pose and answer three key questions:

- Does quantitative integration add to investment performance? (Answer: A little, at least for now.)
- Does qualitative integration add to investment performance? (Answer: A little.)
- Does either help people and the planet? (Answer: No.)

A third wave of sustainability in public equities – engagement – arrived, at scale, in the 2010s. Investors sought greater real-world impact and, to achieve it, used their voice and equity voting rights to advocate for change by engaging constructively with company management.

How engagement processes operate estimates the scope of the strategy in terms of assets before highlighting the challenges created by a lack of third-party validation, as well as the difficulties posed by multiple investors claiming the same successes.

Our Q&A this time addresses the following questions:

- Can just anyone successfully engage? (Answer: No.)
- Does engagement add to investment performance? (Answer: Potentially.)
- Does it help people and the planet? (Answer: A little.)

Before tackling our final equity section, we pause to include an exclusive interview with Catherine Howarth. Since 2008, Catherine has served as the CEO of ShareAction, a charity committed to driving financial system change through regulatory collaboration, the co-ordination of investor engagement and the benchmarking of investors' sustainable practices.

Her insights lead us to look again to the future and consider the potential opportunities and how we might get there.

Chapter 4 – Sustainable public debt markets

Reassuringly we're back to three sections here, each consisting of three subsections. The now familiar strategies of exclusion, integration and engagement are compressed into 'How traditional sustainable public debt market processes operate'. We review exclusionary processes that avoid bonds issued by companies whose activities are deemed unsavoury. Debt's seniority in the capital structure means that sustainability issues have a much smaller impact on debt securities than equity returns. But public debt market investors have ample opportunity to meaningfully engage with corporations as part of the regular issuing and refinancing of debt.

This review leads us to examine traditional sustainable public debt market processes in theory and in practice, and we once more pose and answer three important questions:

- How popular are these processes? (Answer: Not very.)
- How much do they add to investment performance? (Answer: Almost none.)
- Do they help people and the planet? (Answer: No.)

'How sustainable dedicated assets operate' opens with a discussion of public debt market investments that contain features unique to sustainability. Starting with instruments where the issuers' stated mission is sustainability, we profile multilateral development bank debt (such as bonds issued by the World Bank) and microcredit. We highlight a number of challenges related to impact measurement and to ensuring that the funds are used for the intended purposes.

The workings of green bonds and other instruments whose proceeds are ring-fenced for sustainability are addressed next. Several challenges, including the significant issue of sector bias, are looked at. We then explore the most innovative area of sustainable public debt markets: instruments whose cost of debt depends on sustainability, such as sustainability-linked bonds.

These key dedicated assets are then examined in theory and in practice:

- How much do they add to investment performance? (Answer: Almost zero.)
- Do they help people and the planet? (Answer: Yes.)
- Do investors purchasing them do so? (Answer: Not really. Perhaps only as a collective body.)

Our exclusive interview in this chapter features Richard Curtis CBE. In addition to being a renowned screenwriter, producer and film director (whose credits include *Blackadder, Notting Hill* and *Love Actually*), Richard has had an outsized impact upon philanthropy and sustainable investments.

Our final section is, as always, the potential opportunities and how we might get there.

Chapter 5 – Sustainable private markets

A broad swathe of sub-asset classes from venture capital to distressed debt makes up 'The assets that comprise sustainable private markets'. We examine their history from a sustainable perspective and discuss the origins of what we term the 'old world'. In it investors were typically small scale and sought concessionary investment returns. As a result they didn't have a huge amount of positive impact on people and the planet.

The 'new world' dawned in the 2010s. Large-scale, market-rate return funds came to the fore, supported by leading private market investment firms and their considerable resources across the value chain. The investment expertise of these 'big boys' also attracted more institutional capital from pension funds and insurers that otherwise may have been reluctant to support 'untested' smaller impact funds. And their objective decision making, such as refusing to provide follow-on capital for an impactful but economically failing firm, enhanced capital allocation efficiency.

The 'old world', not to be outdone, has sought to reinvent itself through blended finance and new forms of private debt whose return depends upon sustainable outcomes. But we argue that the familiar hurdles of cost, complexity and a lack of standardization simply refuse to go away.

This review sets the stage for examining sustainable private markets in theory and in practice in light of three important questions:

- How popular are sustainable private markets? (Answer: Their popularity is overstated.)
- Do they add to investment performance? (Answer: Only if there is no additionality.)
- Do they help people and the planet? (Answer: Yes, but the effect is often exaggerated.)

In 'The standards that comprise sustainable private markets' we profile the ecosystem that has underpinned their development and the related field of impact investing. We argue that the impact measurement and reporting ecosystem, due to its size and heterogeneity, has created confusion throughout the private market investment industry. As a result, comparing private market firms is difficult and end investors cannot always make informed investment decisions.

Three additional questions are considered:

- Do all private market sub-asset classes embrace sustainability standards? (Answer: No.)
- Do all private market geographies do so? (Answer: No.)
- Do private market firms deploy adequate resources to fulfil sustainability standards? (Answer: In most cases, no.)

An exclusive interview with David Petraeus follows. As of 2022, David chairs Kohlberg Kravis Roberts & Co, LP's (KKR) Global Institute. Prior to assuming this chairmanship, he was the fourth

Director of the US Central Intelligence Agency (CIA), serving under President Barack Obama.

Once more we then look to the future to consider the potential opportunities and how we might get there.

Chapter 6 – Themes and the United Nations Sustainable Development Goals

Having reviewed three primary asset classes we discuss how they can be utilized to boost sustainability.

A section called 'How sustainable themes operate' kicks things off. A brief history lesson leads to a description of, and a nod to, some challenges thematic investors face. We move on to the core premise of thematic investing: that human beings struggle to comprehend exponential growth and often overlook paradigm-shifting technologies and services. We close this section by noting that the potential for exponential growth is not the only desirable thematic trait: network effects, blank slate design, ecosystem development and decentralized technologies all occupy a list of 'what makes a good theme'.

Our review complete, we examine thematic investing in theory and in practice to pose and answer three important questions:

- How popular are sustainable themes? (Answer: Increasingly.)
- Do they add to investment performance? (Answer: Rarely.)
- Should thematic investing be active or passive? (Answer: Active.)

Our second section dives deep into the United Nations Sustainable Development Goals (SDGs). Launched in 2015, the SDGs were designed as a 'blueprint to achieve a better and more sustainable future for all'. Their long-term nature and focus on sustainability make them a popular framework for sustainable thematic investors. We review the basics of the SDGs before considering the extent to which investment capital can help achieve them. The section concludes with a double click on SDG 13 – Climate Action, a highly popular SDG.

Having profiled the UN SDGs, we examine them in theory and in practice and address three key questions:

- Will they be achieved by 2030? (Answer: Almost certainly not.)
- Do public companies significantly contribute to them? (Answer: They align with them more than work to achieve them.)
- Do thematic investors use the SDGs as an investment framework? (Answer: Rarely.)

An exclusive interview with Paul Polman precedes the final section. Paul is a sustainability pioneer who served for 10 years as chief executive officer of consumer giant Unilever and launched the highly impactful Unilever Sustainable Living Plan.

We then conclude with the potential opportunities and how we might get there.

Chapter 7 – Sustainable multi-asset portfolios

Our final content chapter deals with multi-asset sustainable investing, a topic dear to our hearts. Developing innovative solutions that combine the best ideas from across the financial markets and sustainable product providers has been an integral part of our careers.

We open with a look at how traditional approaches to sustainable multi-asset portfolios operate. These approaches, for the most part, existed before we became involved with sustainable investing. We consider three fundamental approaches before posing – and answering – critical questions about popularity, performance and impact upon people and the planet.

The practice of what we term screening is addressed. This method involves comparing a traditional portfolio against one or more sustainable metrics to determine the validity of the investment instrument components. Next, we consider an exclusion approach, which takes a traditional portfolio and removes certain undesirable elements from it. Finally, we review a core-satellite approach in which a traditional portfolio is augmented by specific sustainable assets.

We then ask of traditional sustainable multi-asset portfolios:

- How popular are they? (Answer: Not very.)
- Do they add to investment performance? (Answer: No.)
- Do they help people and the planet? (Answer: No.)

With those uninspiring answers behind us, we move on to 'How modern approaches to sustainable multi-asset portfolios operate' and outline the leaps forward sustainable multi-asset investing has made since the late 2010s.

We consider the entire investment value chain and the role sustainability can play both in macro forecasting and in creating capital market assumptions. We discuss sub-asset class substitutions, such as replacing high-quality government bond exposure with multilateral development bank bonds to enhance portfolio sustainability. We then evaluate the advantages of deploying different sustainable techniques in combination to obtain desired factor and risk-premia exposures.

These modern approaches receive our brief Q&A treatment as we ask and answer:

- How popular are they? (Answer: Their popularity is growing.)
- Do they add to investment performance? (Answer: A little.)
- Do they help people and the planet? (Answer: Only as much as the underlying investments do.)

Before tackling our final multi-asset section, we pause to include an exclusive interview with Rick Lacaille. As of 2022, Rick serves as executive vice president and global head of environmental, social and governance (ESG) initiatives at investment juggernaut State Street. For more than a decade prior to this, he was the global chief investment officer (CIO) at State Street Global Advisors.

Our final multi-asset section looks to the future and assesses the potential opportunities and how we might get there.

Conclusion

Our final chapter consists of three sections.

The first, 'How we might get there', consolidates the various opportunities we've highlighted throughout the book into three aggregated observations. We take the common themes and our repeated asks from our writing and call for *Simplification, Personalization* and *Impact*. These three themes, if adopted, can help us get to a place where sustainable investing's popularity booms, its resilience increases and better outcomes are achieved for people and the planet.

The second section, 'Opportunities', delves deeper and brings together, in sequential order, all our recommendations in one ambitious, hubris-filled place. We hope that this section can act as inspiration for our readers: students, finance professionals, regulators, development practitioners, activists and anyone else waist deep in the subject. While time will undoubtedly prove some of our suggested opportunities to be impractical or outright wrong, we hope the aggregated brainpower of our readers will borrow, adapt and iterate some of these concepts and ideas into power programmes that drive positive change for people and the planet.

The third, and final, section, 'In practice', is the closest we come to offering advice. Unlike the prior sections that concentrate on ideas for the industry, we share here three learnings from our practical experience. We think they have relevance beyond our own careers and can nudge readers into pushing for greater commercial success and into achieving more for the greater good – even if their ideas and identified opportunities differ from ours.

The first, 'What people say and what they do are different', dives into the folly of sustainability-focused surveys and discusses how to adjust your tactics and responses accordingly. The second, 'The importance of the mass middle', cautions against designing solutions that appeal solely to those who hold an overtly enthusiastic view of sustainable investing. In the final observation, 'Creating win-wins', we highlight the power of incentives in order to drive commercial yet credible solutions.

Hopefully you've enjoyed this introduction and continue reading the rest of the book. Thank you for your interest and support.

References

Eccles, R G (2022) A personal message to the cantankerous critics of the International Sustainability Standards Board, *Forbes*, 19 February, www.forbes.com/sites/bobeccles/2022/02/19/a-personal-message-to-the-cantankerous-

critics-of-the-international-sustainability-standards-board/ (archived at https://perma.cc/9S34-98FU)
ESMA (2022) ESMA prioritises the fight against greenwashing in its new Sustainable Finance Roadmap, European Securities and Markets Authority, www.esma.europa.eu/press-news/esma-news/esma-prioritises-fight-against-greenwashing-in-its-new-sustainable-finance (archived at https://perma.cc/EZZ8-KZQ4)
Fancy, T (2021) Financial world greenwashing the public with deadly distraction in sustainable investing practices, *USA TODAY*, 16 March, www.usatoday.com/story/opinion/2021/03/16/wall-street-esg-sustainable-investing-greenwashing-column/6948923002/ (archived at https://perma.cc/P9LA-77QU)
Foster, L (2022) Sustainable investing failed its first big test, A reckoning is coming, Barron's, www.barrons.com/articles/esg-investing-big-test-reckoning-51650041442 (archived at https://perma.cc/CZC7-6JJT)
Goldman Sachs (no date) Marquee, marquee.gs.com/welcome/ (archived at https://perma.cc/J5HE-6AWW)
GSIA (2021) Global Sustainable Investment Review 2020, www.gsi-alliance.org/wp-content/uploads/2021/08/GSIR-20201.pdf (archived at https://perma.cc/B53D-Y9LT)
IIF (2019) The case for simplifying sustainable investment terminology, Institute of International Finance, www.iif.com/Portals/0/Files/content/IIF%20SFWG%20-%20Growing%20Sustainable%20Finance.pdf (archived at https://perma.cc/V25K-EF97)
Langley, W and Miller, J (2022) DWS chief resigns after police raid over greenwashing claims, *Financial Times*, 1 June, www.ft.com/content/50f5c4a1-5ebe-40cc-a89f-2952f58ba324 (archived at https://perma.cc/9LGL-3MCU)
Makortoff, K (2022) HSBC suspends head of responsible investing who called climate warnings 'shrill', *The Guardian*, 22 May, www.theguardian.com/business/2022/may/22/hsbc-suspends-head-of-responsible-investing-who-called-climate-warnings-shrill (archived at https://perma.cc/6HXS-2WCL)
Morningstar (2022) Global Sustainable Fund Flows Report, https://www.morningstar.com/lp/global-esg-flows (archived at https://perma.cc/5P5C-VJBE)
MSCI (2022) MSCI ACWI SRI Index (USD), www.msci.com/documents/10199/c260c2a2-ba71-47b7-a70a-efeb24b8d43c (archived at https://perma.cc/DN4F-MRDG)
Quinson, T (2022) The SEC war on greenwashing has begun, Bloomberg, 15 June, www.bloomberg.com/news/articles/2022-06-15/the-sec-s-war-against-greenwashing-and-esg-misuse-has-begun (archived at https://perma.cc/AR9R-ES2D)
Tett, G (2022) ESG exposed in a world of changing priorities, *Financial Times*, 3 June, www.ft.com/content/6356cc05-93a5-4f56-9d18-85218bc8bb0c (archived at https://perma.cc/2X3P-KGR7)

Thinking Ahead Institute (2021) Top 500 managers see assets hit record $119.5 trillion, www.thinkingaheadinstitute.org/news/article/top-500-managers-see-assets-hit-record-119-5-trillion/ (archived at https://perma.cc/H3XL-3TCJ)

Wall Street Journal (2022) A financier tells some climate-change truths, *Wall Street Journal*, 23 May, www.wsj.com/articles/a-financier-tells-some-climate-truths-stuart-kirk-hsbc-mark-carney-11653340776 (archived at https://perma.cc/KYX6-3X5M)

World Economic Forum (2019) Seeking Return on ESG: Advancing the Reporting Ecosystem to Unlock Impact for Business and Society, www.weforum.org/whitepapers/seeking-return-on-esg-advancing-the-reporting-ecosystem-to-unlock-impact-for-business-and-society/ (archived at https://perma.cc/V6YN-RBKA)

01

What is sustainable investing?

Introduction

Oranges come in many varieties. There are blood oranges, navel oranges and Seville oranges, among 400 other types. They are used in multiple ways: eaten raw, cooked into marmalade, squeezed for juices, added to tea for flavouring, sliced and inserted in cocktails as a garnish, etc. But in essence almost all oranges are round, orange and edible.

Sustainable investments, too, are highly various. In fact, there are over 100 kinds that follow approaches such as exclusion, integration and impact investing (IIF, 2019). Like oranges they are used in many different ways. Investors add them to their portfolios to pursue superior returns, reduce financial risk, align their investment goals with personal values and numerous other things.

Unlike oranges, sustainable investments don't conform to an easy archetype. They often mean very different things to different providers and people (HSBC, 2019). As a result, some investments promoted as sustainable may not seem so to a casual observer.

While a degree of ambiguity prevails throughout financial markets, sustainable investing stands alone as a discipline characterized and defined by it. A group of 'value investors' may calmly question which combination of valuation metrics best capture the nature of 'good value', but sustainable investors will frequently launch into tirades, taxonomies and white papers in defence of a preferred, proprietary definition of the kind of investing they are engaged in.

The consequence of this semantic free-for-all is that when individuals employing a 'value manager' look at the contents of their portfolio, they will likely comprehend the rationale behind the decisions to own the vast majority of the holdings. Individuals who employ a 'sustainable manager', by contrast, may find many of the manager's selections counterintuitive, if not irrational, and question whether their portfolio is sustainable at all.

This chapter kicks off with a section entitled 'The different things sustainable investing can mean'. Although we are as prone to the temptations of hubris as anyone else, we deliberately avoid creating our own definition of the term and instead seek to explain the viewpoints of different market participants.

We delve into the subject by playfully referencing the blockbuster situation comedy *Friends* before getting to the meat of the matter: the fact that sustainable investing is neither a universally acknowledged nor homogeneously defined term. Establishing this unfortunate truth, we move on to consider the implications it has for investors.

The prime one is the uncertainty it creates, which can manifest in everything from misallocated capital to reduced investor confidence and even accusations of mis-selling. We show how two major firms that track the sustainable investing ecosystem differ in their estimates of 'total sustainable assets' by a factor of 1400 per cent – or a cool $30 trillion (GSIA, 2021; Morningstar, 2022a).

The section wraps up by considering the perverse incentives this state of affairs creates. Due to disagreement over definitions, the amount of sustainable assets under management becomes the only common comparator. Investment managers are thus encouraged to inflate their figures, and standard setters are motivated to be liberal in their frameworks. We highlight the difficulty of resolving this situation as it is perpetuated by a human heuristic called 'additive bias'.

With the groundwork (uneasily) laid we move onto 'The ways sustainable investors select sustainable instruments'. We look at two fundamental methods. The first focuses on what companies *do* – for example, a company may transform the transport industry by electrifying automobiles. The second emphasizes how companies *act*

– i.e., a firm may treat its workers well or poorly, its policies may damage the environment or help repair it, etc.

Next, we dive deeper into the debates and challenges sustainable investing gives rise to. We consider the tensions that stem from the decision about whether to refer to a conventional benchmark when selecting financial instruments – a decision that can lead to moves such as buying shares in 'the most sustainable' oil and gas company.

We then introduce the concept of materiality, i.e., the degree to which a topic is relevant or 'material' to the valuation of an investment. This approach is contrasted with values-led selection, which considers how well a topic mirrors the ethics and worldview of the investor. This section concludes with a discussion on whether sustainable investments can create real-world impact and benefits for people and the planet. We tease the theories and practical evidence that we revisit in more depth in subsequent chapters.

Before we tackle our final section, we pause to include an exclusive interview with Gillian Tett. A successful British author and journalist, Gillian currently chairs the editorial board and serves as editor-at-large, US, of the *Financial Times*. Her journalistic career has given her a ring-side seat for the changes sustainable investing has undergone. She has charted its growth and sorted through the ambiguities, contradictions and unresolved debates that define the industry.

The final section puts us to the test. We present 'The potential opportunities and how we might get there'. Here, and in subsequent chapters, we acknowledge our fallibility while drawing on our experience as industry practitioners to highlight pragmatic opportunities whose first promising shoots are already poking into view in the landscape. We seek solutions that align stakeholder incentives and shun ivory tower ideas, utopian visions and overly optimistic hopes for a mass sustainable awakening.

To nudge things in the right direction, we focus on three opportunities that we see and suggest how we might get there.

- The first opportunity seeks to assist retail investors. Taking inspiration from nutritional information food labels, we seek a limited number of sustainable disclosures applicable to companies and investment products. The labels would enable investors to understand exactly what they are purchasing and to choose the instruments appropriately.

- The second is focused on institutional investors. To resolve the vast differences in what rival firms refer to as a 'sustainable' product, a single set of clear definitions is needed, in our view. They would describe different sustainable investing strategies, with financial firms aligning their offerings to them.
- The third looks to regulators. We propose that regulators 'get tough' and introduce clarity into the desired definitions while ensuring that corporate disclosures are supported by strong enforcement.

The different things sustainable investing can mean

Terminology: Differences among Friends

Words mean different things to different people. Take Rachel Greene and Ross Geller from the blockbuster sitcom *Friends*. When Rachel angrily suggests to her partner Ross that they should 'take a break', the two interpret the word 'break' very differently (Longman, 2019). Ross's subsequent hookup with another woman triggers not just an emotional response from Rachel but a comedic plotline that runs for the next seven seasons of the sitcom.

Sustainable investing involves similar ambiguities, nuances and confusions. The term itself has no universally accepted meaning. For example:

- The world's largest asset manager by assets, Blackrock (Thinking Ahead Institute, 2021), says sustainable investing 'is about investing in progress, and recognising that companies solving the world's biggest challenges can be best positioned to grow' (BlackRock, n.d.).

- The world's largest wealth manager by assets, UBS (Burton, 2021), believes that sustainable investing strategies 'aim to incorporate environmental, social and governance (ESG) considerations into investment process and portfolio construction' (UBS, n.d.).
- And the United Nations Principles for Responsible Investment (UN PRI), arguably the world's largest sustainable investment grouping, prefers the term 'responsible' to 'sustainable' and defines it as 'a strategy and practice to incorporate environmental, social and governance (ESG) factors in investment decisions and active ownership' (UN PRI, n.d. a).

While disagreement abounds about what 'it' is, 'sustainable investing' does serve as an umbrella term for a range of similar investment activities. An informative research paper by the Institute of International Finance (IIF), a major trade group for the global financial services industry, discusses the conflation of concepts and the multitude of terms that product providers employ. It finds more than 100 other words used either as sub-categorizations, synonyms or descriptions of activities in closely related fields. A small sampling of them gives a flavour of the word salad: ethical investing, positive screening, socially responsible investing, triple bottom line investing and values-based investing (IIF, 2019).

Terminology: Creating uncertainty

Some conditions and situations require a number of related terms to convey nuance, complexity and specificity. The native Inuit population of Canada has around a dozen words (excluding derivatives) for snow. A further ten describe ice (Schneider, 1985). English, by contrast, uses adjectives to delineate the features of snow and ice.

The Inuit approach is a function of situational necessity. The population must be able to linguistically distinguish between 'aputi' (snow on the ground) and 'pukak' (crystalline snow on the ground) quickly and accurately. The English layering on of adjectives creates only a mild linguistic burden easily tolerated due to the infrequency of their use. That said, climate change might make such episodes more frequent and require more nouns.

In the case of sustainable investing, surveys of investors suggest that a large number of terms with intricately nuanced definitions is not required. In fact, the competing terms may be detrimental to the cause by creating confusion and even erecting a barrier to investment. A survey conducted by consultancy firm Aon indicated that almost 50 per cent of the professional investors questioned called for 'industry agreement on terms and definitions' (Jones, 2018). Meanwhile, in a UBS survey of 5000 high-net-worth investors, around three-quarters of the respondents described themselves as 'not familiar' or 'confused' by the terminology used by the industry (UBS, 2018).

This data points to the broader role of definitions. Their purpose is to enable people to share a common understanding that helps them to think and communicate clearly. What is happening in the area of sustainable investing is, paradoxically, the opposite. Too many definitions with ambiguous overlap have created confusion.

Unfortunately, there is no easy fix. The temptation, when trying to make yourself understood, is to (re)define what *you* mean by sustainable investing. But doing so only adds to the overkill and further muddies the waters. This lesson is one Rachel and Ross from *Friends* learned the hard way. Rachel's attempts to bring clarity and certainty to their relationship via her own written definition of it – an 18-page ('front and back') letter – only exacerbated their difficulties. What works best, we believe, is evolving a small number of widely used, commonly understood, and clearly defined terms. Uncertainty can arise as readily from having too much specialized vocabulary as from having none at all.

Such uncertainty leads to suboptimal outcomes. Famous management consultant Peter Drucker is often quoted as saying, 'You can't manage what you can't measure' (Wolcott, 2016). When it comes to sustainable investing, that holds true even in basic dollar terms. Due to the lack of shared definitions, estimates of the amount of assets invested sustainably vary enormously. At the high end, the Global Sustainable Investing Alliance (GSIA) concluded that, as of year-end

2020, $35 trillion, or 36 per cent of all professionally managed financial assets, was invested sustainably (GSIA, 2021). More conservative figures are provided by the likes of research and data provider Morningstar. It values the market, as of 2022, at closer to $2.8 trillion, less than one-tenth of the GSIA estimate (Morningstar, 2022a). The source of this discrepancy is the wording used to define and group the assets.

THE PERILS OF SELF-IDENTIFICATION

In the absence of definitive definitions, estimates that diverge widely tend to be inevitable to some degree. To demonstrate this idea we'll use the research of Brian Palmer, the Peabody Award–winning journalist, who compared reputably reported figures for the number of Roman Catholics living in the US in the early 2010s. Palmer found the individual survey-based Pew Research set the figure highest – at 75 million – because 'it takes very little effort to self-identify as a Catholic'. At the low end was the US Religion Census, which surveyed local church leaders to approximate the number of their congregants. Its figure came in at just 59 million (Palmer, 2013).

Although Palmer's collated numbers disagree by less than 30 per cent – a far cry from the 1400 per cent variance between GSIA and Morningstar – they illuminate the difficulties involved in establishing consistent figures when definitions are non-standardized. Investment fund managers in most cases are being asked to self-identify as sustainable investors, a description that not only takes very little effort but flatters them.

If we dig into the details, we can see that GSIA data is compiled from the work of four regional members, all of whom 'use a different method to collect the data' (GSIA, 2021). In addition, approximately one-third of the assets originate from Europe, the only region to shun proprietary collection and instead rely upon 'secondary industry data'.

The GSIA defines seven sustainable investing strategies with counted assets that belong to one or more strategies simultaneously. This approach suggests that, structurally, we should expect a lot of sustainable assets. Furthermore, two-thirds of the GSIA-tabulated assets are attributable to two categories, termed 'negative/exclusionary screening' and 'ESG integration'. These categories receive brief, general definitions: ESG integration is described as 'the systematic and explicit inclusion by investment managers of environmental, social and governance factors into financial analysis'. Given the definition's limited detail and broad scope, the categories imply a large degree of variability, subjectivity and a potentially low threshold for determining 'what is sustainable'.

In the case of 'negative/exclusionary screening', an otherwise conventional investment strategy could conceivably claim to be sustainable under the GSIA definition by merely deploying a range of quantitative checks and excluding those companies that fail one or more of them. Definitional ambiguity breeds uncertainty and can distort the amount of assets counted as 'sustainable'. At the extreme, this can cause end investors to question whether their portfolio is indeed sustainable at all.

ILLUSTRATING THE LIMITATIONS OF EXCLUSIONARY POLICIES

To illustrate these points, let's hypothetically build a portfolio of the 40 largest US companies by market capitalization and then deploy the five most popular negative/exclusionary screens. In doing so, we seek to create an exclusionary screened 'sustainable' portfolio and ascertain the extent to which sustainability impacts our investment strategy. While consistent global data about the most commonly deployed negative/exclusionary screens is unavailable, surveys of investor practices provide a degree of transparency we can utilize as a proxy. According to asset manager Schroders, the top five exclusions (excluding groups of exclusions) are, in descending order of prevalence, weapons, tobacco, gambling, pornography and alcohol, so we'll employ them for our illustration (Schroders, 2017).

We run the analysis using data from a leading sustainability data provider (Sustainalytics) and, as per industry practice, set a trigger threshold of 5 per cent of company revenues for any given excluded economic activity to avoid false positives (such as a bank that owns a solitary vineyard). The result is that not a single one of these top 40 US companies would be excluded from the hypothetical portfolio (Sustainalytics, n.d.). This suggests that one could theoretically run a 'negative/exclusionary screening' investment strategy, make no changes to one's holdings, and may still be regarded as investing according to one of the more liberal definitions of sustainable strategies.

Even at the low end of the sustainable asset count, the 2022 Morningstar figure of $2.8 trillion does not come without qualifications. In early 2022, Morningstar culled 40 per cent of its previously listed sustainable investing universe – a huge restatement – after it conducted an 'extensive review' of funds' sustainability credentials (Quinio, 2022). Questions also arise about the validity of the claims made by existing funds that rebadge themselves as 'sustainable' (from 'conventional') via name changes. Over 500 instances of such rebranding occurred in Europe alone in 2021 and sceptics point to the wave of investor inflows into sustainability-branded funds as a reason to be cautious, if not dubious, about them (Blackburn, 2022; Hawker, 2022; Webb, 2022).

These contrasting data points underscore the usefulness of putting oneself in the shoes of investors consulting the various information sources that purport to identify sustainable funds. Based upon the published figures alone, these investors, drawing on the Morningstar data, would conclude that 90 per cent of the universe identified as sustainable by GSIA was not actually so. That's a dramatic conclusion, and one that offers a clue as to just how misleading the vast majority of claimed sustainable investments are.

Terminology: Creating misincentives

Parents of school-age children commonly complain that 'exams are getting easier'. And they are typically right (or should that be correct?!). Using secondary school-leaver (students aged 16) exam data from the UK, we can observe a pattern of continuous annual improvement from 1988 to 2011, with the percentage of students passing a given exam rising steadily from about 42 per cent to almost

70 per cent (Smithers, 2014). Soon after, in part due to concerns about grade inflation, the system was overhauled by the UK government. A new grading scale was installed that sought to differentiate between the achievements of high-attaining students (UK Government, n.d.).

This dynamic illustrates 'Goodhart's law'. In layman's terms, the law says that 'when a measure becomes a target, it ceases to be a good measure' (Strathern, 1997). The desire for superficial improvement is found across our society, including pay increases that merely keep pace with price inflation and the excitement of 'levelling up' in a video game, only to face a proportionally stronger opponent in the next round.

Sustainable investment faces the same problem. Given the absence of a strong, singular definition and an accepted methodology for comparing A with B, the only recognizable comparator is numerical, i.e., two is bigger than one. Consequently, investment firms often race to the top with announcements of ever bigger numbers for their sustainable investing assets and commitments. In doing so, they mechanically race to the bottom with ever lower standards for labelling a strategy 'sustainable'.

It takes a high-integrity CEO to announce an ESG number much lower than that of peer companies by asserting (though such an assertion itself cannot be readily verified due to a lack of common standards) that the quality of the lower number is materially superior to the peers' higher one.

Earlier, we suggested that uncertainty arises as readily from too much terminology as from no shared vocabulary at all, and that the greatest certainty comes from the wide use of a small number of commonly understood, clearly defined terms. It follows that the incentive to inflate sustainable asset figures is largest when uncertainty is greatest. Put plainly, in the absence of clear rules the likelihood of misrepresentation increases.

Unfortunately, the problem extends to the standard setters themselves. They, in effect, compete with one another for industry recognition and media attention. Speaking for tens of trillions of US dollars of assets is preferable to representing a fraction of that amount. Indeed, GSIA's announcements of ever larger sustainable figures are typically covered by major publications (Jessop, 2021), and we too cite them!

INCENTIVES CREATE CHALLENGES EVEN AT THE HIGHEST LEVELS

This dynamic is also evident with the UN-backed Principles of Responsible Investment (UN PRI), which, founded in 2005, has grown into a highly influential sustainable investment organization that represents $120 trillion of assets across almost 4000 signatories (UN PRI, n.d. b).

In its early days, the UN PRI sought legitimacy through greater scale rather than tighter definitions and tougher standards. It encouraged as many investors as possible to sign up to its admirable principles for more responsible investment practices. However, it took until 2020 for the organization to expel one of its signatories for failing to meet its own 'minimum standards' (UN PRI, 2020). And academic studies find that investment managers who sign the PRI neither demonstrate superior sustainable practices compared with those that don't nor improve their practices notably after signing (Kim and Yoon, 2022). None of this is a criticism of the UN PRI per se, for the organization has undeniably attained a position of considerable influence within sustainable investing circles. Its success contrasts with fellow, 'tougher' investor groupings that failed to gain traction and have since faded into obscurity.

The problem of non-standardized definitions and methodologies is, unfortunately, not likely to vanish anytime soon as it is perpetuated by what psychologists term 'additive bias' (*The Economist*, 2021). Humans, when faced with a challenge, typically seek to resolve it by 'adding' rather than 'subtracting'. This bias manifests itself in everything from domestic do-it-yourself projects (add just one more screw to that sagging shelving unit) to initiatives at work that limp along when another steering committee is formed. The natural inclination of investors confronted with a multitude of non-standardized definitions is to sort things out by considering what has come before, identifying the deficiency, and writing a new (slightly different) definition that purports to solve the industry's problems. Despite the good intentions, additive bias has claimed another victim.

The ways sustainable investors select sustainable instruments

Sustainable instruments: Rock and roll

What people *do* and how they *act* are two different things. Throughout history there are countless examples of people who do fantastic public things but act inappropriately in their private lives. Presidents, scientists and artists may each make substantial contributions for the benefit of people and the planet yet fall short when it comes to their actions, engaging in morally suspect behaviour with colleagues or financial chicanery. As a simple thought exercise, think of what your favourite rock star has done for music, and then consider some of their less-than-savoury antics on the road.

There are parallels with sustainable investing. Some companies *do* remarkable things. They invent products and services that transform our lives for the better. However, they may *act* quite differently, working with exploited labourers, for example. When investors consider how to select sustainable investments they are generally considering one or both of what companies do and how they act.

Some sustainable investors emphasize what companies *do*. They seek to build portfolios that reflect themes such as climate action, the circular economy, or health and wellbeing. The companies selected by portfolio managers adhering to this approach are often intuitively understood by end investors, who often recognize the products and services of these firms from their everyday lives and favoured media outlets.

Other sustainable investors focus on how companies *act*. Their goal is to build portfolios by integrating the relevant ESG risks and opportunities to find sustainability leaders. The companies selected by portfolio managers following this approach may not strike end investors as logical, intuitive choices. Interpreting how companies act can be difficult. The underlying data used in the decision-making process is not readily available. It is often quite granular. And it may be at odds with the public image of the company.

For example, when portfolios are constructed based on how companies *act* it is possible that a seemingly unsustainable company, such as an oil exploration company, may be included in them. This firm may have superb relationships with its employees, local communities and regulators; it might boast an impeccable safety and environmental record with strong policies and evidenced action; and it may operate a world-class corporate governance structure to ensure fair pay, diligent financial accounting and objective independent oversight of managerial decisions. Thus, in spite of what the company does, the firm acts in an impeccable manner.

Of the two approaches, the majority of sustainable investors focus on how companies act. According to GSIA data, 'ESG Integration' (a proxy for *act*) is 13 times the size of 'sustainability themed investing' (a decent representation for *do*) (GSIA, 2021). Why this disparity? The vast majority of equity funds have a regional, rather than a global, mandate (Johnson, 2022). In a single country or region it can be difficult to find a sufficient number of companies that perform the desired activity, and the most innovative companies for a given theme may fall geographically outside of the regional mandate. In contrast, all companies within a region can be assessed on how they act. It naturally creates a wider investible universe.

Sustainable instruments: Debates and challenges

If you were asked to name the five most successful opera artists of the past one hundred years you might lead your list with Katherine Jenkins, the Welsh mezzo-soprano, followed by such Italian tenors as Andrea Bocelli or Luciano Pavarotti and even the pop-crossover act Il Divo. If you were tasked with identifying the five most popular musical artists of any genre, it is unlikely that an opera singer would spring to mind. Instead, your list would be dominated by the likes of Elvis Presley, the Beatles, Michael Jackson and Madonna.

Sustainable instruments come in specific, if non-musical categories. Investors can select securities from each sector or they can select those rated as the best overall, irrespective of sector.

Cherry picking the leaders from each sector ensures that the resulting portfolio does not differ markedly from conventional indices. It reduces tracking error and makes the sustainable approach palatable for risk-conscious investors. Plucking 'the best' companies from each sector can result, however, in a portfolio that may confound the end investor, as relatively well-behaved companies in the oil and gas or tobacco sectors may make the grade. If, on the other hand, one selects the best companies overall, without sector considerations, the portfolio may deviate more from traditional benchmarks but the securities in it will likely seem more logical and intuitive to the end investor.

AN ILLUSTRATION OF SECTOR-CONSTRAINTS

To illustrate this point we can use the sustainability ratings – opinions – of two leading providers. MSCI (mostly) sector-neutralizes its headline scores while Sustainalytics does not. This fact explains in large part why 7 per cent of energy companies receive MSCI's prestigious AAA rating for sustainability, while not a single energy company qualifies for Sustainalytics' equivalent score. In fact, if you use Sustainlytics' data, no energy company makes the top quartile of global firms (Sustainalytics, n.d.).

Even sector-unconstrained approaches can yield counterintuitive results if an investor's sustainable focus is solely on how a company acts. The investment approach often favours firms with the strongest policies and controls in place. It is precisely those companies in controversial industries that face the greatest sustainability risks and that therefore create, by necessity, the strictest policy and control frameworks.

Whether to sector-constrain is not the only choice would-be sustainable investors face. They may also decide to weigh data along financial materiality or personal preference lines.

For many institutional investors the concept of materiality is top of mind. Materiality, again, refers to whether a topic is relevant, or material, to an investment's valuation. Carbon emissions, for instance, may serve as a key indicator for understanding an industrial giant's efficiency, technology and likelihood of being on the right side of regulatory change.

The direct carbon emissions of a financial firm, by contrast, are likely to be irrelevant. We might hope its employees all switch off their computers at night and that the electricity used comes from renewable sources, but those factors are unlikely to affect the firm's profits. Instead, governance controls about trading, lending and employee remuneration will offer far more insight into its future success or failure.

WHO USES MATERIALITY?

Materiality is incorporated into the ratings and opinions published by MSCI and Sustainalytics. The industry also generally recognizes the subject-matter expertise of the Sustainability Accounting Standards Board (SASB), which, as of 2022, is merging into the International Financial Reporting Standards Foundation's (IFRS) International Sustainability Standards Board (ISSB) (Fink, 2020).

Yet even selecting sustainable investments based on materiality comes with challenges, as what the market deems material can change (sometimes this is called 'dynamic materiality'). Consider an electric car manufacturer whose valuation has soared due to the market's belief that its products and services represent the future. Now imagine its share price plunging because of a newspaper report that the firm sources its lithium from mines in the Democratic Republic of Congo, whose human rights record is questionable.

Both sustainability topics are material to the value of the company. Both can be reasonably known and understood, with an assessment made about their potential effect on the share price. Yet market participants assign varying degrees of importance to each topic at different times. In short, materiality is rarely fixed and issues are often not considered material – until they are!

While attempting to forecast the materiality of sustainability topics is great fun for institutional investors, retail investors tend to pay more attention to personal preference.

Some have a strong aversion to investing in tobacco stocks. Others do not. Some may consider nuclear power a key technology for a low-carbon future. Others may fear reactors melting like ice lollies in the sun.

Preference-based investing can reflect cultural, religious and political beliefs. Alcohol offers a good example. It is forbidden in some Islamic countries but an integral part of social culture in most of Europe. What seems normal to one individual may abhor another. With values there is rarely any objective right or wrong. As a result of this ambiguity, makers of widely distributed financial products confront difficulties, for the criteria they choose will almost certainly not please all potential customers.

Differences in beliefs and in how financial products are constructed can lead to heated and even acrimonious discussion. Within sustainable investing circles such opposing viewpoints result more and more in accusations of 'greenwashing' (Fletcher and Oliver, 2022). Greenwashing is the practice of deliberately deceiving consumers by presenting a false sustainable image to the public to foster goodwill and increase sales and pricing.

While some greenwashing allegations are valid, the root cause of many of them is simply two individuals or organizations defining what sustainable investing is in different ways. Those investors who buy companies based on how they *act* may take aim at the flawed ESG practices of the firms owned by sustainable investors that prioritize what companies *do*. And sector-unconstrained investors may voice exasperation at the presence of oil and gas companies in the portfolio of investors compelled to select the sustainable leaders from every investible sector.

Quite often, sadly, the argument boils down to the intellectually bankrupt position of 'I don't like 'X' and neither should you'.

Sustainable instruments: Creating impact?

A former colleague our ours used to drive a car to the office. His partner rode a bicycle. They both worked at places the same distance from their house. One day, feeling environmentally conscious, he borrowed his partner's bicycle and pedalled to work. Left unexpectedly without her usual mode of transport, his partner took the car. We remember him sitting at his desk, drenched in sweat, hamstrings cramping, proudly telling us that he had made a positive environmental impact. Only, of course, he hadn't. The same amount of carbon dioxide had been released into the atmosphere, just by someone else who drove his car.

When investors attempt to invest sustainably the same factors are at play. The decision to buy or sell a publicly traded security has little to no real-world impact. If you purchase shares in Apple, no additional money goes to the tech behemoth. Your stock was issued by Apple decades ago and your order merely swaps shares in the secondary market, with you buying them from another investor. Apple is unaffected by your activity.

Following this logic, investors can sell all their 'non-sustainable' oil and gas and tobacco publicly traded shares. They can replace them with the stock of renewable energy giants, corporations with exemplary diversity practices and cutting-edge firms profitably solving critical issues from water stress to rare diseases. These investors can look over their remodelled portfolios and feel good about themselves. But, again, nothing has changed in the real world. For every seller there must be a buyer. Metaphorically, the same number of bicycles and cars exist. They are just operated by different individuals.

Unsurprisingly, this reality can upset many would-be sustainable investors. There are those who argue that these investment decisions do have a sizeable impact. By divesting the security of a company, an investor pushes its value down, which has the follow-on effect, they contend, of restricting the firm's access to capital and making it incrementally harder for it to operate and harm people and the planet. Evidence in support of this well-meaning theory is hard to come by, however.

Academics from Stanford University and The Wharton School of the University of Pennsylvania who looked at this issue concluded that 'current ESG divestiture strategies have had little impact and will likely have little impact in the future'. The reason? Because publicly traded markets are liquid and demand for securities is highly elastic. The researchers found that it would take 80 per cent of all investible wealth to act in a sustainable manner to effect even a 1 per cent change in a firm's cost of capital (Berk and van Binsbergen, 2021).

Further evidence of divesture's limited impact comes from a non-sustainable source – the selling that follows a company's ejection from a major index such as the S&P 500. With over $13 trillion of assets benchmarked to the S&P 500 (S&P Dow Jones Indices, n.d.), a company being removed from it triggers a divestment multiple many times larger than any sustainable investing-derived exclusion. Even with this selling pressure, an abnormal drop in the value of a security lasts on average just 20 days before being reversed – hardly enough time to affect a company's access to capital (Kamal, 2014).

In fact, sustainable investors may even be doing more harm than good. In selling their 'non-sustainable' stock, they reallocate shares from sustainably minded to indifferent investors (Teoh, Welch and Wazzan, 1999). In effect, the new shareholders are far less likely to pressure or incentivize company management to act more responsibly.

A related difficulty for sustainable investors involves the impact linked to purchasing a security and is well summarized by University of Zurich researchers. 'It's not accurate to simply claim a company's impact as your own', they state. 'A company might be doing well by doing good, but your investment only had an impact at the margins, if at all' (Heeb and Kölbel, 2020). In other words, many companies' operations benefit people and the planet enormously, but the act of purchasing their securities does not incrementally increase (or decrease) this impact.

Sustainable investing techniques can (arguably) improve the risk-adjusted returns of a portfolio and align one's investments to one's values. The industry has a tendency to significantly overstate the real-world impact of these actions, however. In doing so, it gives a false sense of progress being made and can divert much needed capital from truly impactful investments.

James sat down to interview Gillian Tett and discuss the challenges, opportunities and nuances of sustainable investing. A successful British author and journalist, Gillian currently chairs the editorial board and serves as editor-at-large, US, of the *Financial Times*. Her journalistic career has given her a ring-side seat for the changes sustainable investing has undergone. She has charted its growth and sorted through the ambiguities, contradictions and unresolved debates that define the industry.

James: As a journalist, how did you first become exposed to sustainable investing?

Gillian: I came from a mainstream journalism tradition that was primed, until recently, to assume that sustainable investing was an awful lot of corporate smoke and mirrors. You had all these companies pumping out hippy-dippy messages that were, we believed, trying to cover up what they were really doing. As journalists we used to say that the only reason why you ever talked to corporations about ESG was to be able to speak with difficult-to-access corporate leaders. I began to change my view around 2016, 2017. I was getting inundated with ESG emails and thought, 'Wow, maybe I'm imposing my prejudice upon the subject matter. I should go and talk to people about what's going on.' So I went out and did a big series of interviews and realized there was a shift in the zeitgeist – companies were looking for purpose. Investors and financiers were seeking more than just profits and wanted to know how those profits were being made. You also had the public sector looking for ways to fund all of the United Nations Sustainable Development Goals. And these three elements were coming together.

James: And what surprised you as you delved deeper into the topic?

Gillian: A big surprise for me was realizing, around 2018, 2019, that we had reached a watershed moment. ESG was truly being seen as a form of risk management by many companies. Managing their reputational risks, their employee risks, the investor risks, the supply chain risk, the regulator risks, all of this was driving sustainability. Of course one could be cynical and say, 'This is hypocrisy. These companies don't really care about changing the world. They just want to defend themselves from lawsuits or losing their employees or their customers.' Or you can say, 'Actually this is the ultimate victory for the original sustainability movement because the zeitgeist has changed to a point where trying to go against the sustainability trend is more dangerous than trying to go with the sustainability trend.'

Another area that surprised me is entirely separate from the wider market. I trained as a cultural anthropologist before I became a journalist. Anthropology is devoted to trying to take a holistic big picture view of any activity and to set things in context. I didn't realize, until quite late in the day, that this is what has happened in the world of economics. And by that I mean that Milton Friedman's vision of capitalism was all about tunnel vision – shareholder-centric. Sustainability is all about the stakeholder and operating with lateral vision, looking at the context of corporate actions and corporations' footprint on the world and the world's footprint on them. And that's kind of what anthropologists do. So, in a funny kind of way, my world has come full circle.

James: Let's talk about the challenges when it comes to sustainable investing. What concerns you?

Gillian: I think one of the areas that concerns me, right now, is the green bubble – too much money flooding into too few assets. The reason there are too few assets is largely because the public sector and the infrastructure around green investing have not caught up. The idea that somehow the corporate sector is going to make up for the deficiencies of public sector policy deeply alarms me. I think in many ways Tariq Fancy, formerly of BlackRock, is correct to point it out – some people are using ESG as a potential excuse to take the pressure off governments. And the reality is that there needs to be a lot of government action. And then last, but not least, I think there is a huge issue around greenwashing and over-promising and over-hype. There needs to be a lot more honesty about the difficulties of the tradeoffs. We are dealing with what I call an olive yield curve, a mixture of green and brown. It's a spectrum of activity. You can't just divide the world into green and brown. That won't work. I think that we, as journalists, need to hold governments' and companies' feet to the fire, but we also need to recognize that we're all on a journey and trying to do the best you can is difficult.

James: Is it fair to say you don't view sustainability as binary?

Gillian: For me it is a bit like eating healthily. In that there isn't one hard and fast way to define what is healthy and what's not healthy. We all think we should eat healthier and we all have slippages, but the direction we should be going in is reasonably clear.

James: Maybe double clicking on companies. What are the changes you've witnessed in the corporate world?

Gillian: Firstly, I think we are seeing company boards wake up to ESG, even though most of them are not trained for it at all. And many might be reacting out of fear and greed rather than any sense of conscience or commitment. But that's fine. That's what business does. And if boards are embracing ESG because of risk management then that's actually a terrific indication of how the zeitgeist has changed. The second thing that impresses me is the degree to which companies are actually moving the Chief Sustainability Officer role or the sustainability function into the mainstream of their operation without ring-fencing it. Previously it's been an awful lot of box ticking and stuff. And now that's changed.

James: I agree, there's been some great progress. How about the areas where sustainable investing can improve?

Gillian: I think we should have a massive expansion of multilateral development bank activity, as well as a massive expansion of related blended finance activity. To get that going, you don't only need better structures, you don't only need willing pools of risk capital, you also need to get much better data monitoring and data awareness. I also think personalization is an interesting topic. I expect to see the rise of customizable investment funds, where one can basically put in one's criteria in a personalized way and end up with a personalized product. It could potentially have a big impact. You would then have the beginnings of a nuanced customer voice, in the same way that people can choose to eat healthier. If you look at what's happened, for example, with consumer choices around, say, dairy products, people can actually choose to switch their consumption behaviour. This could be extended to investment products. I think that's going to be a very interesting theme for the retail market going forward.

James: Even though we're seeing innovation, much as with food, we are also experiencing a wave of sustainable investing regulation. What are your thoughts on these developments?

Gillian: I don't think it's a great idea to create binary structures. You get rigid rules that are backward looking. Such regulations take a very long time to create, they're drawn up by bureaucrats, then they hit the market and they get arbitraged by financiers. I think that's what's going to happen. The market is moving, technology is moving, and what you're looking at most of the time is nasty tradeoffs and very difficult decisions. I think it's better to focus on things like a carbon budget per company or per sector or per investor – if you can get the data. I know that's a slightly controversial view. I think that nuclear and natural gas encapsulate many of the contradictions in all this. Is natural gas green? No. Is it better than coal? Yes. So, these are very difficult decisions right now.

James: Within this complexity what role can the press and journalists play in the development of sustainable investing?

Gillian: I think journalists are beginning to shift from tunnel vision to lateral vision and write about sustainability with greater nuance. First, journalism can take these stories seriously, write about them, and keep a critical and questioning eye to maintain proper oversight. But journalism should not slip into cynicism and seek 'gotcha' moments for their own sake. Second, journalism can help demystify the terms. A lot of the problems stem from the use of acronyms – even ESG itself. A third thing journalists have to do is recognize that a lot of stories are slow moving, which doesn't make them any less important. And a fourth thing is to realize that these stories are by nature silo busting. Historically, media coverage of sustainability has been handled by the section of the media group that covers climate change – the author would usually be the science writer. And the science writer sat in a department that had nothing to do with, say, the political writers or finance writers or technology writers or corporate writers. Sustainability, by its nature, cuts across many different areas of expertise and departments. That's been a challenge for many media companies to deal with.

James: I see a parallel with the corporate world – the growth of the cross-functional chief sustainability officer. Thank you for your time Gillian.

The potential opportunities and how we might get there

When we consider the potential opportunities for sustainable investing we first ask whether there is a need to propose any at all. Hasn't sustainable investing already 'won'? And as Gillian Tett said in our interview, 'The zeitgeist has changed to a point where trying to go against the sustainability trend is more dangerous than trying to go with the sustainability trend.'

But if that is the case, what exactly has won? As evidenced by the stunning 1400 per cent differential between GSIA's and Morningstar's asset count figures, the sustainable investing ecosystem remains highly nebulous (GSIA, 2021; Morningstar, 2022a). And the (literal) 100 attempts to define it have, according to surveys of investors, created little more than aggregate confusion (Jones, 2018; UBS, 2018; IIF, 2019). As authors who have spent much of our professional careers passionately working in the field, even we sometimes find it difficult to put our arms around sustainable investing – what it is and what it is not.

Further progress, we believe, is needed. In that spirit, let's look at three key sets of stakeholders and consider the plausible scenario(s) that could align incentives among them and that may already have a foothold in the real world. These stakeholder groups – retail investors, institutional investors and regulators – are critical for bringing clarity to sustainable investing, in our view.

Retail investors

Retail investors, ultimately, provide financial markets with capital – through their savings, pensions and insurance policies. The problem they face vis-à-vis sustainable investing is that they are often confused both by the terminology used and by the contents of their so-called sustainable portfolios. Consequently, they tend to gravitate toward what companies *do* rather than how they *act*.

This tendency was clearly evidenced in 2022 when the internet exploded with retail investor fury for Tesla being ejected from the S&P 500 ESG index for how it acts (the company faced claims of racial discrimination and lacked published business conduct codes) (Kerber and Jin, 2022). In response, Tesla CEO Elon Musk tweeted, 'Exxon is rated top ten best in the world for environment, social & governance (ESG) by S&P 500, while Tesla didn't make the list! ESG is a scam'. The tweet received over 300,000 likes. The average retail investor, it became clear, does not naturally warm to sector-neutralized benchmarks that evaluate how a company acts (Musk, 2022; S&P Dow Jones Indices, 2022).

The natural temptation is to address this shortcoming by creating a 'sustainable label' for firms or funds. Evidence from the retail sector, however, suggests that sustainable labelling can increase buyer confusion rather than reduce it (Grunert, Hieke and Wills, 2014; Ipsos and London Economics, n.d.). Consumers are not sufficiently familiar with the methodology behind the labelling to fully grasp it, and their own values may differ from those espoused by the standard setters. Consequently, it seems unlikely that terminology – such as the European Union's Sustainable Finance Disclosure Regulation (SFDR), which awards financial products the catchy labels of either Article 6, 8 or 9 (yes, there is no lucky number 7 in this context) – will become discussion topics at the local public house or bridge game.

One potential opportunity for aiding retail investors is to increase the transparency of information to help them make their own informed choices. Nutritional information labels found on food packaging – a consistent, straightforward listing of fat, protein and salt content – is the analogue here. For financial products, we can envisage a set of simple, understandable disclosures on popular sustainable topics such as climate, diversity and waste, issued in a consistent format across companies and funds. The principle would expand on conventional retail investor practices that currently make use of a limited number of financial metrics, such as price-to-earnings ratios, dividend yields and return on equity.

Steps are already being taken in this direction. The groundwork for disclosures about how companies *act* is being laid by the Sustainability Accounting Standards Board (SASB) in its merger into the International Financial Reporting Standards Foundation (IFRS). Meanwhile, the EU's sustainable legislative package includes the

Taxonomy for Sustainable Activities. This classification system publishes lists and thresholds for environmentally sustainable economic activities, essentially defining sustainability for what companies *do*.

An optimal playing field for retail investors will require further regulatory support as well as significant simplification to ensure commerciality.

> OPPORTUNITIES
>
> Seek a limited number of sustainable disclosures applicable to companies and investment products to help investors understand exactly what they are purchasing and enable them to choose the instruments appropriately.

Institutional investors

There is an adage that what investors dislike most is uncertainty (Ellsberg, 1961). Yet when it comes to sustainable investing, uncertainty, as we made clear above, abounds. The crux of the problem for institutional investors, who shift huge sums of capital and have considerable expertise, is the lack of clear definitions and measurement metrics. The result for them is confusion on the part of their clients, a failure to capture the full commercial potential of the discipline and a perverse incentive to lower standards and inflate the figure for sustainable investing assets under management.

The solution we envision relies on incentivizing institutional investors by showcasing the value of their processes and expertise. For it is the latter that justifies their fees. Institutional investors need shared definitions of sustainable investing strategies so that customers can compare like with like and be impressed (or not) with a given institution's approach.

The exact definitions themselves are of secondary importance to their establishment. We do see potential avenues for progress. They could encompass some of the dynamics we've discussed in this chapter, such as enumerating the differences between what a company does and how it acts; clarifying whether these assessments are viewed relative to sector peers or in absolute terms; and detailing whether it is the investor or the company that is generating positive impact.

Alternately, the improvement could be as simple as categorizing fund strategies according to the IIF's proposal as:

- those that 'exclude' securities on sustainable grounds;
- those that 'include' sustainable information to make better investment decisions and;
- those that seek to deliver, and can demonstrate, real-world 'impact' through their investments (IIF, 2019).

The likeliest push will come from regulators. The most advanced effort, as of 2021, is enactment of the EU's Sustainable Finance Disclosure Regulation (SFDR). The definitions are non-commercially called Article 6, Article 8 and Article 9. Article 6 has no sustainability integration. Article 8 broadly resembles the IIF's 'include' terminology. And Article 9 products 'target sustainability as an objective', combining the IIF's 'impact' terminology with thematic funds, i.e., focusing on what companies *do* (Robeco, n.d.). The regulation is immature and investors will interpret the standards in different ways, as evidenced by the vast discrepancy in labelling choices among large asset managers. For example, as of 2022, less than 15 per cent of BlackRock's assets are in the Article 8 and Article 9 category, while almost 75 per cent of JP Morgan's are (Morningstar, 2022b).

Once armed with a consistent set of definitions, institutional investors can spend less time clarifying what they are talking about and more time showcasing their capabilities. This will better align client needs with institutional investor delivery and likely facilitate greater innovation and real-world impact.

OPPORTUNITIES

Align to a single set of clear definitions to describe different sustainable investing strategies.

Regulators

Regulators set the 'rules of the game' and can have considerable real-world impact through the incentives they create. Given that the sustainable investing industry has failed to self-regulate, the answer to the fundamental question 'What is sustainable investing?' unfortunately falls to regulators to mediate and resolve.

Such is the diversity of sustainable investing practices that any regulatory proposal is certain not to please everyone. Yet regulators can take heart from the instructive example of nutritional information labels, as discussed above. Not all interested parties applaud the labels: the orange juice industry would have fiercely advocated for Vitamin C to be included, while the sardine lobby (we truly hope such a body exists!) would have pushed hard for Omega 3's inclusion. Yet despite their shortcomings, the labels provide a robust, consistent basis for consumer comparison.

Faced with this challenge, regulators have the opportunity to draw up minimum standards based on principles rather than all-encompassing, rules-based taxonomies. A small number of well-defined definitions for what is expected from a given sustainable approach (leader, thematic, etc.), combined with a requirement that all sustainable funds disclose certain information and corporations follow suit by making a limited number of mandatory disclosures, would go a long way to assisting retail investor decision-making and clearing up the current disordered state of affairs.

To ensure that such principles align properly with regulatory responsibilities – i.e., that they promote fair industry competition and protect retail investors from mis-selling – simplicity, as with all regulatory actions, should be valued and prioritized.

Any regulatory program also necessitates strict, able enforcement. Financial regulators can take inspiration from the increasingly tough line that the EU has adopted with so-called 'Big Tech'. In 2018, Google was hit with a $5 billion fine for allegedly forcing smartphone manufacturers using its Android operating system to pre-install its search and browser apps on devices. A $2.7 billion penalty was also levied on the tech giant in 2017 for allegedly abusing its dominance of the search engine market. Earlier, in 2009, Intel was fined $1.45 billion for reportedly paying computer manufacturers to delay products that contained chips produced by rival firms (Newell, 2019).

The first major regulatory greenwashing probe of a financial firm was initiated in 2021. The US Securities Exchange Commission (SEC) and the German Federal Financial Supervisory Authority, better known as BaFin, investigated the German asset manager DWS. The original greenwashing accusations were raised by a former DWS employee, Group Sustainability Officer Desiree Fixler.

DWS, in its rebuttal press release, referenced two different proprietary classifications of sustainable assets (one that encompasses a much larger amount of assets than the other) (DWS, 2021). The firm explained the figures it disclosed by referring both to SFDR and GSIA standards. While the nuances of the case are beyond the scope of our discussion here, the episode highlights the absence of standardized definitions and underscores the need for regulators to act at a system level rather than doing so firm by firm.

OPPORTUNITIES

Define a handful of definitions for what is expected from a given sustainable approach. Mandate a limited number of corporate disclosures supported by strong enforcement.

References

Berk, J B and van Binsbergen, J H (2021) The impact of impact investing, *SSRN Electronic Journal*, doi.org/10.2139/ssrn.3909166 (archived at https://perma.cc/42QL-B96N)

Blackburn, N (2022) 16 funds rebrand as sustainable, but how green are they? *Wealth Manager*, citywire.com/wealth-manager/news/16-funds-rebrand-as-sustainable-but-how-green-are-they/a2379823 (archived at https://perma.cc/U5YY-UX84)

BlackRock (no date) ESG investing at BlackRock, www.blackrock.com/ch/individual/en/themes/sustainable-investing (archived at https://perma.cc/9R7M-9FDL)

Burton, J (2021) The world's top 10 wealth management firms by AUM, *Wealth Professional*, www.wealthprofessional.ca/news/industry-news/the-worlds-top-10-wealth-management-firms-by-aum/355658 (archived at https://perma.cc/9U3E-PNFX)

DWS (2021) Media information, www.dws.com/globalassets/cio/dam-us/pdfs/news-and-press/dws-statement-on-current-coverage.pdf?v=6147153 (archived at https://perma.cc/478Y-CC98)

Ellsberg, D (1961) Risk, ambiguity, and the savage axioms, *The Quarterly Journal of Economics*, 75(4), pp 643–669, doi.org/10.2307/1884324 (archived at https://perma.cc/9AW6-TKRJ)

Musk, E [@elonmusk] (2022) Exxon is rated top ten best in world for environment, social & governance (ESG) by S&P 500, while Tesla didn't make the list! ESG is a scam, It has been weaponized by phony social justice warriors, [Twitter] 18 May, twitter.com/elonmusk/status/1526958110023245829 (archived at https://perma.cc/66VK-SRYS)

Fink, L (2020) A fundamental reshaping of finance, BlackRock, www.blackrock.com/us/individual/larry-fink-ceo-letter (archived at https://perma.cc/B4BV-8PTA)

Fletcher, L and Oliver, J (2022) Green investing: the risk of a new mis-selling scandal, *Financial Times*, 20 February, www.ft.com/content/ae78c05a-0481-4774-8f9b-d3f02e4f2c6f (archived at https://perma.cc/VYA2-DHUV)

Grunert, K G, Hieke, S and Wills, J (2014) Sustainability labels on food products: Consumer motivation, understanding and use, *Food Policy*, 44, pp 177–89, doi.org/10.1016/j.foodpol.2013.12.001 (archived at https://perma.cc/ME5Q-WJ54)

GSIA (2021) Global Sustainable Investment Review 2020, www.gsi-alliance.org/wp-content/uploads/2021/08/GSIR-20201.pdf (archived at https://perma.cc/B53D-Y9LT)

Hawker, E (2022) How green are recycled funds? ESG Investor, 9 February, www.esginvestor.net/how-green-are-recycled-funds/ (archived at https://perma.cc/MK29-JTDK)

Heeb, F and Kölbel, J (2020) The Investor's guide to impact: Evidence-based advice for investors who want to change the world, Universität Zürich: The Center for Sustainable Finance and Private Wealth, https://www.csp.uzh.ch/dam/jcr:ab4d648c-92cd-4b6d-8fc8-5bc527b0c4d9/CSP_Investors%20per%20cent20Guide%20per%20cent20to%20per%20cent20Impact_21_10_2020_spreads.pdf (archived at https://perma.cc/HSF4-7N27)

HSBC (2019) Sustainable Finance and Investing Survey 2019: Markets alert to the environment and society, www.gbm.hsbc.com/insights/sustainable-financing/sustainable-financing-and-investing-survey-2019 (archived at https://perma.cc/5CFF-AUF6)

IIF (2019) The case for simplifying sustainable investment terminology, Institute of International Finance, https://www.iif.com/Publications/ID/3633/The-Case-for-Simplifying-Sustainable-Investment-Terminology (archived at https://perma.cc/P34F-5PX9)

Ipsos and London Economics (no date) Consumer market study on the functioning of voluntary food labelling schemes for consumers in the European Union EAHC/FWC/2012 86 04, ec.europa.eu/info/sites/default/files/food-labelling-scheme-final-report_en.pdf (archived at https://perma.cc/Z8NJ-NQLU)

Jessop, S (2021) Sustainable investments account for more than a third of global assets, Reuters, 19 July, www.reuters.com/business/sustainable-business/sustainable-investments-account-more-than-third-global-assets-2021-07-18/ (archived at https://perma.cc/NX5X-DH2F)

Johnson, S (2022) Thematic funds triple share of global investments in a decade, *Financial Times*, 11 April, www.ft.com/content/1db0f968-2175-4434-ba65-c57632b51e02 (archived at https://perma.cc/S9KK-XQNG)

Jones, M (2018) Global perspectives on responsible investing, AON, www.aon.com/getmedia/8bd5172a-ab8b-4aee-aadc-10b59aba426a/Global-Perspectives-On-Responsible-Investing.aspx. (archived at https://perma.cc/7AJK-CLE3)

Kamal, R (2014) New evidence from S&P 500 index deletions, *The International Journal of Business and Finance Research*, 8(2), pp 1–10, www.theibfr2.com/RePEc/ibf/ijbfre/ijbfr-v8n2-2014/IJBFR-V8N2-2014-1.pdf (archived at https://perma.cc/2ED8-SRBR)

Kerber, R and Jin, H (2022) Tesla cut from S&P 500 ESG Index, and Elon Musk tweets his fury, Reuters, 19 May, www.reuters.com/business/sustainable-business/tesla-removed-sp-500-esg-index-autopilot-discrimination-concerns-2022-05-18/ (archived at https://perma.cc/J52M-98TW)

Kim, S and Yoon, A (2022) Analyzing active fund managers' commitment to ESG: Evidence from the United Nations Principles for Responsible Investment, Management Science, doi.org/10.1287/mnsc.2022.4394 (archived at https://perma.cc/2R26-ZWBU)

Longman, M (2019) Friends: were Ross & Rachel really on a break? Therapists, psychics, & fans weigh in, Refinery 29, 20 September, www.refinery29.com/en-us/2019/09/8454587/friends-we-were-on-a-break-ross-cheat-on-rachel (archived at https://perma.cc/LYU9-7RUQ)

Morningstar (2022a) Global Sustainable Fund Flows Report, www.morningstar.com/lp/global-esg-flows (archived at https://perma.cc/5P5C-VJBE)

Morningstar (2022b) SFDR Article 8 and Article 9 funds: Q1 2022 in review, www.morningstar.com/en-uk/lp/sfdr-article8-article9 (archived at https://perma.cc/6VD9-74EQ)

Newell, M (2019) Top 5 largest fines levied on tech companies by the European Commission, TNE, 18 February, www.theneweconomy.com/business/top-5-largest-fines-levied-on-tech-companies-by-the-european-commission (archived at https://perma.cc/Q38J-TBPD)

Palmer, B (2013) One Catholic, Two Catholics, Three Catholics …, Slate, 20 March, slate.com/news-and-politics/2013/03/counting-catholics-how-do-demographers-estimate-the-american-catholic-population.html (archived at https://perma.cc/WR8X-26V8)

Quinio, A (2022) Morningstar cuts 1,200 funds from 'sustainable' list, *Financial Times*, 10 February, www.ft.com/content/9cf8c788-6cad-4737-bc2a-2e85ac4aef7d (archived at https://perma.cc/D9BC-GX8V)

Robeco (no date) Article 6, 8 and 9 funds, www.robeco.com/ch/en/key-strengths/sustainable-investing/glossary/article-6-8-and-9-funds.html (archived at https://perma.cc/CUV7-PVY8)

Schneider, L (1985) *Ulirnaisigutiit: an Inuktitut-English dictionary of Northern Quebec, Labrador and Eastern Arctic dialects*, Presses de l'Université Laval, Québec.

Schroders (2017) Demystifying negative screens: The full implications of ESG exclusions, www.schroders.com/en/sysglobalassets/digital/insights/2018/thought-leadership/demystifying-negative-screens---the-full-implications-of-esg-exclusions.pdf (archived at https://perma.cc/59HB-VBA8)

Smithers, A (2014) GCSE Trends 1988-2014, Centre for Education and Employment Research, University of Buckingham, www.buckingham.ac.uk/wp-content/uploads/2019/02/GCSE14AGS.pdf (archived at https://perma.cc/9WWB-8ULL)

S&P Dow Jones Indices (2022) S&P ESG Index Series Methodology, www.spglobal.com/spdji/en/documents/methodologies/methodology-sp-esg-index-series.pdf (archived at https://perma.cc/H7FT-8QA4)

S&P Dow Jones Indices (no date) S&P 500®, www.spglobal.com/spdji/en/indices/equity/sp-500/#overview (archived at https://perma.cc/S7RL-QKAT)

Strathern, M (1997) 'Improving ratings': audit in the British university system, *European Review*, 5(3), pp 305–321, doi.org/10.1002/(SICI)1234-981X(199707)5:3<305::AID-EURO184>3.0.CO;2-4 (archived at https://perma.cc/92FV-MYRU)

Sustainalytics (no date) Global Access, globalaccess.sustainalytics.com/#/login (archived at https://perma.cc/6XWE-TQR9)

Teoh, S H, Welch, I and Wazzan, C P (1999) The effect of socially activist investment policies on the financial markets: Evidence from the South African boycott, *The Journal of Business*, 72(1), pp 35–89, doi.org/10.1086/209602 (archived at https://perma.cc/Z42Q-PSTM)

The Economist (2021) Why people forget that less is often more, 16 April, www.economist.com/science-and-technology/2021/04/14/why-people-forget-that-less-is-often-more (archived at https://perma.cc/GLN9-NCDT)

Thinking Ahead Institute (2021) Top 500 managers see assets hit record $119.5 trillion, www.thinkingaheadinstitute.org/news/article/top-500-managers-see-assets-hit-record-119-5-trillion/ (archived at https://perma.cc/H3XL-3TCJ)

UBS (2018) UBS Investor Watch: Return on Values, www.ubs.com/content/dam/ubs/microsites/ubs-investor-watch/IW-09-2018/return-on-value-global-report-final.pdf (archived at https://perma.cc/W2Z9-SNGT)

UBS (no date) Sustainable Investing, www.ubs.com/global/en/wealth-management/sustainable-investing.html (archived at https://perma.cc/825U-BV5M)

UK Government (no date) Why have GCSEs in England changed, newgcses.campaign.gov.uk/ (archived at https://perma.cc/SX6J-9WFW)

UN PRI (2020) Signatories delisted for not meeting the minimum requirements, Principles for Responsible Investment, www.unpri.org/reporting-and-assessment/signatories-delisted-for-not-meeting-the-minimum-requirements/6480.article (archived at https://perma.cc/CBQ7-5BVW)

UN PRI (no date a) What is responsible investment? Principles for Responsible Investment, www.unpri.org/an-introduction-to-responsible-investment/what-is-responsible-investment/4780.article (archived at https://perma.cc/M2LB-2BMY)

UN PRI (no date b) What is the PRI? Principles for Responsible Investment, www.unpri.org/about-us/about-the-pri (archived at https://perma.cc/H6KB-5HJE)

Webb, D (2022) SFDR reclassifications raise 'legitimate' greenwashing concerns, warns Morningstar, *Responsible Investor*, 8 February, www.responsible-investor.com/sfdr-reclassifications-raise-legitimate-greenwashing-concerns-warns-morningstar/ (archived at https://perma.cc/MB7J-Z432)

Wolcott, R C (2016) Don't be tyrannized by old metrics, *Harvard Business Review*, 23 September, hbr.org/2016/09/dont-be-tyrannized-by-old-metrics (archived at https://perma.cc/V662-VZJS)

02

Sustainable data and ESG ratings

Introduction

When we financial types want a new suit we visit a tailor. Fortunately, we happen to know a great guy in Hong Kong from when we used to live there! He uses a floppy tape measure to size, in inches, our chest and neck circumferences, shoulder widths, and a dozen other critical measurements. Mr Cheng is meticulous and the information about our bodies that he collects is fully standardized and consistent.

Possessed of individual data points, what Mr Cheng does next differs depending on the client. James might ask for two centimetres extra on his left cuff to accommodate the watch his ex-girlfriend bought him. Others (not James...) might opt for a tailored waist to show off their toned physique. These choices are personal and the output created by the consistently collected data points will differ from person to person.

With sustainable investments things are a little different. Firstly, financial tailors can't agree on what should be measured. Even when they do, they often use non-standardized units, and many measurements may be missing entirely. Consequently, when financial tailors work with sustainability data, a large number of assumptions, estimates and approximations are required to create something that just about, metaphorically, resembles a suit.

This chapter kicks off with a section that surveys 'How sustainable data originates, is measured and is disclosed'. We look first at the obstacles that arise when originating sustainability data, which is frequently self-disclosed by corporations and often lacks third-party audit or assurance.

We move on to the issue of measurement and, again, difficulties abound. Companies often measure things immaterial to the future of their business. When they do measure useful things, the results are often given in non-standardized units or with a unique scope. Comparison of the data reported by one company to that of another becomes problematic for investors. The final part of this section concerns disclosure. We cover the surfeit of disclosure standards that compete for corporate and investor attention, and the hurdles this creates.

With the fundamentals of sustainable data established, we proceed to a discussion on its use. Often, data is aggregated into environmental, social and governance (ESG) ratings. Appropriately, this section is entitled 'How sustainable data is aggregated to form ESG ratings'. We start by considering the inputs – aggregation methodologies that combine sustainability data into ESG ratings. Next, we look at the outputs: we review how and why ratings and scores diverge among providers. The final part of this section drills down into whether the sustainable data ecosystem and ESG ratings create real-world impact and whether they catalyse positive change for people and the planet.

Before we tackle the final section, we pause to include an exclusive interview with Professor Robert G Eccles, whose career in, and contribution to, sustainability are unmatched. He was a tenured professor at Harvard Business School and is, as of 2022, the Visiting Professor of Management Practice at Saïd Business School, University of Oxford. As the founding chairman of the Sustainability Accounting Standards Board (SASB), he co-founded the International Integrated Reporting Council (IIRC) and, as of 2021, has served as chair of Kohlberg Kravis Roberts & Co, L P's (KKR) Sustainability Expert Advisory Council.

The final section peers into the future and considers 'The potential opportunities and how we might get there'. The ecosystem of sustainable data and ratings has developed over thirty years. As of 2022 it was worth, according to Substantive Research, one billion US dollars a year (Carrodus, 2021). When contemplating the opportunities this presents, we look for ways to increase consistency and align incentives for multiple stakeholders. In all cases, we take inspiration from existing embryonic practices.

- The first opportunity calls for simplicity to aid retail investors. We borrow from the practice of placing nutritional information on food packaging and want to see financial offerings advertise a limited number of commonly produced sustainable data points.
- The second opportunity acknowledges that institutional investors require deeper, more complex datasets and urges support for a single sustainability reporting standard. We highlight the positives of the International Sustainability Standards Board (ISSB), formed from the merger of the Sustainability Accounting Standards Board (SASB) into the International Financial Reporting Standards Foundation (IFRS).
- The final opportunity focuses on corporations and goes further. In addition to supporting ISSB, we would like sustainability information integrated into conventional financial accounts and a monetary value placed on corporations' real-world impacts, both positive and negative.

How sustainable data originates, is measured and is disclosed

Data originations: To infinity and beyond

The 21st century has been characterized by unprecedented access to data. As of 2021, over four billion people own or make use of a smartphone (Mawston, 2021). They can browse a great deal of humankind's knowledge and data in the palm of their hand (though many still choose to look at cat videos instead).

Data is big business. And the amount of data in the world has been growing at an exponential rate. In 2010, humankind had produced two zettabytes of data, a figure that rose to 44 zettabytes by 2020 (Raconteur, n.d.). For context, a zettabyte is 10^{21} bytes: if a byte was represented by a pound or euro coin, a single zettabyte stack of coins would stretch from Earth to Alpha Centuri and back 300 times (Vopson, 2021).

Despite the explosion in the availability and storage of information and its ever-increasing role in decision making, sustainable data has lagged behind. Largely self-reported, unregulated and confined to an annual update cycle, it is highly heterogeneous. And while there is plenty of it, sustainability data often creates greater confusion than clarity.

The good news is that corporations are increasingly originating sustainability information. KPMG reports that, among the largest 250 companies worldwide, 96 per cent issued a sustainability report in 2020. This figure was up from 83 per cent in 2008 and 35 per cent in 1999 (Threlfall et al, 2020). This tsunami of publications generates an astronomical number of data points. Refinitiv, a sustainable data provider and aggregator, proudly states that it draws on up to 500 different metrics per company (Refinitiv, 2020). The figure is so large that an unedited dataset is unlikely to be digestible by, or useful to, the typical investor.

Part of the reason so many data points are originated is because sustainable data is mostly reported by companies themselves. This raises several questions about objectivity, conflicts of interest and reliability. While voluntary disclosure frameworks, such as the UN-backed Global Reporting Initiative (GRI) and the Sustainability Accounting Standards Board (SASB), exist, there is little in the way of regulatory-required sustainability reporting in much of the world as of 2022.

Research from the Investor Responsibility Research Centre Institute (IRRCI) found that 97 per cent of S&P 500 company sustainability reports chose 'customization and a unique style over following any one reporting framework closely'. Furthermore, about 25 per cent of US companies 'did not reference a specific framework' at all (Kwon, 2018). As a result, sustainability reports vary wildly in form and substance. Their length (not necessarily a proxy for quality) tells the story. Work by Teneo, a CEO advisory firm, found that the sustainability reports put out by large US companies in 2021 ranged from 12 to 243 pages (Teneo, 2021). Essentially, companies are choosing what they want to report.

Sustainable data can originate in many different places, and company practices vary greatly. A 2021 report by the International Organization of Securities Commissions (IOSCO) found that sustainable data may be spread across multiple reports, for example, the annual report, corporate sustainability report and individual webpages (IOSCO, 2021). By originating and publishing data in different places, the risk arises that interested parties will not be able to collect all relevant information.

With self-reported data scattered in multiple locations and issued without reference to common templates, it is no surprise that the data comes with only limited assurances. Superficially, the use of third-party verification has been rising. According to KPMG, 71 per cent of the world's largest 250 companies undertook some form of external verification of their figures in 2020, up from 40 per cent in 2008 (Threlfall et al, 2020). But digging into the details reveals that assurances are typically limited.

The IRRCI found that 90 per cent of assurances dealt only with partial data. While greenhouse-gas emissions were verified most frequently, there remains significant ambiguity due to varying corporate language and inconsistent levels of transparency (Kwon, 2018). Consequently, investors can have only limited confidence that the sustainability data being self-reported is accurate. Should it be erroneously reported, in most jurisdictions, investors have little recourse and the company itself faces few consequences.

Interestingly, investors and executives differ on whether sustainability reports should receive the same scrutiny as conventional financial statements. According to a McKinsey survey, 67 per cent of surveyed investors said that 'sustainability reports should undergo full audit, similar to a financial audit'. Just 36 per cent of corporate executives agreed (Bernow et al, 2019).

Sustainable reporting, it is clear, compares unfavourably with conventional financial reporting. While in the latter a degree of interpretation exists for such elements as the timing of revenue recognition, current sustainable reporting remains in its infancy and is beset by conflicts of interest and operational risks.

Data measurement: Different things get measured in different ways

When a tennis player sits down with a potential sponsor the two sides may differ in their assessments of the player's marketing worth. The player may point to their increased win percentage that year, while the sponsor nitpicks at their lack of Chinese language skills, which would be useful in penetrating the lucrative Far East market. Even if they both see eye to eye on topics, they may measure success in different ways. The player might cite their exceptional victory at the US Open, while the sponsor might remind them of their mid-match profanity-laden rant at the umpire, which ended up being replayed on sports shows worldwide.

When it comes to sustainable data, things are eerily similar. Despite the aforementioned abundance of reporting, two companies rarely report on the same topic, let alone use the same format. So comparing them and integrating them into financial modelling is demanding.

The challenge begins with what is reported. A financial firm may be able to accurately measure its water consumption, but this data is not very useful to investors. The figures are unlikely to be large or a good indicator of the firm's financial health. For a fast-fashion retailer or a brewer, by contrast, water data is highly meaningful. An investor would want to understand not only how much water is being used in operations, but also the water stress that exists where production facilities are located. Such information can indicate the extent of operational efficiency, risk management and potential constraints on organic growth.

The scale of the challenge that publishing immaterial data points poses is highlighted by Danske Bank's analysis of 100 Nordic companies. The Danske analysts identified over 20,000 individual sustainable data points, of which just 28 per cent were deemed material to an investment case. Much of corporate reporting is largely pointless for a financial audience, it appears (Hakola, Poll and Vannefors, 2020).

Furthermore, despite the blizzard of data, many key indicators still went missing. Just 17 per cent of firms disclosed enough information to enable stand-alone analysis on all material sustainability issues, Danske found. Interestingly, better disclosure rates often prevail in industries considered suspect in terms of sustainability, such as the mining sector (Hakola, Poll and Vannefors, 2020). The Sustainability Accounting Standards Board (SASB) reinforced Danske's findings about the limited validity to end investors of the sustainability data being reported. SASB analysis concluded that companies use 'generic boilerplate language' and 'vague, non-specific information' more than 50 per cent of the time (SASB, 2017). Quantity is not the same as quality.

Danske's researchers shed light on how sustainable data is often useless for comparing firms. On average, 50 per cent of the data produced is not suitable for comparative analysis, they found, because it is in some way idiosyncratic. When one attempts to use such datasets in practice further issues emerge. Data points that have the potential to be comparable often suffer from 'scope mismatches' – the same topic is reported in different ways or to different extents. Scope mismatches force analysts to estimate, extrapolate or assume in an attempt to align data. At the end of this arduous process, Danske's analysts concluded that, for any given sector or topic, only 1–10 per cent of them yielded truly comparable data for all required data points (Hakola, Poll and Vannefors, 2020).

Danske Bank's disillusioning findings are confirmed by investment bank Goldman Sachs. Goldman found that across the global equity universe the single most common ESG metric (the existence of a 'community involvement policy') was only available for 85 per cent of companies. The most common numeric metric (the 'percentage of women employees') was available for just 58 per cent of companies, and only 20 per cent of the approximately 180 metrics supplied by Goldman's data provider had a disclosure rate, across companies, in excess of 50 per cent. Concerningly, Goldman's analysis was conducted on a cleaned dataset, where the provider had already adjusted the data to minimize scope mismatches (Tylenda, 2020).

CHALLENGES WHEN COMPARING COMPANIES

To illustrate how arduous it is to compare companies, let's take two real world examples. The first looks at carbon emissions by technology giants Apple and Samsung and was first highlighted by Deutsche Bank (Reid, Templeman and Mahtani, 2018). Under the Greenhouse Gas Protocols, greenhouse gas (GHG) emissions are categorized into 'scopes'. Scope 1 captures direct GHG emissions – those produced on site and by vehicle fleets, for instance. Scope 2 includes indirect GHG emissions that result from the consumption of purchased electricity. Scope 3 includes other indirect emissions within the value chain, such as those generated by the production of purchased materials, outsourced activities and waste disposal (Greenhouse Gas Protocol, n.d.).

Given the difficulty of measuring Scope 3 emissions, many corporations fail to report them. MSCI estimates that less than 20 per cent of listed companies worldwide lay out Scope 3 data, despite, in the typical case, over 70 per cent of a company's attributable carbon emissions belonging to Scope 3 (MSCI, 2020). In the case of Apple and Samsung, Apple in 2017 appeared to be 150 times more environmentally friendly than Samsung – but only if Scope 1 and 2 emissions alone were considered. Many sustainable investors, as well as popular financial benchmarks, solely use Scope 1 and 2 data, so their willingness to invest in Samsung would have been materially influenced by the reported figures. Yet if Scope 3 emissions had been factored in, emissions that took account of Apple's outsourcing operations in China, the two firms would have had approximately the same levels of GHG intensity, which is logical given their similar operating models.

The second example centres on gender diversity in the fast-moving consumer goods (FMCG) sector. While certain sustainability topics are clearly sector-specific and subject to broad interpretation, such as Scope 3 emissions calculations, others, such as gender diversity, should theoretically permit straightforward, consistent reporting. Yet due to a lack of standards and protocols this isn't the case in practice.

Analysis by the World Economic Forum of 15 peers in the FMCG industry revealed that, collectively, companies reported 22 different, non-comparable employee gender classifications. Of these, 16 were for equivalents of senior management. A further seven geographic classifications, 'all of which were structured differently', made comparison impossible. Interestingly, the lack of consistency and comparability occurred despite 13 of the 15 firms referencing use of the Global Reporting Initiative (GRI) standards to disclose their data (World Economic Forum, 2019).

Data disclosure: There should only be one

Many of us have experienced the pain associated with signing up for – or worse cancelling – a new service or product. We first enter our details into an online form, only to be told that we must verify our identity via physical means. We wait a week and receive paper forms in the post that request information nearly identical to what we provided in our electronic submission. After carefully filling in these forms using CAPS and a black ballpoint pen, we finally receive a written code that grants us access to the online portal, where we need to create a user profile and again input many of our personal details, now for the third time.

For corporations seeking to disclose sustainability data, a similar experience is par for the course. They publish extensive sustainability reports but neglect to standardize the information. So some stakeholders, such as third-party data aggregation firms, request that bespoke questionnaires be filled in. The combination of multiple standards and multiple data seekers creates a diverse if not chaotic reporting architecture.

In addition to the aforementioned Global Reporting Initiative (GRI) and Sustainability Accounting Standards Board (SASB), numerous other standards exist. They include the Taskforce on Climate-Related Financial Disclosures (TCFD), rankings and accolades such as the Dow Jones Sustainability Indices (DJSI), and stock exchange-specific requirements mandated by dozens of bourses from Botswana to Vietnam (SSE initiative, n.d.).

According to The Reporting Exchange, an online tool developed to help corporations navigate the landscape of sustainability reporting requirements, the number of voluntary reporting frameworks, mandatory reporting requirements, methodologies and protocols for company measurement and disclosure of sustainable information exceeds 2,000. Even if we only take a tiny sample of just nine voluntary reporting frameworks that The Reporting Exchange identified, there are more than 1,400 potential indicators that companies could use to disclose their sustainability performance (Arabesque, n.d.).

It hardly comes as a surprise then that corporate managements feel exasperated by the current situation. According to the IOSCO survey, the majority of corporate respondents 'expressed concerns' that data requests are overly time-consuming (IOSCO, 2021).

Furthermore, a McKinsey survey revealed that 58 per cent of corporate executives 'agreed' or 'strongly agreed' with the statement: 'There should be one sustainability-reporting standard.' This discontent is shared by investors. When asked by McKinsey what the 'top challenges associated with current sustainability-reporting practices' were, their most frequent response was 'inconsistency, incomparability, or lack of alignment in standards' (Bernow et al, 2019). A damning assessment indeed.

Nonetheless, some frameworks are more popular than others. Many corporations do in fact reference the GRI, albeit with fluctuating adherence. Data compiled via a GRI and SASB-sponsored 2021 survey found that, in a sample of over 130 corporates, 39 per cent were making efforts to reference both standards, 33 per cent focused solely on the GRI and 10 per cent solely on the SASB (GRI and SASB, 2021).

The GRI benefits from its longevity, having been launched in 2000. It is commonly considered a multi-stakeholder (or 'double materiality') reporting framework: the data it requests often concerns environmental and social topics not of direct relevance to profit-seeking investors. So its figures may interest some stakeholders while not being financially material to the investment case (Sustainability Knowledge Group, 2021).

SASB's growth has been remarkable since it published its 77 industry-specific standards in 2018. SASB has focused on the disclosures most relevant in determining the value of a firm ('single materiality'). As such, it has found favour with investors, most notably BlackRock CEO Larry Fink, who, in his 2020 letter to

CEOs, stated, 'BlackRock believes that the Sustainability Accounting Standards Board (SASB) provides a clear set of standards for reporting sustainability information across a wide range of issues, from labour practices to data privacy to business ethics' (Fink, 2020).

As of 2022, SASB is merging into the International Financial Reporting Standards Foundation's (IFRS) International Sustainability Standards Board (ISSB). The alignment between SASB and one of the two major global accounting standards will likely ensure that subsequent iterations of SASB's standards continue to gain in popularity.

A third noteworthy framework is the Taskforce on Climate-Related Financial Disclosures (TCFD). It was released in 2017, supported by the G20 Financial Stability Board, and chaired by billionaire financial data pioneer Michael Bloomberg (TCFD, n.d.). TCFD has ridden the climate wave generated by the likes of Greta Thunberg and benefited from the advanced state, relative to other sustainability topics, of GHG emission reporting.

TCFD has a narrow focus: to establish 'climate-related financial disclosures that would be useful to investors and others in understanding material risks'. As of 2020, across its eleven requested disclosures, and based on a sample size of over 1,500 of the world's largest public companies, 50 per cent of them disclosed in alignment with at least three of the eleven TCFD recommendations. Reporting frequency for each recommended disclosure ranged from 13 per cent to 53 per cent of companies, an increase of eight percentage points on average from the 2019 assessment (TCFD, 2021).

TCFD now cites more than 2,500 supporters, of which over 1,000 are financial institutions. Perhaps most importantly for its future adoption, TCFD is increasingly being enshrined in current or forthcoming regulation. It is becoming a mandatory reporting requirement for many stock exchanges and territories, including the United Kingdom and Switzerland (TCFD, 2021).

A final action worthy of note is the EU's plans for the Corporate Sustainability Reporting Directive (CSRD). The CSRD updates the Non-Financial Reporting Direction (NFRD), among other legislation. By the late 2020s, it will require in the neighbourhood of 50,000 companies to disclose information on strategy, policies, risks, targets and due diligence related to environmental, social and employee matters, respect for human rights, anti-corruption and bribery issues, and diversity (European Commission, 2021a; CDSB, n.d.).

In sum, from an outside vantage point it is easy to look at the data disclosure landscape and want to demand, in a (mis)quote of the 1986 fantasy epic *Highlander*, that 'there should only be one' standard. In practice, though, differing stakeholder incentives make alignment tough to achieve. Corporations want to continue to select metrics that paint their operations in a flattering light, while standard setters often argue that their solution is optimal.

Tellingly, some investors also favour a proliferation of standards. When McKinsey inquired about the potential for streamlining sustainability reporting, 34 per cent of respondents said that harmonizing standards would weaken their proprietary insights or reduce the differentiation of their investment products (Bernow et al, 2019). Therefore, as the regulatory and voluntary standard setters, independent data aggregators, rankers and accolade givers all go on jostling for position, neither corporates nor investors are likely to enjoy any certainty about corporate sustainability reporting anytime soon.

How sustainable data is aggregated to form ESG ratings

Rating inputs: Construction challenges

The 2022 incarnation of the wildly successful EA Sports computer game franchise 'FIFA' gives Lionel Messi a headline rating of 93 out of 100, making him the 'best player' in the game. His long-time rival, Christiano Ronaldo, rates a 91. So is the case closed? Lionel Messi is a better football player than Christiano Ronaldo?

Aficionados of the game will tell you that it's not that simple. Despite an inferior headline rating, the Portuguese playmaker beats his Argentine counterpart on Pace (87 vs 85), Physicality (75 vs 65), and Shooting (93 vs 92) (Goal, 2021). If your playing style requires any of these attributes you may regard Ronaldo as a superior addition to your virtual team. Furthermore, the overall ratings appear to have little relationship to six publicly visible attributes, where the simple average for both players is a measly 77. The explanation is that each player is actually rated on over 30 attributes, which are weighted differently depending on the position they play, with various other bonuses applied (Sohns, 2021).

This situation mirrors that of sustainable investing data. Investors, or third-party data aggregators, collect individual data points and aggregate them via proprietary methodologies into a single headline sustainability rating. The allure of crunching and reducing complex datasets to a single number is a strong one. Hence, aggregate sustainability ratings are popular within the financial industry, and providers such as MSCI and Sustainalytics operate sizeable businesses that employ hundreds of people (Sustainalytics, n.d.). These headline ratings can be integrated into financial models or strategies that exclude all firms with a sustainability rating lower, or higher, than 'X'.

Constructing headline sustainable ratings that distil into a single integer is not unproblematic. All of the issues raised in 'Chapter 1 – What is sustainable investing?' must be considered. Decisions have to be made about many issues. They include but are not limited to:

- the relative importance of how a company *acts* vs what it *does*;
- whether to sector neutralize the ratings or not;
- the extent to which financial materiality is employed;
- what is deemed financially material; and
- the integration or not of personal preference and values.

Depending on how each issue is resolved, companies will score better or worse, and the resulting conclusions as to 'what is sustainable?' will be very different.

Further challenges and considerations, not explicitly covered in Chapter 1, also arise. For example, because larger companies tend to have greater corporate sustainability resources, they are better placed to respond to reporting requests. Therefore, they often score higher on third-party sustainability ratings (Akgun, Mudge and Townsend,

2021). This phenomenon is a function of the emphasis that many ratings place on policy and disclosure rather than action.

Another difficulty stems from the lack of comparability between reported sustainability data. Shoehorning heterogeneous information from different corporations into consistent categories creates many issues. A prominent one is the problem of 'missing' data, termed a 'plague' by sustainable-focused asset manager NN Investment Partners (Reinders, Choong and Lanchenko, 2021). Missing data can be estimated, assigned a zero score to the detriment of the company, or given a sector-average figure, depending on the rating provider. Which only further complicates sustainable ratings and dilutes their value.

Rating outputs: Divergences between providers

Simon and I (James) disagreed about many things. When it came to beer he preferred XXXX (pronounced four-ex), a lager from his Australian homeland. He found it 'cost effective' and also appreciated the company's largesse: XXXX once gave him a free 'stubby holder' (a small sleeve made out of a wetsuit that keeps your beer cold). I, on the other hand, as a clichéd millennial, favour flavourful, overpriced India Pale Ales, ideally produced by a remote microbrewery whose hops, sourced from a hippy commune, are fertilized by genuine llama dung.

Both views are based on reasonably logical rationales. What makes beer good and bad might find some general agreement among drinkers, but the preference for a specific brand is an opinion, not a fact.

Because the entities that publish sustainable ratings face the numerous challenges outlined above, their outputs are also opinions, not facts. The ratings, like those of beer, tend to trend in the same direction, with, for example, controversial weapons normally being seen as 'bad' and renewable energy production as 'good'. But beyond broad trends, two rational individuals are well within their rights to form different opinions based on the same (or similar) datasets.

When comparing ratings released by providers, researchers find that the correlations of provider pairings are positive yet far from one. They usually rest in the 0.4–0.8 range (Bender and Maffina, 2022; Berg, Kölbel and Rigobon, 2022). This lack of agreement upsets some commentators (Mackintosh, 2018; Shifflett, 2021), perhaps due to the heuristic known as 'ambiguity aversion' first documented by Daniel Ellsberg (Ellsberg, 1961). Proponents of this view often cite credit ratings, whose correlations between providers get close to 1.0, as an optimal model (Mayor, 2019).

Credit ratings bear a similarity to sustainability ratings in that both share the word 'rating' and often use an AAA to D scale. But that is where the similarities end. A credit rating expresses the probability of default – a discrete, concrete event that can be forecast using historical observations and statistically significant financial data points (such as a free cash flow-to-interest payment ratio). By contrast, a sustainability rating measures intangible performance, is subject to the interpretation of individuals and relates to nothing discrete or historical; there is no standalone observation from which the statistical significance of variables can be derived.

WHAT THE REGULATORS SAY

While the differences in output may not be a problem *per se*, a 'fact finding' exercise from the International Organization of Securities Commissions (IOSCO) highlights the concerns. Chief among them are:

- a lack of alignment on definitions, including what the ratings intend to measure;
- a lack of transparency about the methodologies underpinning the ratings; and
- the need for better communication with the companies that are the subject of ESG ratings in order to ensure that the ESG ratings are based upon sound information (IOSCO, 2021).

These concerns are underpinned by an unfortunate reality. There are incentives for sustainable rating providers to be deliberately opaque in order to keep a proprietary hold on their methodology and revenue streams

(Bender and Maffina, 2022). Because of these challenges and the divergences, regulatory scrutiny on sustainable data aggregators will almost certainly increase in the coming years.

Digging deeper into the topic of divergence, we can add quantitative analysis to our qualitative explanations. An informative paper published by researchers at MIT Sloan School of Management decomposed the differences in sustainable headline ratings into three contributing factors, which we've renamed 'What', 'How' and 'Aggregation' for ease of understanding. The three terms are defined as follows:

- What: the chosen attributes that constitute sustainability performance.
- How: the chosen indicators that yield numerical measures of the attributes.
- Aggregation: the weighting that combines the indicators into a single rating.

When comparing the source of divergence between rating providers, the MIT researchers found that 'What' (37 per cent) and 'How' (50 per cent) were the dominant variables. Differences in aggregation methodologies accounted for just 13 per cent of the rating deviation (Berg, Kölbel and Rigobon, 2022). Their work implies that the differences arise not because two rational individuals assess a common dataset in different ways, but because the individuals are looking at very different datasets to begin with. The bulk of the difficulty, it appears, is 'upstream' and concerns how sustainable data is originated, measured and disclosed.

To understand the consequences for investors let's leave the MIT Sloan School of Management but stay in Boston and turn to Harvard Business School research. The latter work finds that greater ESG rating disagreement between providers is associated with investment return volatility and larger absolute price movements in stocks (Christensen, Serafeim and Sikochi, 2021). Although eye opening, this finding is quite logical.

The popular efficient market hypothesis theory states that security prices incorporate all known information (Fama, 1970). Hence, when information is unknown or subject to debate, market participants are likelier to be surprised or proven incorrect. They adjust their investment positions accordingly by buying or selling securities and creating price volatility.

The paper also identifies some interesting dynamics. The researchers reveal that 'greater ESG disclosure actually leads to greater ESG rating disagreement'. This finding appears counterintuitive at first reading. Having more information should create a fuller picture of a company's sustainability operations and leave less room for ambiguity and estimation. In reality, when it comes to sustainability data, less can be more, as a deluge of data muddies the water and creates a breeding ground for differing interpretations. This research complements the work of Danske Bank, which concluded that barely one-quarter of disclosed sustainability data points are material to an investment case (Hakola, Poll and Vannefors, 2020).

A third finding by the Harvard researchers is that rating providers often agree on topics such as the existence of policies and often disagree on the resulting company outputs and actions. Again, this finding conforms with logic and common sense. Discovering that a human rights policy exists doesn't require an abundance of skill. That said, even on 'straightforward' metrics, ESG rating providers can still disagree. The 'yes/no' answer to a basic governance data point – whether the CEO and chairperson are the same individual or not – results in a correlation between data providers of less than 0.6 (Mayor, 2019).

Given the divergence in third-party sustainability ratings, the fact that many institutional investors choose to go it alone comes as no shock. Some will integrate individual sustainable data points into their modelling and investment process and others will create their own sustainability ratings after drawing on a range of data sources. The former involves treating sustainable data points similarly to conventional financial metrics. A company with a strong track record on diversity, inclusion and employee treatment, for instance, may be expected to have lower staff turnover and lower staff costs than peers. This, in turn, may feed into lower operating costs and higher margins. Alternately, strong governance practices and an excellent track record in supply chain management may reduce operational risk and give sheen to a discounted-cash-flow model valuation by means of a lower weighted average cost of capital.

Proprietary sustainability ratings remain very popular with institutional asset managers. Research from consultants SquareWell Partners looked at the 50 largest asset managers and found that 60 per cent have developed their own sustainable rating systems for internal use. Furthermore, 40 per cent draw on four or more sustainable data provider services (SquareWell Partners, 2021).

Rating impacts: People and the planet

When you log in to your favourite social media platform you are bombarded by posts that reflect your political persuasion and personal echo chamber. As you scroll you can click the 'thumbs up' button to show support for 'X' or 'Y.' Yet, despite your noble intentions, your contribution will not have a real-world impact. At most, the advertising algorithm will note your choice and fairly soon you'll be offered a Che Guevara tee shirt or Pepe the Frog mug.

ESG ratings constitute a multi-million-dollar business. Extensive time and effort go into collating the inputs and creating the outputs. Yet their real-world benefits for people and the planet are limited. Viewed in a positive light, the ESG rating ecosystem has resulted in better data and greater awareness of sustainability topics. Increased use of the ratings has paralleled a wave of regulatory actions, such as the EU's Green Deal (European Commission, n.d.). These actions change economic incentives and legality, so their impact is concrete. But despite the correlation between the growth in ESG ratings and the regulatory agenda, no evidence that ESG ratings themselves have produced a measurable impact exists.

Some commentators even argue that the flowering of the sustainable investing data ecosystem has been counterproductive for the sustainability movement. Kenneth P Pucker, former chief operating officer of footwear firm Timberland and current lecturer at Tufts University, observed in the *Harvard Business Review*, 'It turns out that reporting is not a proxy for progress.' His subsequent assessment noted many of the challenges that we've highlighted and, insightfully, suggested that 'reporting may actually be an obstacle to progress'. Pucker argues that reporting consumes bandwidth, often exaggerates progress and can even be a distraction that protects the status quo and masks a lack of underlying change in mindsets and corporate behaviour (Pucker, 2021).

Pucker's view finds support across the sustainable ecosystem. A survey by asset-management giant Fidelity of their in-house financial analysts found that the analysts thought that 40 per cent of companies overstated their sustainable credentials to some degree (Fidelity International, 2021). While at the 2019 UN Climate Change Conference, commonly known as COP25, teenage activist Greta Thunberg made an impassioned claim that 'The biggest danger is not inaction. The real danger is when politicians and CEOs are making it look like real action is happening when in fact almost nothing is being done' (Reuters, 2019).

In response to these criticisms, investors have increasingly shifted their attention from data and ratings based on disclosure to information that evidences real-world change. They are also changing tack by using sustainable data and ratings not solely as a metric to decide whether to invest but as a starting point for deeper engagement with company management. The data becomes the basis for catalysing change (GSIA, 2021). (We discuss the topic of engagement in more detail in 'Chapter 3 – Sustainable public equity markets'.)

An ambitious attempt to bring impact measurement into the sustainable data ecosystem comes from the Harvard Business School and its 2020 proposal, 'Framework for Product Impact-Weighted Accounts' (Serafeim and Trinh, 2020). The Harvard approach involves assigning monetary values to the environmental and social impact of a company's products and services across seven pillars. By expressing all impacts, both positive and negative, with a common denominator – money – the Harvard approach blends accounting profit with the real-world impact achieved by each company. The result is a single impact-adjusted profit figure, which, due to its singular nature, is, in effect, a form of ESG rating.

This academic work used two automobile companies as a case study. It utilized the Sustainability Accounting Standards Board (SASB) framework and combined it with firm-specific data, such as the sales-weighted average passenger fleet fuel economy. Additional industry metrics such as Federal Highway Administration data for average distance driven were also included. These figures were used to calculate dollarized emissions impacts along with metrics such as dollarized necessity and satisfaction impacts.

The expanded Harvard dataset includes 1800 companies. In an analysis reported on by Barron's, the university researchers found that 250 businesses create more environmental damage a year than profit (Cohen, 2021). This method of impact accounting may also have investment consequences. The 'Framework for Product Impact-Weighted Accounts' judged Proctor and Gamble's palm oil use to have created environmental damage equal to 10 per cent of firm profits. Proctor and Gamble would later face a shareholder revolt due to its contribution to deforestation and degradation of intact forests (Gray and Temple-West, 2020).

Harvard is not alone in seeking to put monetary values on externalities to better understand corporate impact. Another notable example comes from private equity giant TPG, which established a measurement firm called Y Analytics that created an indicator term, the Impact Multiple of Money (IMM). This monetization of positive and negative impacts is employed to 'manage, measure and track impact results' from investments held by the successful, impact-focused TPG Rise funds (The Rise Fund, n.d.).

In summary, while drawing a direct link between the sustainable data ecosystem and real-world benefits is difficult, the industry is developing tools that better incorporate externalities as well as the positive and negative impacts caused by corporations into ESG rating frameworks.

In this interview, James sat down with Professor Robert G Eccles, whose career in and contribution to sustainability are unmatched. He was a tenured professor at Harvard Business School and is, as of 2022, the Visiting Professor of Management Practice at Saïd Business School, University of Oxford. As the founding chairman of the Sustainability Accounting Standards Board (SASB), he co-founded the International Integrated Reporting Council (IIRC) and, as of 2021, has served as chair of Kohlberg Kravis Roberts & Co, L P's (KKR) Sustainability Expert Advisory Council.

James: Thank you for taking the time. Let's start by asking how you became so involved with sustainable investing, particularly data and measurement.

Robert: It's a long story. I've always been interested in measurement, starting with two undergraduate degrees at MIT in pure math and history.

I then got my PhD at Harvard in sociology and joined the faculty at the Harvard Business School. My first research project was on transfer pricing, a very complex and controversial issue inside companies. You could do market price or cost or cost plus. And it became clear to me that there was no one right answer. In the end it depended on the firm's overall strategy.

I wrote a book entitled the *Transfer Pricing Problem: A theory for practice*, and afterward I wandered around looking for my next research project. I ended up doing a case study at a bank on transfer pricing. And that was my first foray into the capital markets.

It led to a work on investment banks that's called *Doing Deals: Investment banks at work*. And it was really the first book that applied network notions to organizational design. After writing it I got tenure and I remember interviewing this guy at Citibank, who told me, 'I need to have a different way of measuring things. All this financial stuff is rear-view mirror. I want something that will give me a sense of what the performance is going to be in the future, like maybe what our customers think.'

I thought, 'Oh, that's interesting,' and then I bumped into this idea a few more times. In 1991, I wrote an article in *Harvard Business Review* called 'The Performance Measurement Manifesto'. The basic thesis was that companies should start measuring non-financial performance – though I didn't use the term at the time. I also had a sense that maybe this was a topic the Securities Exchange Commission (SEC) would get involved in someday.

Later, with Sarah Mavrinac, I created a survey we had not seen done by anyone before. We sent out questionnaires to the sell-side, the buy-side and companies. It was a list of 10 things, very generic, about human capital, intellectual capital, R&D, etc. We asked the companies, 'Do you measure this? And do you think it's important to report on it?' We also asked the sell-side and the buy-side analysts, 'Do you think it's important?' and 'Do you get the information you need?'

And everybody said, 'Yeah, it's important.' And the analysts responded, 'No, we're not getting the information we need.' While the companies themselves said, 'Well, we agree it's important but we're not really reporting it. We're not sure how to do it.' So that led to an article called 'Improving the Corporate Disclosure Process' that was published in MIT's *Sloan Management Review*.

James: So at this point you've caught the measurement bug and you've encountered the financial ecosystem. How did sustainability data and ratings first begin to get codified?

Robert: After 10 years at Harvard, I earned tenure and then left four years later to start a company. Needless to say, this was a big shock to many. One of our clients was Price Waterhouse who later became PwC. They'd read my article in *Sloan* and were working on something called 'ValueReporting'. Together, we replicated the aforementioned survey in other countries and got the same results. More interestingly, we replicated this survey with industry and tailored the topics per sector – foreshadowing the SASB. Out of this research we published a book called *The Value Reporting Revolution: Moving Beyond the Earnings Game*.

You can see how non-financial reporting was beginning to emerge. In the book there was a chapter on the Global Reporting Initiative (GRI). The GRI had just started and, soon after, non-financial metrics became very relevant. The internet bubble ended – a bubble built on intangible assets – and there were the big accounting scandals at WorldCom and Enron. I thought, 'Okay, maybe we should reissue this book.' But instead we wrote another one.

It was a tight little work called *Building Public Trust: The Future of Corporate Reporting*. The crux was a three-tier model. For the base tier we argued the need for convergence between US Generally Accepted Accounting Principles (US GAAP) and the International Financial

Reporting Standards (IFRS). Then there were industry-specific, non-financial metrics in what was the middle section. And the top tier was company-specific disclosures relevant to the strategy.

James: But that's not the end. How did integrated reporting come about?

Robert: When I returned to teaching at Harvard I encountered 'integrated reporting' and a light bulb went on. I recall that Natura, a cosmetics and fragrances company in Brazil, and Novo Nordisk, a pharmaceutical company based in Denmark, published integrated reports in the same year. And they called them integrated reports, too. The language and the reasoning of the two companies were the same as well. It was like, 'The world is changing and this sustainability stuff is really important. We've got to pay attention to it. So we're going to have these integrated reports.'

That was the impetus for the book, *One Report: Integrated Reporting for Sustainable Strategy* with Mike Krzus. And through connections at PwC I was introduced to The Prince's Accounting for Sustainability Project. They convened a little get together at Prince Charles' place – Clarence House. All the great and the good from the reporting community attended, which was how the seeds were sown for the International Integrated Reporting Council (IIRC). A meeting followed that next summer. Mervyn King came, as did Sir Michael Peat. I remember a big table and the meeting being run like the British court. Anyway, the idea [for IIRC] was formed, a press release was issued and we experienced some difficulties ensuring that these sharp-elbowed NGOs all agreed. But we got there.

James: Can you tell me how this led to SASB, an organization Simon and I have been strong supporters of?

Robert: I first met Jean Rogers [the founder and first CEO of SASB] at a conference. But we didn't talk a lot. I ran into her again when she was at Arup and my Harvard colleague Amy Edmondson and I were doing research on sustainable cities. Later, though, out of the blue, I got an email from her saying, 'Hi, Bob, I'm going to start this thing called 'The Sustainability Accounting Standards Board'. Do you want to chat?' So we do and I end up being the [SASB] chair. We went into Bloomberg and met with Daniel Doctoroff, who was CEO at the time. We've got a little PowerPoint presentation. And we're nervous. 'Please, can we have a million dollars?' we ask and he answers, 'Sure, here's a million dollars.' We were shocked. The reason that it happened so easily was that they were thinking about doing something similar. But as a commercial organization they couldn't be a credible standard setter.

So SASB was formed. And in the early days GRI and SASB engaged in some head butting. GRI are like, 'What do we need you for? We've been around for a long time.' I was like, 'Look you define materiality as basically an externality for stakeholders. And it's important.' However, SASB's focus was narrower and centred on the materiality to investors.

James: Even with SASB, the regulators were not yet onboard. How did that come about?

Robert: For the longest time when you talked to investors, they said sustainability was important, but they didn't act on it. Then things started changing and the decision makers – portfolio managers – started getting involved. They were trying to do ESG integration at the portfolio manager level, but the data was very inconsistent.

The accounting standard setters and the regulators weren't yet interested, however. They said: 'We get that. But it's not the job of the regulators to pick the winning pony. Market forces will sort it out.' And I thought, 'That's complete rubbish. Market forces didn't get us accounting standards.'

So my Oxford colleague Professor Richard Barker, now a member of the International Sustainability Standards Board (ISSB), and I went to the International Accounting Standards Board (IASB) office and talked to Hans Hoogervorst, the chairman. We told him, 'We've got a great idea. You guys are standard setters. Why don't you set standards for non-financial indicators?'

Let's just say that idea didn't go over very well.

So instead we published a green paper entitled 'Should FASB and IASB Be Responsible for Setting Standards for Nonfinancial Information?' And we had this big debate at Oxford Union. It was a wonderful production. People came in their tuxedos. And the vote was two to one in favour of standards set by regulation. That was 2018.

Through Sir Ronald Cohen I then met a woman named Clara Barby, who had been seconded from Bridges Fund Management to run the Impact Management Project (IMP). She was trying to get NGOs – the likes of CDP, CDSB, UNDP, SASB, GRI, etc. – to sit around a table.

And I joined her in New York for three hours. Representatives of one NGO would beat their chest and the reps of another NGO did the same. Finally the meeting ended and Clara asked me, 'What did you think of that?' And my response was 'This is the biggest waste of three hours in my life so far.' But she said, 'Bob, you don't understand. Had we called this meeting a year ago, these people would have been killing each other. So it's progress.'

A year later we had another meeting, at the Organisation for Economic Co-operation and Development (OECD) headquarters outside Paris. Remarkably, tentatively, the NGOs started talking about how they could collaborate on things.

Then in 2020 it all came together. The IFRS foundation launched its consultation paper to establish the ISSB. At the same time the IMP published a paper about a common framework and the World Economic Forum published one on stakeholder metrics. A great idea's time had finally come. With tremendous support from investors (and others) the IFRS Foundation established the ISSB. Along the way, SASB and the IIRC merged to become the Value Reporting Foundation and it has since been absorbed into the ISSB. GRI and the IFRS Foundation have formally announced a collaboration and the ISSB committed to build upon great work of the Task Force on Climate-related Financial Disclosures (TCFD). The groundwork laid by many NGOs helped lay the foundation for a formal regulator to take the reins on establishing standards for sustainability reporting.

James: But not everyone is happy with ISSB, correct?

Robert: Yes. There are people who vehemently oppose its formation.

To oversimplify, you have the 'single materiality' crowd – that's SASB, CDP, CDSB, TCFD, etc. And you have the 'double materiality' proponents such as GRI and the European Financial Reporting Advisory Group (EFRAG).

A debate broke out about whether ISSB should do double materiality. The position we took was, 'No, that's not their job.' Others don't agree. They don't seem to understand what ISSB's competency and remit are. It's a challenge to create standards relevant for investors. Creating multi-stakeholder standards is quite a different process. That's what the GRI does, and they do it well, I think.

James: And what do you see as the optimal outcome?

Robert: What I'd like to see happen is the establishment of a so-called 'global baseline'. That would be the single materiality stuff – with the ISSB taking care of it. For the double materiality side, it's less clear. What you don't want is GRI and EFRAG covering the multi-stakeholder topics and all of the single materiality data points too. That would result in competing standards and different ways of reporting on the same thing, which wouldn't be helpful.

I think you'd like to have that global baseline. But there'd always be adjustments. Think of how Chinese GAAP is like IFRS but with custom Chinese stuff. When it comes to sustainability reporting, some jurisdictional differences should be permitted. It's not as cut and dried even in financial accounting and reporting as people think.

Historically, creating standards for financial accounting received a lot of pushback, and there were assertions that it was not possible. 'My situation is unique' was a common refrain. 'I can't possibly do this.' 'It's as much art as science.' I'm now hearing similar statements about sustainability reporting.

So it will be messy. It'll be ongoing and contested. There will be haters. But you'll finally get a baseline. I hope enough jurisdictions will mandate it.

James: Will adoption of common standards ultimately help people and the planet?

Robert: Maybe. You need real people to act.

I'll tell you a funny story. A couple months ago I was thinking about doing a video series on climate change and the role of the financial sector. I went to my hair salon and sat down.

I said to my hair stylist, 'Lori, we're not going to have our usual pleasant chitchat. You're going to be a focus group for me.'

She responded, 'Oh, that's great.'

And I questioned her, 'You know what I do, right?'

'Not really,' she answered. 'You sort of fly around and talk to people.'

'Yeah, that's kind of what I do,' I answered before explaining my role in a little more detail. Then I pressed on, 'You know what 'Net zero by 2050' is, right?'

There was a long pause. 'By 2050 everything will be crypto?' she said.

So I asked the hair stylist next to her. 'Net zero by 2050?' She also didn't have a clue. Neither did a couple of the clients.

You and I live in this weird financial and sustainable world. We think, 'My God, we've got to deal with these things.' You're even writing a book about it. But many people kind-of know, kind-of don't know that climate change is occurring. They don't live in the bubble we do.

In our highly contested domain people argue and call each other names because someone uses ESG and sustainability interchangeably. All these other people in the world are just trying to lead their lives and get by. Sometimes it's good to get out of our bubble and recognize that.

James: I think that's a very good perspective to adopt. Thank you, Robert, for your time.

The potential opportunities and how we might get there

The ecosystem of sustainable data and ratings has developed over thirty years. As of 2022, it was worth, according to Substantive Research, one billion US dollars a year (Carrodus, 2021). However, the landscape is vast and a lack of standardization has led to far too many non-comparable, idiosyncratic data points. The challenge associated with sustainable data and ratings is well summarized by British philosopher and House of Lords member Onora O'Neill, whose words, on another topic, hold true. O'Neill mused that 'increasing transparency can produce a flood of unsorted information and misinformation that provides little but confusion unless it can be sorted and assessed. It may add to uncertainty rather than to trust' (O'Neill, 2002).

When we look at opportunities in this sphere we look for ways to increase consistency and align incentives across multiple stakeholders. In all cases, our opportunities take inspiration from existing embryonic practices. In turn, we consider three crucial stakeholders: retail investors, institutional investors and finally corporations.

The first opportunity calls for simplicity for retail investors. It borrows from nutritional information found on food packaging and asks for a limited number of commonly produced sustainable data points.

The second opportunity acknowledges that institutional investors require deeper, more complex datasets and sees an opportunity to support a single market reporting standard – namely, the ISSB, which was formed by the SASB and IFRS merger.

Our final opportunity, for corporations, goes further. In addition to supporting the ISSB, we seek to integrate sustainability information into conventional financial accounts and to place a monetary value on corporations' real-world impacts, both positive and negative.

Retail investors

Let's start with non-professional investors. There is simply too much sustainable investing data being produced for them to digest. Confusion and indecision abound. As demonstrated by the FIFA football game, the average person doesn't require hundreds of data points to make a decision. A half dozen is often enough.

Nutritional information labels on packaging offer a good parallel for what is needed in the sustainable data world. Developing a small number of consistent indicators across all companies, regardless of materiality, would improve the general population's understanding of, engagement with, and ultimately investment in sustainability.

Exactly which sustainability indicators should be selected is of secondary importance to establishing them. Armed with key sustainability information, similar to the way in which dieters, reading labels, can count the calories on the products they consume, one retail investor could focus their investments on water, while another could emphasize diversity.

Small practical steps have already been taken. A 2020 World Economic Forum (WEF) report tamed its own additive bias and sought to simplify the existing reporting architecture rather than add new complexity. The WEF paper identified 'a set of 21 more-established or critically important metrics and disclosures' for all companies. Importantly, the quantitative metrics they chose were 'already being reported by many firms (albeit often in different formats)' (World Economic Forum, 2020).

The 21 metrics covered 14 themes across governance, people, planet and prosperity. The themes could be condensed to just 10 if governance (which typically scores low on retail investor preference surveys) (UBS, 2018) were condensed into a single theme.

A set of consistent metrics would enable wealth managers to pursue mass customization of retail portfolios that focus on investors' specific values and preferences. Each metric could also be weighted to create a single overall personalized score. Variants of this approach have already been tested in the market. Fin-tech firm Ethic (Ethic, n.d.) (which incidentally maintains a high-profile partnership with the Duke and Duchess of Sussex) has pioneered it in the US. And in Europe wealth manager, UBS, has an advisory product that creates personalized sustainability scores across six dimensions (UBS, n.d.). To take the approach mainstream, regulators will have to step in and mandate such disclosures as part of non-financial reporting. Even with the EU's development of the CSRD, the current trajectory still favours complexity over simplicity.

OPPORTUNITIES

Agree on a small number of sustainability metrics, reported consistently by all companies, to enable mass customization of retail investors' portfolios and increase retail investor engagement and adoption.

Institutional investors

In the institutional sphere, although a limited number of consistent sustainable data points provides a good base, the degree of fundamental analysis undertaken by these more sophisticated investors requires greater sector-specific information reported and presented in a consistent manner.

Institutional investors could wait for regulators to decide what data they will receive, but we'd encourage them to actively shape the future and back a proverbial horse. In our opinion, that horse is the integrated ISSB, formed by the coming together of SASB and IFRS. ISSB combines what is arguably the most preferred corporate reporting framework with a broader, more established accounting standard.

Having easy access to consistently reported corporate data that is material to the financial value of their investments, institutional investors could focus their research resources on interpreting it rather than collating it. Their investment decision-making process would improve, their credibility when engaging with corporate reporting on real-world issues would increase, and ultimately their financial products would become more attractive to investors.

To get there, institutional investors will have to make their voices heard by lobbying corporates and regulators alike to align to a common set of standards.

> OPPORTUNITIES
>
> Actively shape the future by pressing for consistent, sector-specific disclosure regulations that enable sustainability factors to be fully integrated into the investment process.

Corporations

Of all stakeholders, corporations are in the toughest position. They are constantly pulled in different directions as regulators, stock exchanges, data aggregators and accolade givers all clamour for information. It's no wonder that 58 per cent of executives want a single sustainability reporting standard and 66 per cent are prepared to support mandatory, legally binding issuance of sustainability reports (Bernow et al, 2019). Too much is being asked of them and, incentivized to make themselves look attractive to potential customers and providers of capital, they are simply unable to say 'no'.

Like their institutional investor counterparts, they too can take an active role in shaping the future by supporting the SASB and IFRS combination. They can also accelerate real-world impacts by adopting integrated reporting, which involves including sustainability information into pre-existing financial reports with the same rigour as audits do. They can also support impact-focused initiatives such as the Harvard-designed Product Impact-Weighted Accounts.

Some progress is being made. According to KPMG, 22 per cent of the largest 250 companies worldwide attempted integrated reporting. And according to Harvard over 50 companies have experimented with impact-weighted accounts (Harvard Business School, n.d.).

Getting to where we need to be will likely require a regulatory nudge. But continued work from academia to demonstrate the commercial value of ISSB, integrated reporting and impact-weighted accounts may accelerate the trend.

OPPORTUNITIES

Align to a single reporting framework, further integrate sustainability information into financial accounts and focus on real-world impacts, both positive and negative.

References

Akgun, O T, Mudge, T J and Townsend, B (2021) How company size bias in ESG scores impacts the small cap investor, *The Journal of Impact and ESG Investing*, 1(4), pp 31–44, doi.org/10.3905/jesg.2021.1.022 (archived at https://perma.cc/64MF-T9M6)

Arabesque (no date) The Reporting Exchange – The global resource for sustainability reporting, www.reportingexchange.com/ (archived at https://perma.cc/MQ7L-Y26Y)

Bender, J and Maffina, S (2022) The ESG data challenge: Importance of data quality in ESG investing, SSGA, www.ssga.com/sg/en/institutional/ic/insights/the-esg-data-challenge-importance-of-data (archived at https://perma.cc/SST5-2AFL)

Berg, F, Kölbel, J F and Rigobon, R (2022) Aggregate confusion: The divergence of ESG rating, *Review of Finance*, p. rfac033, doi.org/10.1093/rof/rfac033 (archived at https://perma.cc/Y7C5-NAVW)

Bernow, S *et al* (2019) More than values: The value-based sustainability reporting that investors want, McKinsey Sustainability, www.mckinsey.com/business-functions/sustainability/our-insights/more-than-values-the-value-based-sustainability-reporting-that-investors-want (archived at https://perma.cc/KSP6-GWS6)

Carrodus, M (2021) How to combat greenwashing? Find the right data partner, Substantive Research, 10 September, substantiveresearch.com/matter/how-to-combat-greenwashing-find-the-right-data-partner/ (archived at https://perma.cc/TFH6-UAQL)

CDSB (no date) EU Corporate Sustainability Reporting Directive (CSRD), www.cdsb.net/what-we-do/policy-work/eu-sustainability-reporting (archived at https://perma.cc/LR2C-RMFU)

Christensen, D M, Serafeim, G and Sikochi, A (2021) Why is corporate virtue in the eye of the beholder? The case of ESG ratings, *The Accounting Review*, 97(1), pp 147–175, doi.org/10.2308/TAR-2019-0506 (archived at https://perma.cc/JJE5-SULE)

Cohen, R (2021) Corporate impact is woefully opaque. Biden can change that, Barron's, www.barrons.com/articles/how-biden-can-make-corporate-impact-a-force-for-good-51613158420 (archived at https://perma.cc/D382-E4YG)

Ellsberg, D (1961) Risk, ambiguity, and the savage axioms, *The Quarterly Journal of Economics*, 75(4), pp 643–669, doi.org/10.2307/1884324 (archived at https://perma.cc/9AW6-TKRJ)

Ethic (no date), www.ethic.com/ (archived at https://perma.cc/2U87-PD73)

European Commission (2021a) Questions and Answers: Corporate Sustainability Reporting Directive proposal, ec.europa.eu/commission/presscorner/detail/en/QANDA_21_1806 (archived at https://perma.cc/V588-G3M7)

European Commission (no date) A European Green Deal, ec.europa.eu/info/strategy/priorities-2019-2024/european-green-deal_en (archived at https://perma.cc/348U-CJN4)

Fama, E F (1970) Efficient capital markets: A review of theory and empirical work, *The Journal of Finance*, 25(2), p 383, doi.org/10.2307/2325486 (archived at https://perma.cc/47BY-FRMZ)

Fidelity International (2021) ESG Analyst Survey 2021: A world of opportunity, euissmultisiteprod-live-8dd1b69cadf7409099ee6471b87c49a-7653963.s3-eu-west-1.amazonaws.com/filer_public/f9/92/f99274b6-288c-4cf9-a0de-6bd42d2968af/fidelity_analyst_survey_esg_2021.pdf (archived at https://perma.cc/MTV8-WTHG)

Fink, L (2020) A fundamental reshaping of finance, BlackRock, www.blackrock.com/us/individual/larry-fink-ceo-letter (archived at https://perma.cc/B4BV-8PTA)

Goal (2021) Best FIFA 22 rating: Cristiano Ronaldo or Lionel Messi? Sporting News, 10 January, www.sportingnews.com/us/soccer/news/best-fifa-22-rating-cristiano-ronaldo-lionel-messi/pdoqk3tn72v71fk5vmxrf0utq (archived at https://perma.cc/U4CL-7DX7)

Gray, A and Temple-West, P (2020) Investor rebellion at Procter & Gamble over environmental concerns, *Financial Times*, 14 October, www.ft.com/content/1dd92502-e95b-4c21-be1c-c18a598acf1a (archived at https://perma.cc/5NXX-DSV2)

Greenhouse Gas Protocol (no date) Greenhouse Gas Protocol, ghgprotocol.org/ (archived at https://perma.cc/H7JP-BZHY)
GRI and SASB (2021) A practical guide to sustainability reporting using GRI and SASB standards, www.globalreporting.org/media/mlkjpn1i/gri-sasb-joint-publication-april-2021.pdf (archived at https://perma.cc/9WYJ-7G32)
GSIA (2021) Global Sustainable Investment Review 2020, www.gsi-alliance.org/trends-report-2020/ (archived at https://perma.cc/MN2M-44GD)
Hakola, R, Poll, J N and Vannefors, J (2020) In search of quality ESG data: An investment view on corporate sustainability disclosures. Danske Bank, danskebank.com/-/media/danske-bank-com/file-cloud/2020/5/in-search-of-quality-esg-data---an-investment-view-on-corporate-sustainability-disclosures.pdf?rev=2560aff2dc3f4a6eb85db2b9d863443a (archived at https://perma.cc/DPJ8-U6BF)
Harvard Business School (no date) Impact-weighted accounts, www.hbs.edu/impact-weighted-accounts/Pages/default.aspx (archived at https://perma.cc/VG9U-AV7K)
IOSCO (2021) Environmental, Social and Governance (ESG) Ratings and Data Products Providers: Consultation Report.
Kwon, S (2018) State of Sustainability and Integrated Reporting 2018, IRRCI, www.weinberg.udel.edu/IIRCiResearchDocuments/2018/11/2018-SP-500-Integrated-Reporting-FINAL-November-2018-1.pdf (archived at https://perma.cc/Z87Y-BKKJ)
Mackintosh, J (2018) Is Tesla or Exxon more sustainable? It depends whom you ask, *Wall Street Journal*, 17 September, www.wsj.com/articles/is-tesla-or-exxon-more-sustainable-it-depends-whom-you-ask-1537199931 (archived at https://perma.cc/HC7H-Z4KE)
Mawston, N (2021) Four billion people use a smartphone, Strategy Analytics, www.strategyanalytics.com/strategy-analytics/blogs/devices/smartphones/smart-phones/2021/06/24/four-billion-people-use-a-smartphone (archived at https://perma.cc/Y6FS-LC87)
Mayor, T (2019) Why ESG ratings vary so widely (and what you can do about it). MIT Sloan, 26 August, mitsloan.mit.edu/ideas-made-to-matter/why-esg-ratings-vary-so-widely-and-what-you-can-do-about-it (archived at https://perma.cc/HZL5-MJXE)
MSCI (2020) Scope 3 carbon emissions: Seeing the full picture, 17 September, www.msci.com/www/blog-posts/scope-3-carbon-emissions-seeing/02092372761 (archived at https://perma.cc/X8TP-PD8E)
O'Neill, O (2002) The Reith Lectures: Onora O'Neill – A question of trust [Radio Broadcast], BBC Radio 4, www.bbc.co.uk/programmes/p00ghvd8 (archived at https://perma.cc/JT42-YN9Q)
Pucker, K P (2021) Overselling sustainability reporting, *Harvard Business Review*, hbr.org/2021/05/overselling-sustainability-reporting (archived at https://perma.cc/V56F-UAQM)

Raconteur (no date) A day in data, www.raconteur.net/infographics/a-day-in-data/ (archived at https://perma.cc/6SSH-WTSY)
Refinitiv (2020) Environmental, social and governance scores from Refinitiv, www.refinitiv.com/content/dam/marketing/en_us/documents/methodology/refinitiv-esg-scores-methodology.pdf (archived at https://perma.cc/32Q5-R75S)
Reid, J, Templeman, L and Mahtani, S (2018) Big data shakes up ESG investing, Deutsche Bank, www.dbresearch.com/PROD/RPS_EN-PROD/PROD0000000000478852/Big_data_shakes_up_ESG_investing.PDF?undefined&realload=rtq4tBNQLeFaMvKWklfjow4P9HtOUhEuWYPgcqZNy~K2xEmbWhrjA8moNJtjqwG3 (archived at https://perma.cc/59YX-UFXU)
Reinders, S, Choong, Y T and Lanchenko, A (2021) ESG-Net: Finding the missing ESG data in EM corporate debt, NN Investment Partners, www.nnip.com/en-CZ/professional/insights/articles/esg-net-finding-the-missing-esg-data-in-em-corporate-debt (archived at https://perma.cc/477U-DRYU)
Reuters (2019) Activist Thunberg denounces 'clever accounting' in climate fight, 11 December, www.reuters.com/article/climate-change-accord-idUKL8N28L1RE (archived at https://perma.cc/87ZJ-72LM)
SASB (2017) State of Disclosure 2017: An analysis of the effectiveness of sustainability disclosure in SEC filings, www.sasb.org/knowledge-hub/state-of-disclosure-2017/ (archived at https://perma.cc/XA3E-AM7N)
Serafeim, G and Trinh, K (2020) A Framework for Product Impact-Weighted Accounts, Harvard Business School Working Paper, No. 20-076, www.hbs.edu/faculty/Pages/item.aspx?num=57580 (archived at https://perma.cc/JJQ5-Y79Y)
Shifflett, S (2021) How ESG stocks perform depends on who ranks them, *Wall Street Journal*, 11 June, www.wsj.com/articles/how-esg-stocks-perform-depends-on-who-ranks-them-11623403803 (archived at https://perma.cc/LB7E-36EF)
Sohns, J (2021) FIFA ratings explained: How is the overall rating created? EarlyGame, earlygame.com/fifa/fifa-ratings-explained-overall-rating (archived at https://perma.cc/99AA-RAGM)
SquareWell Partners (2021) The playing field: Look at the world's largest 50 asset Managers, higherlogicdownload.s3.amazonaws.com/GOVERNANCEPROFESSIONALS/a8892c7c-6297-4149-b9fc-378577d0b150/UploadedImages/2021_-_SquareWell_-_Top_50_-_Asset_Managers_Approach_to_ESG.pdf (archived at https://perma.cc/H6T9-HYYT)
SSE initiative (no date) ESG guidance database, sseinitiative.org/esg-guidance-database/ (archived at https://perma.cc/4GWV-L6YZ)
Sustainability Knowledge Group (2021) GRI and SASB Reporting Standards: Working together, 5 May, sustainabilityknowledgegroup.com/gri-and-sasb-reporting-standards-working-together/ (archived at https://perma.cc/TK5E-MP89)

Sustainalytics (no date) About us, Morningstar, www.sustainalytics.com/about-us (archived at https://perma.cc/76ZM-Q9BH)
TCFD (2021) Task Force on Climate-related Financial Disclosures: 2021 Status Report, www.fsb.org/2021/10/2021-status-report-task-force-on-climate-related-financial-disclosures/ (archived at https://perma.cc/Z2SY-MSAR)
TCFD (no date) Task Force on Climate-Related Financial Disclosures, www.fsb-tcfd.org/ (archived at https://perma.cc/U2P9-3TZC)
Teneo (2021) We are living in a material world: The state of 2021 U.S. sustainability reporting, https://www.teneo.com/app/uploads/2021/09/Teneo_The-State-of-U.S.-Sustainability-Reporting.pdf (archived at https://perma.cc/RK5E-QQWD)
The Rise Fund (no date) Measurement, therisefund.com/measurement (archived at https://perma.cc/N867-PD54)
Threlfall, R et al (2020) The time has come: The KPMG survey of sustainability reporting 2020, KPMG, assets.kpmg/content/dam/kpmg/lu/pdf/the-time-has-come.pdf (archived at https://perma.cc/9KVV-T6UX)
Tylenda, E (2020) GS Sustain: The PM's guide to the ESG revolution 2: ESG building blocks.
UBS (2018) UBS investor watch: Return on values, www.ubs.com/content/dam/ubs/microsites/ubs-investor-watch/IW-09-2018/return-on-value-global-report-final.pdf (archived at https://perma.cc/W2Z9-SNGT)
UBS (no date) UBS advice [Sustainable Investing], www.ubs.com/ch/en/wealth-management/investment/solutions/advice-si.html (archived at https://perma.cc/YF4Z-ENHK)
Vopson, M M (2021) The world's data explained: how much we're producing and where it's all stored, The Conversation, 4 May, theconversation.com/the-worlds-data-explained-how-much-were-producing-and-where-its-all-stored-159964 (archived at https://perma.cc/NER2-LN4L)
World Economic Forum (2019) Seeking Return on ESG: Advancing the reporting ecosystem to unlock impact for business and society, www.weforum.org/whitepapers/seeking-return-on-esg-advancing-the-reporting-ecosystem-to-unlock-impact-for-business-and-society/ (archived at https://perma.cc/V6YN-RBKA)
World Economic Forum (2020) Measuring Stakeholder Capitalism: Towards Common Metrics and Consistent Reporting of Sustainable Value Creation, www.weforum.org/reports/measuring-stakeholder-capitalism-towards-common-metrics-and-consistent-reporting-of-sustainable-value-creation/ (archived at https://perma.cc/LQP6-YZTC)

03

Sustainable public equity markets

Introduction

The size of a house is typically defined by its floor area. The size of a factory is commonly expressed either by referencing its production in physical volume or its dollar output. And the size of a country's economy is usually quantified as Gross Domestic Product (GDP), which, if you recall your first-year university economics lessons, means private consumption + investment + government spending + exports – imports.

But what is the size of sustainable investing in global listed equity markets? The answer turns out to vary greatly depending on who you ask, the equity market you are asking about and how sustainable investing is defined. To help answer this question of size, in this chapter we look at three popular approaches to sustainable investing in public equity markets, namely, exclusion, integration and engagement.

We start with a section that considers 'How exclusion processes operate'. Historically, sustainable investing initially focused on 'exclusion' – the practice of removing companies, sectors or economic activities from an investment universe or portfolio based on an investor's preferences, moral or social values and/or risk tolerance. We then assess exclusion's estimated size in terms of assets, the operational hurdles facing investors and the cultural differences that can lead investors to exclude activities that differ markedly from one another.

With this review complete, we will examine exclusion of public equities in theory and in practice to pose and answer three important questions:

- Does the practice of exclusion add to investment performance? (Answer: No.)
- Does it detract from investment performance? (Answer: It can.)
- Does it help people and the planet? (Answer: No.)

Exclusion interprets sustainability in a negative way – prescribing what you can't do – and it later (partially) gave way to 'integration'. A more positive concept, integration seeks to demonstrate what sustainability can do for investment portfolios by including sustainability information in the investment decision-making process.

Our second section goes on to examine 'How integration processes operate'. We begin by assessing integration's estimated size in terms of assets. We then address a line of argumentation that suggests that the 'mainstreaming' of integration has blurred the lines about it to such an extent that the term no longer refers to a discrete investment strategy. A short discussion on the incentives that can entice firms to overstate the extent of their integration processes concludes this section.

Having profiled integration, we examine it in theory and in practice to put forward and answer three key questions:

- Does quantitative integration add to investment performance? (Answer: A little, at least, for now.)
- Does qualitative integration add to investment performance? (Answer: A little.)
- Does either help people and the planet? (Answer: No.)

A third wave of sustainability in public equities – engagement – arrived, at scale, in the 2010s. Investors sought greater real-world impact from their investments and, to achieve it, used their voice and equity voting rights to advocate for change by engaging constructively with company management. In our third section, we look at 'How engagement processes operate'. We once again assess the estimated size of the strategy in terms of assets before highlighting the challenge created by a lack of third-party validation and the difficulties posed by multiple investors claiming the same successes.

After conducting this review, we examine engagement in theory and in practice in light of three central questions, which we answer:

- Can just anyone successfully engage? (Answer: No.)
- Does engagement add to investment performance? (Answer: Potentially.)
- Does it help people and the planet? (Answer: A little.)

Before we tackle our final equity section, we pause for an exclusive interview with Catherine Howarth to discuss sustainable investing and active ownership. Since 2008, Catherine has served as the CEO of ShareAction, a charity committed to driving financial system change through regulatory collaboration, the coordination of investor engagement and the benchmarking of investors' sustainable practices. A board member of the Scott Trust, the owner of *The Guardian*, Catherine was recognized in 2014 by the World Economic Forum as a Young Global Leader.

Our final equity section gazes into the future and considers 'The potential opportunities and how we might get there'. Of all asset classes, equities have, arguably, the longest and most developed relationship with sustainable investing. Abundant intellectual capital has been brought to bear on the discipline over the years, overcoming many challenges and seizing many opportunities. We suggest concrete actions to exploit three more opportunities that we see and provide suggestions on how we might get there.

- The first focuses on exclusion and integration. We acknowledge the difficulties caused by a lack of homogeneity in industry processes and standards, particularly as regards the heterogeneous state of corporate data. We see an opportunity to standardize corporate reporting that would enhance both exclusion's and integration's effectiveness.
- The second addresses engagement and calls for an increase in the number of shareholder proposals at annual and extraordinary

general meetings. Getting there, we argue, will require legislative intervention in certain jurisdictions to ensure that well-thought-out proposals make it on the ballot.

- The final opportunity involves the lack of impact that public market equity investors are having on people and the planet. The evolution of financial markets has reached the point, we argue, where inserting innovative features that achieve tangible, evidenced-based real-world impact is possible. We cite an example of a climate fund that not only deploys exclusion, integration and engagement but measures the carbon emissions associated with its equity investments and commits to climate neutrality by funding counterbalancing activities such as reforestation projects.

How exclusion processes operate

Exclusion: Get yourself better friends

If you don't like something, it often makes sense to have nothing more to do with it. Not a fan of meat? Eliminate it from your diet and become vegetarian. If your best mate from school has become a toxic bully, ban them from your life and meet better friends. Exclusion is a simple way of distancing yourself from the activities, products and people you regard as unhelpful, undesirable or downright wrong.

Within public equities, exclusion targets what an investor doesn't like. The process, in this case, typically removes companies, sectors or economic activities from an investment universe, rendering them ineligible for any subsequent investment portfolio.

While it is difficult to define just how many public equity products utilize exclusions, the Global Sustainable Investing Alliance (GSIA) estimates that, as of year-end 2020, $15 trillion, over 15 per cent of professionally managed assets, did (GSIA, 2021). As we argued in 'Chapter 1 – What is sustainable investing?', using a small handful of exclusions is probably insufficient to credibly refer to an investment product as sustainable. A similar view has led Goldman Sachs to attribute just $2 trillion to exclusion-led sustainable strategies, a fraction of GSIA's estimates (Bingham et al, 2022).

Exclusion: Agreeing to disagree

While school officials may suspect that some of their students are smoking something they shouldn't behind the bike sheds, they can't force these offenders to leave school until they have proof. In short, in order to exclude something you have to first know that it exists, that it is happening. Unfortunately, this is easier said than done.

To put an exclusionary approach into effect an investor will often rely on a third-party sustainable data provider such as MSCI or Sustainalytics. Such providers often offer upwards of 50 different exclusion criteria collated from company reports and third-party sources (MSCI, 2019). However, providers often disagree on whether an activity is occurring or not.

Analysis of sustainable data providers by asset manager Schroders found that, for some popular exclusions such as nuclear or fur, there was just 40 per cent agreement about the activity in question. In other words, companies were simultaneously cited as being involved, and not being involved, in certain business activities (Schroders, 2017). Such huge discrepancies in the data the providers offer come about because companies rarely report their share of revenue generated by such business activities. The data providers must estimate company exposures, and these estimates can yield highly different results. This issue of input data is a fundamental one and calls into question the very validity of exclusion as an investment approach.

DIFFERENT TYPES OF EXCLUSIONS

The practice of exclusion traces its roots as far back as the 17th century, when religious groups such as the Quakers and Methodists avoided companies whose operations were not consistent with their values. It gathered pace when the first ethical mutual fund was launched at the height of the Vietnam War in 1971. This fund refused to invest in companies involved in producing nuclear and conventional military weapons (Copay et al, 2021). Today, many public equity funds employ exclusions, which range from steering clear of firms tied to controversial weapons to niche areas such as avoiding companies that trade in Angora wool or produce asbestos.

Exclusions may be based on what are frequently termed international norms. They may target violators of common international frameworks such as the International Labour Organisation (ILO) Conventions, the Universal Declaration of Human Rights and the United Nations Global Compact. They may also reflect investor preferences or values by avoiding 'sin' companies linked to alcohol, tobacco, gambling, adult entertainment and so forth (Belsom and Wearmouth, 2020).

In the case of norms-based screening, the approach is usually binary. Either a company is deemed to be in violation of the framework or it is not. In the case of preference and value-based exclusions, the approach tends to involve a threshold, such as 10 per cent of sales (MSCI, 2021). This calculation is done to determine whether the activity is material to company operations or not. For example, if a large renewable energy firm owned a single vineyard, it would be harsh to exclude it from the investment universe due to its exposure to alcohol.

Investors may also exclude companies due to so-called controversies. Here the focus is on how firms act, and they can be excluded whether they sell renewable energy or fur. A controversy references a significant negative event, such as a reprimand from a regulator or a news report alleging malpractice. Sustainable data providers such as MSCI or Sustainalytics normally categorize controversies on a severity scale (MSCI, 2020) and adjust it as controversies are rectified or fade from public consciousness.

Exclusion: The world is an unsavoury place

The average Argentine consumes 36 kilograms of beef per year, almost 50 per cent more per capita than is the case for citizens of any other country. By contrast, beef consumption in India totals less than 1 kilogram per person, largely due to the cow being a revered animal in its majority religion, Hinduism (OECD and FAO, 2021). Social and cultural norms differ markedly worldwide and few, if any, economic activities are universally esteemed. It is therefore unsurprising that a zealous sustainable investor may take issue with a large swathe of the public equity universe.

Some exclusions are more popular than others. Common ones in Western portfolios centre on companies whose activities are tied to fossil fuels or tobacco. Taken individually, exclusions can fence off as much as 5 per cent of global equity market capitalization. When taken together, however, depending on the combination, exclusions can eliminate upwards of 20 per cent of an investable equity universe (Schroders, 2017).

Theoretically, all US-domiciled companies could be off limits for the portfolios of investors who reside in countries that have a particularly tense relationship with US authorities. That would eliminate about 60 per cent of the global investable universe (MSCI, 2022a).

Given the large impact exclusions can have on the investment universe, sustainable investors who favour the practice are left either to materially restrict their investable options or to implement only a small subset of potential exclusions. Selecting the former option inevitably creates decided portfolio biases and risks. Choosing the latter may compromise an investor's sustainable ideals.

Having reviewed how exclusion processes operate, we now examine them in theory and in practice by asking and answering three key questions.

Exclusion: Does the practice of exclusion add to investment performance?

Short answer: No.

IN THEORY

Proponents of exclusion in public equities advance theories as to why it should boost investment performance. For one, it has the potential to prevent elevated operational risks caused by controversial management behaviour or non-adherence to international norms from seeping into a portfolio (Konqui, Millet and Darolles, 2019). The practice could also enhance returns by shunning the shares of companies whose operations are vulnerable to changing societal views, which may render their products and services less appealing or obsolete. Excluding them could get investors ahead of the curve.

Improved performance could also stem from currently unpriced externalities that become tangible costs under new regulation. For example, thermal coal miners and utilities might be required to pay for their emissions under a carbon tax or trading scheme (Andersson, Bolton and Samama, 2016; Caldecott, 2018). By avoiding such stocks, exclusion investors could be anticipating these regulatory changes and avoiding the poor investment performance.

IN PRACTICE

Studies supporting the notion that systematic exclusion increases investment returns are few and far between. The lack of evidence is in itself compelling and leads to the inference that exclusion fails to contribute to performance.

A rare study that suggests otherwise is an MSCI-authored paper. This research found that excluding companies with 'the worst' controversies generated a small rise in returns. The authors also noted, though, that a number of other factors added to the outperformance. The caveats to their findings caused them to conclude that 'exclusions based on alleged wrongdoing are a blunt instrument' (Lee, Nagy and Eastman, 2017).

The lack of evidence is unsurprising. To mechanically exclude securities is to act before thinking. Doing so would require accepting the quality of the input data without question. It would also deny an investor the opportunity to consider mitigating circumstances, to weigh information and consider it through a sustainable integration process. Such a process might still persuade the investor to decline to invest in a given company, but only if the data was deemed accurate, material and highly detrimental to the investment case.

Due to the large number of participants in public equity markets, a mechanical exclusion process is unlikely to reliably produce excess returns since prolonged investment outperformance implies a persistent mispricing of securities. Public equities are a liquid financial market, so it would be highly unusual for market participants to fail to correct a mispricing despite evidence of its existence.

Finally, exclusions, by definition, shrink the investment universe and reduce the number of investment options available. Over the past 50 years, investment orthodoxy has held that the optimal risk-adjusted investment return is realized via a combination of the widest possible selection of assets, which achieves the so-called efficient frontier (Markowitz, 1952). If, through exclusion, investors limit themselves to a subset of securities, then the investment options can, mechanically, only ever be as good as the full investment universe.

Exclusion: Does it detract from investment performance?

Short answer: It can.

IN THEORY

Critics of exclusion in public equities theorize about why it should detract from investment performance. The most straightforward hypothesis is that excluding a large number of stocks can create cyclical exposures that lead to periods of portfolio underperformance. A more expansive application of the same logic suggests that excluding numerous equities will undermine portfolio diversification to such an extent that structural underperformance is unavoidable (Pizzutilo, 2017).

A related theory argues that if several investors excluded the same equity, then they would materially alter the supply–demand dynamic. Desired by a reduced number of buyers, often-excluded stocks would be priced cheaper than their peers. These cheap stocks would then offer superior future returns that could be exploited by sustainability-agnostic investors choosing between them and those of peer companies. A portfolio that excludes equities would, by this logic, underperform (Zerbib, 2019; Pedersen, Fitzgibbons and Pomorski, 2020; Pástor, Stambaugh and Taylor, 2021).

IN PRACTICE

Studies demonstrate that exclusion may cyclically detract from investment performance. Structural underperformance, however, only occurs when there is an excessively large number of exclusions.

It is well documented that various 'sin' stocks have outperformed over certain time periods. Unsurprisingly, exclusionary investment strategies, during this same time, suffered cyclical underperformance. Notably, the global tobacco sector bettered the wider market by over 250 per cent in the ten years starting 2001. Many studies in the early twenty-first century attributed the differences in performance to the use of exclusions or sustainability factors (Fabozzi, Ma and Oliphant, 2008; Hong and Kacperczyk, 2009; Statman and Glushkov, 2009).

As of 2022, this view has been debunked. While there is no doubt that tobacco and other 'sin' stocks have shone at certain times, their outperformance is now attributed to factors unrelated to exclusions or sustainability. This conclusion was reached by decomposing equity returns into so-called factors – quantifiable firm characteristics common across multiple companies.

Factors such as intra-sector size – differences in market capitalization between companies within the same economic sector – explain the performance deviations without any need to reference exclusions or sustainability (Adamsson and Hoepner, 2015; Blitz and Swinkels, 2021). Yet, regardless of explanation, excluding a large number of public equities without taking appropriate portfolio construction countermeasures can create tracking error and result in periods of cyclical investment underperformance.

The evidence suggesting that exclusions cause structural underperformance is scant. Research shows that a well-constructed portfolio, which takes into account factor biases such as those mentioned above, may consist of little more than 100 stocks (Evans and Archer, 1968; Fisher and Lorie, 1970; Statman, 1987; Campbell et al, 2002; Domian, Louton and Racine, 2007). Such a relatively concentrated portfolio can replicate the economic sensitivities and mimic the investment performance of the wider market. Consequently, provided their portfolios are well constructed, investors can exclude multiple stocks – even entire sectors – and retain their risk-adjusted investment performance.

This finding is taken as gospel across the fund management industry. The vast majority of investment portfolios, whether actively or passively managed, hold a mere fraction of the 40,000 public companies available to investors globally (De La Cruz, Medina and Tang, 2019). Passive portfolios, in particular, have long been explicitly designed to use a smaller number of stocks to mimic a larger index, a process known as stratified sampling.

A notable sustainable example is the MSCI All-Countries World Low Carbon Target index. This index excludes companies based upon their reported, or estimated, carbon emissions and uses just two-thirds of the stocks found in the parent index, the MSCI All-Countries World index. Relative to its parent, the Low Carbon Target index reduces the portfolio's carbon footprint by 70 per cent yet operates with a tracking error (a measure of performance deviation) of just 0.3 per cent annually (MSCI, 2022b). Through diversification and proper portfolio construction, exclusions can be profitably employed and structural underperformance avoided.

The evidence in support of the theory that exclusions have significantly altered the demand and price for stocks is also limited. Demand for public equities has been shown to be highly elastic (Kaul, Mehrotra and Morck, 2000; Wurgler and Zhuravskaya, 2002; Ahern, 2014). When exclusionary-focused investors avoid or divest from a company, sustainability-agnostic investors quickly fill the void with minimal price impact.

To create a demand–supply imbalance large enough to make excluded equities 'cheap' and thus ensure underperformance for exclusionary-focused investors, the percentage of investors shunning the same stocks would have to be impractically large, research has shown. Without this factor being fulfilled, a security's long-term price or a company's cost of capital is barely affected (Heinkel, Kraus and Zechner, 2001; Berk and van Binsbergen, 2021).

Notwithstanding the evidence cited above, many sustainable funds do not actually pursue large-scale exclusions. Instead they adjust their investment universes in minor ways. A survey of exclusion-focused funds found that a little over half applied a 'sin' screen that included tobacco, alcohol, gambling and pornography. Yet this combination affected only about 5 per cent of global market capitalization (Schroders, 2017).

What would have a far greater impact on the investment universe – excluding, for example, all fossil fuel-related stocks – is pursued by less than 5 per cent of exclusionary portfolios (Schroders, 2017).

Because many self-proclaimed exclusionary strategies target only a small handful of activities deemed unsavoury, they are, arguably, not undertaking a credible sustainable exclusionary strategy at all.

Exclusion: Does it help people and the planet?

Short answer: No.

IN THEORY

Proponents of exclusion in public equities advance theories for why exclusion should help people and the planet. The benefits could originate from exclusionary-focused investors increasing the cost of capital for unsavoury firms by excluding them from their portfolio. This action would make it incrementally harder for targeted firms to do business and could lead, ultimately, to them ceasing operations.

By refusing to purchase or by divesting securities, the theory suggests, exclusionary-focused investors push down equity prices and thereby raise a company's cost of capital (Rohleder, Wilkens and Zink, 2022). A higher cost of capital will make some projects economically unprofitable and cause them to be vetoed by company management. For example, if a new oil pipeline is forecast to return 10 per cent annually in profits, but the cost to finance it is 12 per cent, the pipeline will almost certainly not be built. Conversely, if the cost to finance it is 8 per cent, then the likelihood of the company going ahead with the project is high.

IN PRACTICE

Despite the best of investor intentions there is little evidence that this theory works in real life. The concepts of investor return and corporate cost-of-capital are intricately linked. A higher cost of capital for a company mechanically implies a higher return for an investor (Asness, 2017). As previously discussed, exclusions do not materially alter the price of equities, so exclusionary-focused investors do not increase the cost of equity for targeted corporations. This creates an awkward dynamic for proponents of exclusion, who would need their investments to mechanically underperform to have the impact they desire (Blitz and Swinkels, 2021).

A 2021 paper by researchers from Stanford University and The Wharton School of the University of Pennsylvania illustrated just how far exclusionary-focused investors are from having a beneficial effect on people and the planet. It would take 80 per cent of all investable wealth acting in a sustainable manner, the authors showed, to create a 1 per cent change in a firm's cost of capital. They concluded 'that current ESG divestiture strategies have had little impact and will likely have little impact in the future' (Berk and van Binsbergen, 2021). Billionaire philanthropist Bill Gates has been even more damning. In relation to climate change, he concluded that 'Divestment, to date, probably has reduced about zero tonnes of emissions. It's not like you've capital-starved [the] people making steel and gasoline' (Edgecliff-Johnson and Nauman 2019).

How integration processes operate

Integration: Knowledge is power

When new information that can improve your decision making is offered, it's logical to make use of it. Richard Thaler's 2017 Nobel Prize in economics, bestowed on him for his behavioural finance insights, owes much to the integration of psychology into traditional economic paradigms (Nobel Prize Organization, n.d.). Integrating machine learning and image recognition into various forms of cancer screening has improved detection rates (Shen et al, 2019). Listening to your co-author's constructive feedback and integrating it into the final copy undoubtedly improves the quality of a chapter. Integration takes information, weighs it for relevance and materiality, and uses it to contest, confirm and improve upon the original assessment of a situation.

Within public equities, the process of integration involves applying relevant sustainability data to the investment case. It is an approach that expands the range of information brought to bear on investment decisions.

The GSIA estimates that, as of year-end 2022, $25 trillion, or more than 25 per cent of professionally managed assets, make use of integration (GSIA, 2021). As we argued in 'Chapter 1 – What is sustainable investing?', self-identified or rudimentary integration practices are insufficient in most cases to credibly refer to an investment product as sustainable. A similar view has led Goldman Sachs to attribute just $1.7 trillion to integration-led sustainable strategies (Bingham et al, 2022).

HOW INTEGRATION PROCESSES TYPICALLY FUNCTION

The United Nations Principles for Responsible Investment define integration as 'the explicit and systematic inclusion of environmental, social and governance issues in investment analysis and investment decisions' (Orsagh, Sloggett and Georgieva, 2018).

Within public equities, integration typically starts with an assessment of materiality, which considers on a granular level the sustainability factors most relevant. For example, when it comes to a fast-fashion retailer, topics such as the fair treatment of employees, supply chain management and water stress have the potential to affect company value. By contrast, for a bank, loan exposure to climate change-sensitive locations, employee remuneration governance and staff turnover in control functions may be more significant topics.

Investors may be guided by a range of sources, including third-party materiality frameworks such as those developed by the Sustainability Accounting Standards Board (SASB). An assessment would factor in the financial metrics potentially affected by the identified topics, namely, margins, revenues, cost-of-capital, etc., as well as the likelihood and/or extent in various scenarios of the effect.

An investor would then seek consistent data points and key performance indicators related to the topics identified. Quality checks would typically be conducted to ascertain, just as with financial data, whether any idiosyncratic, geographic or other adjustments are required. Subsequent peer comparisons would seek to identify sector norms, peer dispersion and potential outliers (Orsagh, Sloggett and Georgieva, 2018). Armed with this information, an investor would adjust financial projections made in the absence of sustainability data or, in the case of more coordinated processes, create forecasts with sustainability factors fully incorporated into the assumptions and modelling.

Integration may also be applied during portfolio construction. Sources of risk attributable to sustainability, such as exposure to physical factors or transitional climate change, may be considered in a portfolio context to avoid concentration issues when sizing positions. Other portfolio-level integration techniques are also possible. They might include environmental or social stress tests or scenario analysis, such as the portfolio risk caused by rising sea levels or an increase in minimum wages or corporate taxes worldwide.

Integration: Going mainstream

In the early 20th century, a handful of swimming strokes were used in the freestyle category at the Olympics. The most popular was the so-called Trudgen stroke – a hybrid of front crawl arm technique and breaststroke leg kick. Today, swimmers are still allowed to use any competitive swimming stroke (front crawl, breaststroke, butterfly, backstroke) when racing freestyle, although front crawl is so widely adopted that there is no need for a discrete front crawl race.

The spectrum of what constitutes integration is so broad it has been argued that integration has 'gone mainstream' (Bernow, Klempner and Magnin, 2017; Patel, 2018) and has now been adopted by a large number of public equity investors. This has blurred the lines to such an extent that the term integration may no longer refer to a discrete investment strategy.

The diffusion of integration practices across the investment industry can be partially attributed to integration being a process rather than a set of rules. Practices can vary widely from firm to firm and can differ markedly between a firm's stated activities and their procedures in reality. It can therefore be difficult to identify legitimate integration as opposed to tokenism.

Legitimate integration impacts all aspects of an investment case – from long-term margin and cost-of-capital assumptions to terminal growth rates. Unable to perform due diligence on an investment manager's practices, a retail investor is hard pressed to confirm whether the manager is practicing credible integration by using public information alone.

Furthermore, there are few incentives for institutional investors, who seek to attract capital to manage, to publicly denounce integration's value. Integration adds information to the investment decision-making process, so investors must be prepared to state that they consciously do not consider all material issues when making investment decisions. This admission would seemingly cause them to violate their fiduciary duty and certainly could tarnish the attractiveness of their investment firm to potential allocators of sustainable capital.

As a consequence, an ever-growing number of strategies claim to integrate sustainability into their investment process, regardless of the reality. Retail investors are left wondering who really does what.

Integration: Same, same, but... same

Incentives are powerful motivators. Within athletics, national governing bodies are usually responsible for conducting drug tests on their athletes. There is often little incentive for the drug testers to catch the cheats, as doing so would deprive their country of a medal hope. Giving the impression of conducting thorough testing while essentially allowing the athletes to continue doing what they've always done is much easier and tends to be what some unscrupulous governing bodies default to.

A similar dynamic can play out within sustainability. When an analyst discusses the topic with a battle-hardened portfolio manager, the career interests of both can be furthered by making it appear to superiors that a serious process is being followed, even if the portfolio managers continue to do what they've always done.

For example, portfolio managers may be happy to superficially endorse sustainability issues in exchange for not having to significantly change their process. This can take the form of stating, 'I am already looking at the key ESG issues.' Or by offering soundbite examples such as, 'That CEO who smoked marijuana on social media exemplified poor governance.' Or by claiming to factor in environmental risk ex post: 'I didn't own the oil company responsible for the big oil spill that wiped billions off its market capitalization.'

Forced to choose between testy interpersonal conflict and a high five from management, the two protagonists have incentive to agree, respectfully ignore one another or conduct an unengaged training session.

The United Nations Principles for Responsible Investment (UN PRI), the largest body of sustainable investors in the world, gives credence to this unfortunate reality by stating that integration 'does not mean major changes to your investment process are necessary' (Orsagh, Sloggett and Georgieva, 2018).

As a result, two firms purporting to integrate sustainability may, in fact, feature vastly different processes and maintain contrary credibility.

These dynamics are, to an extent, visible in the holdings of sustainable funds. In some cases, the resultant portfolios that purport to integrate sustainability differ little from those that do not. Researchers from UK bank Barclays combed through two decades worth of fund holdings data and concluded that 'ESG funds are not really different from conventional funds in terms of holdings, risk exposures and therefore performance' (Barclays, 2020).

In sum, it is illogical to suggest that by changing nothing in the investment process, integration can be value additive. While some integration processes are highly effective and credible, others are same, same, but… same.

Having reviewed how integration processes operate, we now examine them in theory and in practice by asking and answering three key questions.

Integration: Does quantitative integration add to investment performance?

Short answer: A little (at least for now).

IN THEORY

Proponents of quantitative integration in public equities advance theories as to why exclusion should contribute to investment performance. They posit that financial markets are not fully efficient and that not all public information is incorporated into a security's current price. A superior understanding of a company's competitive position, therefore, can improve investment returns.

In this paradigm, understanding sustainability trends and material sustainability factors can give an investor an edge. Proponents will argue that sustainability considerations are often relatively under-researched by market participants and that ESG investing is a relatively immature investment discipline (Howard-Grenville, 2021; Varley and Lewis, 2021).

Investors seeking to verify that quantitative integration can aid performance often use quantitative methods to create a number of robust time series for analysis. For example, popular data provider MSCI runs a range of rules-based 'Socially Responsible Investing' (SRI) indices that can be compared with conventional benchmarks. The SRI indices compile a huge swathe of sustainable data that is computed based on its financial materiality to form a headline rating. Only the resulting top 25 per cent of companies are included in the index (MSCI, 2021).

IN PRACTICE

Several hundred studies have assessed how the quantitative integration of sustainability has influenced investment performance. The most comprehensive meta-study was conducted by researchers at the University of Hamburg. It found that studies that focused solely on investment performance demonstrated a positive relationship between ESG adherence and performance far more frequently than those that indicated a negative relationship (Friede, Busch and Bassen, 2015).

Individual studies that have focused on sustainability through the lens of financial materiality have also buttressed quantitative integration's reputation. A Harvard University study determined that equities ranked in the top quartile on material sustainability issues outperformed their bottom quartile peers by more than 2.7 per cent annually, on a sample size of 2,000 US companies over two decades (Khan, Serafeim and Yoon, 2016).

This sanguine view has not gone unchallenged. In the (almost) entertainingly titled 2021 paper *'Honey, I Shrunk the ESG Alpha': Risk-adjusting ESG portfolio returns*, the authors noted that '75 per cent of outperformance is due to quality factors that are mechanically constructed from balance sheet information' (Bruno, Esakia and Goltz, 2021). Such research, which does not deny that sustainable integration strategies have outperformed their conventional peers, explains the outperformance as a product of conventional financial factors. These academics argue that the observed outperformance can be replicated without reference to sustainability (Madhavan, Sobczyk and Ang, 2021).

The challenge has some merit. Since public equity markets are highly liquid it is unlikely that a widely available set of rules would be able to generate consistent investment outperformance. That would imply a persistent mispricing of equity securities and a failure by market participants to correct it despite evidence of its existence.

The historic outperformance achieved by quantitative integration strategies is possibly cyclical, not structural. Financial equilibrium models demonstrate that rising share prices result in a lower implied cost of equity and thus lower future returns (Pedersen, Fitzgibbons and Pomorski, 2020). The recent outperformance enjoyed by companies that exhibit a strong quantitatively identified sustainability profile would, according to this logic, later give way to longer-term underperformance (Pastor, Stambaugh and Taylor, 2021). Academic estimates as to how long such cyclical dynamics persist vary. Typically, the proposed period is five to six years (Avramov et al, 2021). Interestingly, as of 2022, the aforementioned quantitatively integrated MSCI SRI global index has outperformed its conventional counterpart in six consecutive years (MSCI, 2022c).

In sum, the practical evidence points to quantitative integration producing mild outperformance. But legitimate questions remain about whether conventional factors or sustainability explain it. There is also considerable debate as to whether quantitative integration will remain a persistent source of excess return.

Integration: Does qualitative integration add to investment performance?

Short answer: A little.

IN THEORY

Proponents of qualitative, or process-based, integration in public equities put forward theories for why it should increase investment performance. They argue that markets are not perfectly efficient and superior investment processes can yield superior investment results.

Unlike quantitative approaches, qualitative integration processes can evolve. They do not mechanically process data and can therefore benefit from investor judgement and skill. Understanding material ESG factors contributes to the investment process, according to this thinking. By qualitatively integrating and adapting to changing circumstances, sustainable investors can develop deeper insights into how shareholder value will be created (CFA Institute, n.d.).

IN PRACTICE

There is less research about qualitative than quantitative integration. Academic studies typically require long time series compiled objectively and with minimal hindsight bias. By qualitative integration's very nature, an evolving process will create a time series in which ESG criteria are inconsistently applied.

A robust way of assessing qualitative integration is to look at its performance in practice. This entails examining the track record of public equity funds that purport to use the approach. We can determine whether these funds have added to investment performance or not.

In 2020, fund-data provider Morningstar undertook a study of more than 4,000 equity funds. It concluded that 'a majority of surviving sustainable funds (those that existed 10 years ago and still exist today [in 2020]) outperformed their average surviving traditional peer'. A full 58 per cent of sustainable funds boasted outperformance, Morningstar found, with global and US sustainable funds edging their conventional peers by 60 and 100 annual basis points, respectively. Sustainable funds also had a higher survivorship rate than their conventional peers, perhaps demonstrating their persistent appeal to investors (Bioy, 2020).

Since 2020, more qualitative integration studies have been published. Morgan Stanley noted that, in 2020, across a sample of 3000 equity funds, sustainable equity funds outperformed their traditional peer funds by a median total return of 4.3 percentage points (Morgan Stanley, 2021). Morningstar found that, in 2020, 42 per cent of sustainable equity funds had first-quartile performance relative to peers with just 6 per cent of sustainable equity funds producing fourth-quartile performance (Hale, 2021b). This trend continued, though in milder form, in 2021 when 56 per cent of sustainable funds claimed top-half performance compared with peers (Hale, 2021a).

Integration: Does it help people and the planet?

Short answer: No.

IN THEORY

Proponents of integration in public equities theorize about why it should help people and the planet. By integrating it into the investment case, investors may improve their ability to forecast the fair value of public equities. By buying undervalued and selling overvalued securities, they may claim to be influencing the share prices of companies and helping them settle at their fair value.

Theory links the share price to the cost of capital. A share price closer to fair value will result in a more accurate cost of capital and ensure that only appropriate projects, with all sustainability risks and opportunities considered, will be funded.

Another theoretical impact that integration could have stems from the so-called signalling effect. Through the process of integration, investors publicly declare which sustainable topics are important for an investment case. They raise awareness of what constitutes 'good' and 'bad' corporate behaviour. Proponents of integration may claim to be having a signalling effect and affecting a company's social licence to operate, potentially impacting the company's relationship with its customers, suppliers and regulators (Impact Management Project, 2018; Asset Management Association and Swiss Sustainable Finance, 2021).

IN PRACTICE

As with exclusion, there is scant evidence that integration has any meaningful real-world impact. At the margin, superior investment returns from sustainable funds imply that investee companies benefited from higher share prices and may have enjoyed incremental cost-of-capital benefits. But evidence related to this transmission mechanism is far from conclusive (La Torre et al, 2020).

The concept of signalling has not been rigorously tested, as of 2022, by academics (Kölbel et al, 2020). Sustainability's popularity has undoubtedly soared in recent years, but it is not possible to say why: whether it's because of investor action or due to investors reacting to the wider trend. Some practitioners of it have been sceptical about the signalling effect. Former BlackRock Sustainability Chief Investment Officer Tariq Fancy refers to the practice as little more than wishful thinking. It is akin to a placebo, in his view, and enables the investment industry to claim impact and action while failing to fundamentally alter their practices (Bisnoff, 2021). An ever so slightly more favourable view is espoused by University of Zurich researchers. They argue that, by virtue of scale, ESG integration 'maybe' impacts the real economy 'a little bit' (Heeb, Kellers and Kölbel, 2022).

How engagement processes operate

Engagement: It's good to talk

In the mid 1990s, British Telecom ran a successful marketing campaign with the slogan 'It's good to talk' (IPA, n.d.). In many cases, talking can resolve conflict, whether of the Cuban Missile Crisis or The Troubles in Northern Ireland variety. It also works well with your significant other.

Try ignoring your upset partner after you have left the towels on the floor (again) or didn't clean the sink or shower after shaving. It's far better to engage, to talk, to use your influence as a loved one to defuse and then rectify the situation. Engagement employs constructive dialogue as well as status and influence to create mutually beneficial outcomes.

A subset of investors sought to apply the lessons learnt from leaving towels on the bathroom floor to the sustainable investing industry. They noted the lack of real-world impact created by traditional exclusion and integration approaches and hoped to flip public equity sustainable investing on its head. Rather than excluding companies with suboptimal sustainability profiles or penalizing them through integration, they purchased the securities of select firms with the intent of using their influence to constructively engage with them (Investment Week, 2020; Davies, 2021; Phillipps, n.d.).

The GSIA estimates that, as of year-end 2022, $10 trillion, or over 10 per cent of professionally managed assets, engage in engagement (GSIA, 2021). As we argued in 'Chapter 1 – What is sustainable investing?', self-identified or rudimentary engagement practices are unlikely to suffice to credibly refer to an investment product as sustainable. This view is supported by the actions of Goldman Sachs' sustainability research team. In late 2021, analysts at Goldman Sachs removed several sustainable funds from their market analysis due to the funds' only undertaking token engagement (Bingham et al, 2021).

Huge swathes of the institutional investor community now publish 'active ownership' reports detailing their engagement and voting records. In our experience of running multi-billion US-dollar sustainable investing programs, however, only a small number of funds actually put engagement at the centre of their investment strategy and use it as a tool to catalyse sustainability momentum, generate corporate operational improvements and achieve investment outperformance.

HOW ENGAGEMENT PROCESSES TYPICALLY FUNCTION

Within public equities the process of engagement is, typically, a constructive dialogue between investors and company management. It includes, but goes beyond, using voting rights at corporate meetings and seeks a deeper relationship where the shareholder provides support in the form of monitoring, constructive challenge and the provision of subject matter expertise (Hermes Investment, n.d.).

Engagement may start with either a top-down or bottom-up process. In a top-down process, an investment firm defines its engagement priorities. These tend to be values-led ones and may relate to a global framework such as the UN Sustainable Development Goals (SDGs). The investment firm under this model will raise these topics with company management in order to influence policy and actions. The firm, in certain circumstances, may proactively seek out investments in companies whose operations have particular relevance to the engagement topics.

A bottom-up process begins with an analysis of existing portfolio holdings. Similar to the process of integration, a materiality assessment may be undertaken to identify potentially relevant risks and opportunities at a stock-specific level. When a topic is identified, the investment firm may consider whether it has adequate resources and expertise to succeed with an engagement.

In either case, after a topic and target company are identified, an engagement strategy will be drawn up. It normally consists of objectives and milestones that serve as progress indicators. Who to engage with, whether investor relations, the head of corporate sustainability or a C-level executive, will be considered.

Engagement may take place through private dialogue, such as bilateral calls and letters. It may also occur through public forums, e.g., by asking questions at an annual general meeting or publishing open letters in the press. It may be undertaken alone or conducted collectively. In the latter case, an investor alliance such as Climate Action 100+ or ShareAction can be joined or formed. A collective engagement could also be spearheaded by an engagement service provider such as Federated Hermes EOS or BMO Reo. Such firms maintain a large team of professionals and provide an outsourced service for smaller investors without the resources to engage public companies directly.

Engagement strategies will likely include escalation measures in the event that progress cannot be made. These measures may include, but are not limited to, contacting a more senior corporate executive, migrating collective action from the private to the public sphere to increase public pressure, raising a shareholder proposal at an annual general meeting or staging a protest vote, against, for instance, the reappointment of a board member. Should engagement fail, investors may consider divestment and exclusion (Robeco, n.d.).

Engagement: I have a feeling

Olympic boxing has endured numerous scoring controversies in its history, perhaps none more 'outlandish' than the legendary Roy Jones Jr's unfathomable 1988 loss to Park Si-hun. Jones landed 86 punches on his South Korean opponent, who only connected with 32 of his own (Ashdown, 2012). The core issue that the sport has faced (apart from instances of outright corruption) is that boxing scoring is largely subjective. Aggression, punch accuracy and ring generalship can all play a role in a judge's scoring, meaning that the resultant scores are often a product of a judge's 'feeling'.

Measuring success for corporate engagements can also create difficulties as defining milestones and progress is inherently subjective. What constitutes progress on gender diversity, for example? Is it a fundamental shift in management composition, the announcement of a new hiring target, a 'productive' meeting with the CEO or the topic being acknowledged as 'relevant' by investor relations? Faced with such complexities, some investors may default to requests that are easier to definitively measure, such as 'stop doing X' or 'start publishing Y'.

Such a binary approach to engagement, however, risks debasing the value of it, especially if an investor measures success in percentage terms. Being content to publish the share of engagements that have brought a milestone nearer may limit changes to small, incremental ones immaterial to company value and of little benefit to people and the planet. Examples of such irrelevant 'success' include management agreeing to make a minor disclosure or announcing that it will formally 'consider' an opposing point of view.

Other investors, recognizing the limitations of binary requests, may seek to trigger more substantial and complex change. In these cases assessing an engagement's efficacy is a heterogeneous exercise and can, without suitable oversight, lead to investors creating self-aggrandizing narratives.

For example, was mining giant Anglo American's exit from its South African coal operations (Reuters, 2022) due to engagement from sustainable investors, a reflection of changing demand patterns, a calculated financial step, or a combination of all three? As of 2022, despite a plethora of new players launching engagement services (Sharma, 2021; Morningstar Sustainalytics, n.d.), investors can call on no significant third-party assessors or auditors of engagement programs. Consequently, whether engagement is deemed to be working can often be a case of 'I have a feeling'.

Engagement: Jumping on the bandwagon

In a corporate setting, when something good happens, many individuals come out of the woodwork to link themselves to the success. On the day a big account is signed, the senior manager will insist on sending out the company-wide email on behalf of the salesperson responsible for the triumph. The account manager previously tasked with wooing the client (but sidelined after failing to make progress on it) will proudly speak of the solid foundations that were laid. And the marketing team will reference how the new client once complimented the colours in a pitch book. When something goes well, people are only too happy to share in the credit.

Many of the highest profile successes have resulted from collective engagement – numerous investors binding together to present a common view to a company. Examples include Climate Action 100+ pushing chemical giant BASF to commit to net zero by 2050 and reduce emissions 25 per cent by 2030 (Climate Action 100+, 2021). And ShareAction persuading HSBC to end coal financing by 2040 and within the OECD by 2030 (ShareAction, 2022).

Collective engagement can be a powerful instrument as it can generate significant media attention and drum up public pressure. However, such exercises can also lead some collective engagement signatories to freeload and claim each success as their own, even if they only played a minor role in the engagement. Dozens of investors using the same engagement as an example of their excellent stewardship can mislead end investors and results in a case of jumping on the bandwagon.

Having reviewed how engagement processes operate, we'll now examine them in theory and in practice by asking and answering three important questions.

Engagement: Can just anyone successfully engage?

Short answer: No.

IN THEORY

Proponents of engagement in public equities advance theories for why it should be an option for all investors. Any shareholder in a public company can, in theory, make their opinions known to management. They can send the CEO a letter, ask questions on quarterly earnings conference calls and request an audience with management.

IN PRACTICE

Size, in terms of your holdings in the company, matters. Retail and smaller institutional investors have less access to corporate management than larger investors do. In many cases small, individual investors have no access at all. This curtails their ability to engage.

When it comes to voting, investors seeking to file a shareholder resolution to be considered at an annual general meeting face differing requirements by country. In the US, the dollar value of stock holdings required for an investor to file is relatively low at $25,000 (As You Sow, n.d.). But the process is complex and companies often contest the potential resolution at the Securities Exchange Commission (ICCR, 2017). The technical nature of the process effectively excludes many smaller investors.

Analysts from universal bank Credit Suisse note the constraints and state that 'most shareholders own a small proportion of the shares and therefore have limited formal power'. Credit Suisse goes on to suggest that 'shareholders can consider building coalitions and pool their influence to send a stronger signal to companies' (Credit Suisse, 2020). This view is echoed elsewhere, with collaborative engagement said to yield greater 'legitimacy' (Gond and Piani, 2013) than individual actions.

The importance of sizeable holdings is evidenced in academic studies. A paper by University of Cambridge researchers looked at a sample of engagements and found that collaborative engagement increased the success rate by more than 25 per cent. The study also found that investors holding a larger percentage of the shares had greater success and that domestic investors wielded more influence than foreign ones (Dimson, Karakaş and Li, 2015). Although there are always exceptions (Herbst-Bayliss, 2021), barriers to entry for investors seeking to use their voice to make a tangible impact on corporate behaviour tend to be considerable.

Engagement: Does it add to investment performance?

Short answer: Possibly.

IN THEORY

Proponents of engagement in public equities expound on why it should increase investment performance. They suggest that investors are able to identify deficiencies that have a material impact on corporate financial wellbeing. It follows then that a company which listens to them and then fixes the problem will improve its operations, financial health and share price.

A practitioner view from Federated Hermes EOS (EOS) states 'that companies with informed and involved shareholders are more likely to effectively manage risk and achieve superior long-term performance' (Hermes Investment, n.d.).

Some practitioners have gone further in recent years. They have sought to create investment alpha by catalysing corporate sustainability improvement (BMO, 2019; UBS, 2019). When a company betters its sustainability practices, they theorize, it concurrently enhances the quality of its operations and competitive position (Clark and Lalit, 2020). Engagement in their view is a tool to catalyse sustainability improvement. They prefer not to passively wait for it to occur unaided.

IN PRACTICE

Because of the heterogeneous nature of engagement, obtaining robust datasets that cover it being consistently performed and measured is difficult. Furthermore, proving causation between engagement and subsequent management action, as well as assigning the appropriate degree of attribution to the investor's actions, is highly problematic. These dynamics also make assessing the impact of the investor's engagement on the share price, while controlling for other variables such as factor performance or exogenous causes, extremely challenging.

Thus, only a handful of academic studies exist. They typically rely on non-public information provided by (self-interested) asset managers. So the papers may suffer to an extent from the conflicts of interest of their authors. What they suggest is that engagement adds huge value to an investment process.

A 2012 study led by Cambridge University researchers with a dataset spanning more than 600 US companies between 1999 and 2009 found that engagement on environmental and social topics succeeded in triggering a cumulative size-adjusted abnormal return of 7.1 per cent over the subsequent 12 months (Dimson, Karakaş and Li, 2015). These findings were echoed by a study of almost 300 companies between 2005 and 2014, which determined that value-at-risk was 20 per cent lower for engaged firms compared with a control group (Hoepner et al, 2021).

A further study, published in 2021, used data from a European asset manager and supported this positive view. It assessed 660 engaged companies and peer matched them using a four-factor adjustment in an attempt to isolate the effects of engagement. The researchers discovered that excess returns from targeted firms were

2.7 per cent higher than those of non-targeted peer firms over the six-month period following the engagement. Interestingly, the results were especially strong for firms that had exhibited poor sustainability practices, as measured by third-party ESG ratings. Specifically, targeted firms in the lowest ESG quartile outperformed their matched peers by 7.5 per cent in the year subsequent to the engagement, suggesting the efficacy of sustainable improvement as an investment strategy (Barko, Cremers and Renneboog, 2021).

These studies provide some support for the case that engagement can add to investment performance. Given the studies' structural limitations though, no definitive view on its value in the investment process can realistically be formed.

Engagement: Does it help people and the planet?

Short answer: A little.

THE THEORY

Proponents of engagement in public equities offer theories for why engagement should benefit people and the planet. The argument is straightforward. If an investor identifies a sustainability deficiency within a target firm, which is then subsequently fixed, this change will almost certainly prove beneficial. If the investor can prove a direct cause-and-effect relationship between their engagement and the resultant action, then they can claim additionality – a change that would not have occurred had it not been for their intervention.

A less expansive interpretation of the theory states that the concerns raised by an investor form part of a mosaic of information that may progressively shift a topic up a corporate agenda and lead to improvements.

IN PRACTICE

There is at least anecdotal evidence to support these claims. Investors frequently publish case studies that document the purported real-world impact of their actions (Federated Hermes, 2021). And academic studies have shown that successful engagement can lead to changes in a company's third-party ESG rating (Dyck et al, 2019; Barko, Cremers and Renneboog, 2021). Improved ESG ratings, while typically focused on financial materiality, could be interpreted as a company accepting responsibility to act more consciously on behalf of people and the planet.

But proving cause and effect between the engagement and the outcome is difficult. In practice, a company could have changed course for any number of reasons, such as customer or supplier pressure. Even when the link between engagement and action is explicit, such as when a company appoints a director from a historically underrepresented background, no meaningful real-world impact may result. Companywide management representation may not change nor pay gaps narrow.

Interestingly, studies show that social engagements tend to have a higher success rate than environmental engagements (Dimson, Karakaş and Li, 2015). Attempting to explain this discrepancy, researchers have found that engagements succeed more frequently when the cost of change to the corporate is lower (Barko, Cremers and Renneboog, 2021). Sadly this implies that engagements, in general, only influence minor elements of corporate strategy and that their impact is similarly limited.

In this interview, James sat down with Catherine Howarth to discuss sustainable investing and active ownership. Since 2008, Catherine has served as the CEO of ShareAction, a charity committed to driving financial system change through regulatory collaboration, the coordination of investor engagement and the benchmarking of investors' sustainable practices. A board member of the Scott Trust, the owner of *The Guardian*, Catherine was recognised in 2014 by the World Economic Forum as a Young Global Leader.

James: Thank you for taking the time, Catherine. How did you become part of the sustainable investing ecosystem?

Catherine: I got into the field in an unusual way. Before ShareAction I spent eight years working for a remarkable organization called London Citizens, which used a very disciplined and interesting methodology for building power in powerless communities. And as part of that, 20-something years ago, we started the Living Wage Campaign in the UK.

And at the time, HSBC and Barclays were both building their new headquarters at Canary Wharf, and we were working in the East End of London. So, to bring this concept of living wages to life, we engaged the banks. I bought shares in HSBC, just five shares, actually. And I had shares from my grandmother in Barclays. So, I could therefore go to the annual general meetings (AGMs).

My first taste of shareholder action was at Barclays' general meeting, putting a question to the board about living wages. I also attended HSBC's AGM, although there we went with a cleaner who was due to begin work at HSBC.

We ended up playing Barclays and HSBC off against each other, which was a valuable lesson for me in how to take the competition in capitalism and make it a force for good. Anyways, after some initial resistance, Barclays became the first FTSE100 company to become an accredited living wage employer in the UK. Once that happened, HSBC rapidly followed suit.

And I thought, these shareholder tactics are really interesting, but how did I get into the field? So, I stood for election to the board of my own pension scheme and was elected by its members. It was a big multi-employer scheme for the UK's not-for-profit sector, which was established in the late 1940s, and had very democratic governance. Once elected, I then got an incredible education in investment matters and fiduciary obligation. So, that's how I got into it all.

James: I like this idea of harnessing the capitalist urge to create positive competition. Would you say that that is the biggest positive surprise you've encountered?

Catherine: I think what's been unexpectedly positive is that, right across the financial system, we encounter people who really get sustainability, and they get it at a personal as well as a professional level. It becomes quite motivating for them. Those people drive change from within, pushing against the constraints and the incentive systems that don't reward sustainability.

James: Let's do the other side as well. What has been the biggest negative?

Catherine: The way fiduciary duties of investors are set out in law is hugely problematic. Indeed, it's not fit for purpose in the 21st century. We all know that investee companies can have significant negative impacts on the environment and on society and these impacts can and do harm beneficiaries of the pension schemes that invest in such companies. Yet pension scheme fiduciaries are only permitted in law to take a narrow view of sustainability as it affects the enterprise value of the companies in a pension portfolio. Although the duty of a pension fiduciary is to act in the best interests of their beneficiaries, the law as it stands inhibits fiduciaries from fulfilling that duty. Why? Because any action by a fiduciary investor to challenge a company's negative impact on society and the environment is prohibited if taking that action conflicts with maximising financial returns. So, investment law, in effect, places a huge brake on meaningful action to achieve sustainable business behaviour.

James: In this book, Simon and I focus not only on challenges but opportunities too. What do you see as the biggest opportunity within sustainability?

Catherine: We would unlock more change if we had more democratic structures in capital markets. I talked earlier about my pension scheme, which was established in the 1940s, and its democratic design. I, as an ordinary scheme member, without a background in finance, could stand to be on the board. That's hugely unusual now.

Indeed, we have actually gone backwards in terms of the democratic governance of fiduciary institutions. These days you hand your earnings over to a pension scheme and have almost no way of knowing where it's going, what happens to it. If we gave end investors more voice and power, that would catalyse deeper change. This matters greatly in a world where we know that young people recognize the relevance and value to them of sustainability.

Then, taking a different angle, ShareAction does a huge amount of work to encourage institutional investors to be more active owners and become engaged as stewards of companies. Most of that happens in the public equities space. I see a huge opportunity to adopt that responsible stewardship mindset in the fixed income space and in private markets too.

James: Let's go deeper into active ownership then. How do you see the interplay of exclusion and engagement?

Catherine: I very much see them as part of the same toolkit. It's a false dichotomy to present engagement as in opposition to divestment. That said, a lot of engagement activity needs to sharpen up. Credible engagement means setting clear asks of companies and adopting an escalation pathway. Ultimately, if the asks are not met, this may result in you divesting. But even having divested, you can continue to engage. If these are, for example, systemically important high-carbon companies, you have an interest in them even when they're not in your portfolio. They might come back in at some other time having acted to adopt a credible low-carbon transition plan. So, it's not like divestment is always the end of engagement.

James: One of the criticisms of engagement is that it ends up shifting assets from the public to the private markets, as public companies respond to investor pressure. Is that a valid criticism or a bit of a misdirection?

Catherine: I think it is a valid challenge. But there may be a somewhat limited set of buyers for potentially high-risk assets. The idea that private equity wants to lap up a whole lot of dodgy high-carbon assets is possibly a bit naive.

In order to achieve the carbon transition, we need a far greater allocation to green assets, and we don't see it on nearly the scale that's required at the moment. So, while I believe engagement with the high-carbon sectors is a critical part of the picture, we also need to focus on what capital allocators should be doing about green sectors and technologies. We have to put capital to work to create abundant, cheap, clean energy for industries that can then grow and thrive.

James: A criticism of collective engagement is that by grouping investors together, you create potential freeloading – investors claiming to have a positive impact when in fact they are not.

Catherine: That's a real issue. While collective action is critical, it does create the conditions in which much of the heavy lifting of engagement can be left to a small number of players while others just drift along. Indeed, sometimes those quieter players only exercise their influence when they want to slow things down, which is depressing.

So, asset owners need to smarten up about what credible engagement by asset managers looks like, and then insist on it from their managers. The challenge is that stewardship is not obviously rewarded in markets. We need to reimagine incentive structures within asset management to truly reward stewardship activity. Compared to portfolio management, it's not as richly rewarded, and that's a problem.

James: What does the optimal collaborative engagement look like then?

Catherine: ShareAction did a piece of work last year about the role of the food retail sector in public health. And we filed a shareholder resolution at Tesco, which has over a quarter of the UK's grocery market. Following the resolution, Tesco made some fantastic commitments, and then everybody else in the UK's food retail sector piled in and followed suit. I found that an interesting lesson. You can achieve systemic shifts across a sector if you identify the right initial corporate target to focus on. Furthermore, there is an interplay between the actions of sector leaders and the regulatory trajectory. Once a sector leader has made significant sustainability commitments, they have an interest in regulatory standards reaching the same bar, as do their investors. That's an important part of what good investor stewardship looks like, namely, to address public policy as well as directly engaging companies to act on a voluntary basis.

James: Let's look to the future. Where do you see the key sustainable investing debates taking place?

Catherine: The sustainable investing industry has largely – not entirely – won the battle that says: 'sustainable issues can be financially material, and when they are financially material, investors should manage them actively.' But there is still insufficient investor consideration of how sustainability considerations impact the real world and thus the lives of millions of people whose assets are put to work by professional investors. There continues to be a huge tension within the investment industry around this question.

At the more ambitious end of sustainable investing, people completely get it, but sometimes they have to do what they do on sustainability under cover of darkness almost, because of the constraints imposed by the prevailing legal standards of fiduciary obligation. It's almost like on the sly you get some good impacts. But you better be hush-hush about it because you might be clobbered for not paying sole attention to financial outcomes.

It is time to openly acknowledge that impact outcomes are relevant to all of us, including each of us as pension savers, or indeed retail investors. If we can make that leap then we move into a new, better dimension as far as sustainability outcomes are concerned. That's still a battle that hasn't been won.

My previous example of the living wage is pertinent. If companies don't pay decent wages then perhaps they make more profits and an individual's pension would be worth a little more. However, in aggregate that individual could be worse off due to stagnating wages. We need to connect the dots and acknowledge that these topics are highly material to the lives of people whose assets we look after. Short term, that might be a bit detrimental to so-called 'shareholder interest'. But who are the shareholders? They're millions and millions of working people whose lives are impacted by corporate decision-making. We don't yet have frameworks in sustainable investing that allow us to fully consider investment impacts but that is, surely, the next generation of change in this dynamic field of practice.

James: Catherine, thank you very much for your time.

The potential opportunities and how we might get there

Of all asset classes, equities have, arguably, the longest and most developed relationship with sustainable investing. Significant intellectual capital has been invested, with many obstacles overcome and many opportunities seized.

Yet, historically, equity investments have failed to deliver significant real-world benefit for people and the planet. In addition, approaches to exclusion, integration and engagement can be highly heterogeneous, which can make it difficult for retail investors to find products that align with their values and objectives.

To rectify this situation we'll focus on three opportunities with suggestions on how we might get there. The first focuses on exclusion and integration and seeks to address the current inconsistencies by pushing for standardized corporate reporting. The second tackles engagement and calls for an increase in the number of shareholder proposals at annual and extraordinary general meetings.

Our final opportunity concerns the lack of impact currently being created by public market equity investors. We argue that financial markets have evolved to the point that it is now possible to insert innovative features that achieve tangible, evidence-based real-world impact. We cite an example of a climate fund that commits to climate neutrality by counterbalancing reforestation projects.

Exclusion and integration

Exclusion and integration face significant hurdles. In this chapter, we have referenced a lack of homogeneity across industry processes and standards, difficulty in communicating processes clearly to end clients and a lack of real-world benefits.

The first two deficiencies can be addressed by applying standardized sustainable data and consistent strategy labelling. In 'Chapter 1 – What is sustainable investing?', we highlighted an appealing concept derived from nutritional information labels on packaged goods. Nutritional information offers a limited amount of data, measured consistently and presented clearly. A consumer can make quick, informed decisions based on it. For example, the bodybuilder might focus on protein and carbohydrate content while the traditional dieter will count calories.

Public equity products could deploy a similar approach. This would build on the consistent corporate reporting we advocated for in 'Chapter 2 – Sustainable data and ESG ratings'. If public equity products disclosed consistent metrics for all their holdings on popular topics, such as water and waste, a clear picture with a clear thread running through it would emerge throughout the sustainable investing industry. This consistent approach would start with corporate activities, be present in corporate reporting, form part of public equity product disclosure and finally would enable retail investors to act in an informed way upon their preferences.

Once public equity funds report a set of consistent metrics, it would be possible to pursue mass customization of retail investor portfolios, focusing on their specific values and preferences. Retail investors would also be able to assign a weight to each metric that would create a single overall personalized score. A bonus of acting on this opportunity would be that investors' aggregate preferences would function as a 'weighing machine'. Their choices would definitively define what retail investors truly care about. Corporations, fund managers and regulators could adapt accordingly.

Seizing this opportunity would not preclude institutional investors from operating additional, more complex exclusionary or integration processes. The proposal would merely create a tangible entry point for retail investors to demonstrate their preferences and understand the holdings within their portfolio, as well as the activities of the companies in which they invest.

OPPORTUNITIES

Define a small number of sustainability metrics and ensure that all public equity products report them consistently. This would enable mass customization of retail investors' portfolios and increase the adoption of sustainable investing practices.

Engagement

While engagement is generally considered to be more impactful than exclusion or integration (RBC Global Asset Management, 2021), this tool is not available to most retail investors. Data shows that public equity voting rights are significantly underutilized by retail investors and often go to waste. Data from voting facilitator Broadridge shows that institutional investors vote more than 90 per cent of their holdings, while retail investors vote less than 30 per cent of theirs (Proxy Pulse, 2020).

We believe that engagement can be made more effective by adopting a more authoritative position. Practitioners of sustainable engagement can take inspiration from activist shareholders and seek to reorient corporate business models to a more sustainable and profitable future. Such an opportunity, we acknowledge, may require an infusion of traditional activist talent. Our view finds support from hedge fund activist manager and billionaire philanthropist Chris Hohn who, in 2022, stated 'if you want to achieve change, you need a harder mechanism'. He suggested, in its current form, 'engagement achieves nothing' and, instead, was preparing to file numerous climate resolutions at corporation's annual general meetings (AGMs) in a more aggressive activist style (Pham and Marsh, 2022).

A less ambitious opportunity is to further the rights and reach of shareholders by expanding shareholder resolutions at AGM. According to Morningstar data, the number of social and environmental resolutions that pass in the US has increased dramatically, from less than five in 2015 to more than 35 in 2021 (Cook and Solberg, 2021). Institutional investors can step up their activity further and retail investors can pool their efforts through organizations such as As You Sow, which attempt to 'seed' change and rally retail shareholders. Such an approach has the potential to be far reaching, as countless companies, regardless of sector or economic activities, can be subject to shareholder resolutions.

Importantly, to get there, further regulatory support is needed. For example, in the US, a public company can petition the US Securities Exchange Commission (SEC) to strike would-be shareholder proposals off its AGM agenda (Johnson and Kerber, 2021). In 2021, guidance from the SEC reversed several practices of the Donald Trump era and made it harder for companies to obtain SEC approval to delete would-be agenda items. In late 2021, Apple failed in its efforts to erase a shareholder proposal asking it to provide greater transparency about its efforts to keep forced labour out of its supply chain (Nellis, 2021).

OPPORTUNITIES

Institutional investors could position engagement in increasingly activist terms. They could fight to increase the number of shareholder proposals at AGM and, in jurisdictions where it's necessary, alter legislation to ensure that well-thought-out proposals make it to the ballot.

Impacting people and the planet

As discussed earlier in the chapter, public equities suffer from a lack of real-world impact. Buying and selling securities in a liquid secondary market has limited-to-no impact on a company's cost of capital, so allocation decisions have little impact on people and the planet. Furthermore, although engagement has the potential to change corporate behaviour, its impacts, in its current incarnation, are sporadic rather than system-changing.

A sizeable opportunity lurks. A public equity product needs to be defined that has tangible real-world impact while maintaining its risk-adjusted return and the liquidity profile (typically, daily or intraday), which is a prerequisite for retail investor participation.

A rudimentary attempt at creating real-world impact would be to donate part of the management fees from a public equity product to charity (Perron, 2020; Kennedy, 2022). In such a model, the greater the assets in the fund, the greater the charitable donation, which could demonstrably benefit the world. But retail investors could legitimately wonder why the management fee isn't simply lower to begin with, allowing them to choose which charity, if any, they'd like to support.

A more advanced approach linked to fund assets has been pioneered by Belgium asset-manager Candriam (Schroeder, 2019) and the Luxembourg bank Quintet (Quintet Private Bank, n.d.). In both cases, the managers operate thematic climate funds that use a combination of exclusion, integration and engagement strategies to select securities that either support climate mitigation or climate adaptation. They then go one step further and measure the carbon footprint of their investments, acknowledging responsibility for their ownership share of each investee company's emissions.

Armed with this figure they offset or sequester the same amount of carbon through concrete actions, such as reforestation. A simple message can be communicated to their retail clients, for example, 'More fund assets, more trees planted.' The real-world benefits are directly linked to their funds' holdings and investment process. If the fund manager invests in carbon-intensive public equities, the cost of offsetting increases, thereby decreasing the firm's profits.

This innovation has parallels in the retail sector. When shopping for goods online or buying an airline ticket, a customer is often presented with the option of offsetting the CO_2 associated with the purchase. The Candriam and Quintet approach hints at a future where all financial products may either offer retail investors an opportunity to impact the real world or even default them into being financially accountable for the emissions of the companies they invest in. As financial markets become more sophisticated, the mechanisms for combining impact with liquid public equity products are likely to proliferate and migrate to other areas such as water and waste.

OPPORTUNITIES

Develop public equity financial products that deliver tangible, evidence-based real-world impact. They may include climate funds that deploy exclusion, integration and engagement, along with a commitment to climate neutrality through counterbalancing activities such as reforestation projects.

References

Adamsson, H and Hoepner, A G F (2015) The 'Price of Sin' aversion: Ivory tower illusion or real investable alpha? SSRN Electronic Journal, doi.org/10.2139/ssrn.2659098 (archived at https://perma.cc/D6S6-LL6P)

Ahern, K R (2014) Do common stocks have perfect substitutes? Product market competition and the elasticity of demand for stocks, *Review of Economics and Statistics*, 96(4), pp 756–766, doi.org/10.1162/REST_a_00414 (archived at https://perma.cc/M93M-3Q9A)

Andersson, M, Bolton, P and Samama, F (2016) Hedging climate risk, *Financial Analysts Journal*, 72(3), pp 13–32, doi.org/10.2469/faj.v72.n3.4 (archived at https://perma.cc/QJ3U-Z392)

As You Sow (no date) Shareholder advocacy, www.asyousow.org/shareholder-advocacy (archived at https://perma.cc/LW5W-EUTH)

Ashdown, J (2012) 50 stunning Olympic moments No14: Roy Jones Jr cheated out of gold, *The Guardian*, 15 February, www.theguardian.com/sport/blog/2012/feb/15/olympic-moments-roy-jones-jr (archived at https://perma.cc/F6BS-UVNU)

Asness, C (2017) Virtue is its own reward: Or, one man's ceiling is another man's floor [Blog] AQR, www.aqr.com/Insights/Perspectives/Virtue-is-its-Own-Reward-Or-One-Mans-Ceiling-is-Another-Mans-Floor (archived at https://perma.cc/3A2N-BCTS)

Asset Management Association and Swiss Sustainable Finance (2021) How to Avoid the Greenwashing Trap: Recommendations on transparency and minimum requirement for sustainable investment approaches and products, Switzerland: Asset Management Association and Swiss Sustainable Finance, www.greenfinanceplatform.org/guidance/how-avoid-greenwashing-trap-recommendations-transparency-and-minimum-requirement (archived at https://perma.cc/S7C6-3AG9)

Avramov, D et al (2021) Dynamic ESG equilibrium, SSRN Electronic Journal, doi.org/10.2139/ssrn.3935174 (archived at https://perma.cc/N3DG-MKN6)

Barclays (2020) ESG funds, www.cib.barclays/our-insights/3-point-perspective/esg-funds-looking-beyond-the-label.html?cid=3PPESG_120820_PR (archived at https://perma.cc/M76W-GAUW)

Barko, T, Cremers, M and Renneboog, L (2021) Shareholder engagement on environmental, social and governance performance, *Journal of Business Ethics*, 180, pp 777–812, doi.org/10.1007/s10551-021-04850-z (archived at https://perma.cc/VA2H-QVRT)

Belsom, T and Wearmouth, C (2020) An introduction to responsible investment: screening, UNPRI, www.unpri.org/an-introduction-to-responsible-investment/an-introduction-to-responsible-investment-screening/5834.article (archived at https://perma.cc/A7JL-Z9A6)

Berk, J B and van Binsbergen, J H (2021) The impact of impact investing, SSRN Electronic Journal, doi.org/10.2139/ssrn.3909166 (archived at https://perma.cc/42QL-B96N)

Bernow, S, Klempner, B and Magnin, C (2017) From 'why' to 'why not': Sustainable investing as the new normal, McKinsey & Company, www.mckinsey.com/~/media/McKinsey/Industries/Private%20Equity%20and%20Principal%20Investors/Our%20Insights/From%20why%20to%20why%20not%20Sustainable%20investing%20as%20the%20new%20normal/From-why-to-why-not-Sustainable-investing-as-the-new-normal.ashx (archived at https://perma.cc/BUJ2-U29E)

Bingham, D R et al (2021) GS SUSTAIN: ESG tracker: ESG sturdy vs a retrenchment in broader equity flows, Goldman Sachs

Bingham, D R et al (2022) GS SUSTAIN: ESG tracker: ESG flows and share gains remain positive in the face of market stress, Goldman Sachs

Bioy, H (2020) Do sustainable funds beat their rivals? *Morningstar*, 16 June, www.morningstarfunds.ie/ie/news/203248/do-sustainable-funds-beat-their-rivals.aspx (archived at https://perma.cc/TW79-4KD6)

Bisnoff, J (2021) Free markets and ESG investing won't fix the climate crisis, says former blackrock sustainability chief, *Forbes*, 30 March, www.forbes.com/sites/jasonbisnoff/2021/03/30/free-markets-and-esg-investing-wont-fix-the-climate-crisis-says-former-blackrock-sustainability-chief/ (archived at https://perma.cc/Q2HB-8RDE)

Blitz, D and Swinkels, L (2021) Does excluding sin stocks cost performance? SSRN Electronic Journal, doi.org/10.2139/ssrn.3839065 (archived at https://perma.cc/FE7B-5XHY)

BMO (2019) BMO launches a unique responsible investing fund with small and mid-sized businesses around the world, about.bmo.com/blog/bmo-launches-a-unique-responsible-investing-fund-with-small-and-mid-sized-businesses-around-the-world/ (archived at https://perma.cc/EF63-WNU4)

Bruno, G, Esakia, M and Goltz, F (2021) 'Honey, I Shrunk the ESG Alpha': Risk-adjusting ESG portfolio returns, *Scientific Beta*, pp 45–61, joi.pm-research.com/lookup/doi/10.3905/joi.2021.1.215 (archived at https://perma.cc/8JAH-3ZW3)

Caldecott, B (ed) (2018) *Stranded Assets: Developments in finance and investment*, Routledge, Abingdon.

Campbell, J Y et al (2002) Have individual stocks become more volatile? An empirical exploration of idiosyncratic risk, *The Journal of Finance*, 56(1), pp 1–43, doi.org/10.1111/0022-1082.00318 (archived at https://perma.cc/HXP8-5TNK)

CFA Institute (no date) Sustainable investing & investment management, www.cfainstitute.org/en/research/esg-investing/sustainable-investing (archived at https://perma.cc/4AMZ-UUUF)

Clark, C and Lalit, H (2020) ESG improvers: An alpha enhancing factor, Rockefeller Capital Management, rcm.rockco.com/wp-content/uploads/2020/09/ESG-Improvers-Whitepaper.pdf (archived at https://perma.cc/6HT4-LYUA)

Climate Action 100+ (2021) CA100+ investors engage with BASF on climate neutrality, www.climateaction100.org/news/ca100-investors-engage-with-basf-on-climate-neutrality/ (archived at https://perma.cc/BYS7-UXF5)

Cook, J and Solberg, L (2021) The 2021 proxy voting season in 7 charts, *Morningstar*, www.morningstar.com/articles/1052234/the-2021-proxy-voting-season-in-7-charts (archived at https://perma.cc/A3YV-MAK2)

Copay, V et al (2021) To exclude or engage, Quintet Private Bank, www.quintet.com/en-gb/articles/to-exclude-or-engage (archived at https://perma.cc/3C8B-Q7HB)

Credit Suisse (2020) Shareholder engagement for ocean sustainability, www.credit-suisse.com/about-us-news/en/articles/news-and-expertise/shareholder-engagement-for-ocean-sustainability-202009.html (archived at https://perma.cc/YD2L-YUN3)

Davies, H (2021) ESG engagement over exclusion: How you can do well by doing good, Campden FB, www.campdenfb.com/article/esg-engagement-over-exclusion-how-you-can-do-well-doing-good (archived at https://perma.cc/HL8J-VLX3)

De La Cruz, A, Medina, A and Tang, Y (2019) *Owners of the World's Listed Companies, Paris*: OECD Capital Market Series, Paris, www.oecd.org/corporate/ca/Owners-of-the-Worlds-Listed-Companies.pdf (archived at https://perma.cc/CH9P-BEYH)

Dimson, E, Karakaş, O and Li, X (2015) Active ownership, *Review of Financial Studies*, 28(12), pp 3225–3268, doi.org/10.1093/rfs/hhv044 (archived at https://perma.cc/6HB9-J8MA)

Domian, D L, Louton, D A and Racine, M D (2007) Diversification in portfolios of individual stocks: 100 stocks are not enough, *Financial Review*, 42(4), pp 557–570, doi.org/10.1111/j.1540-6288.2007.00183.x (archived at https://perma.cc/4J5Z-F3FN)

Dyck, A et al. (2019) Do institutional investors drive corporate social responsibility? International evidence, *Journal of Financial Economics*, 131(3), pp 693–714, doi.org/10.1016/j.jfineco.2018.08.013 (archived at https://perma.cc/BT37-LN3F)

Edgecliff-Johnson, A and Nauman, B (2019) Fossil fuel divestment has 'zero' climate impact, says Bill Gates, *Financial Times*, 17 September, www.ft.com/content/21009e1c-d8c9-11e9-8f9b-77216ebe1f17 (archived at https://perma.cc/FS9B-ZTEC) [Last accessed 01 July 2022].

Evans, J L and Archer, S H (1968) Diversification and the reduction of dispersion: An empirical analysis, *The Journal of Finance*, 23(5), pp 761–767, doi.org/10.1111/j.1540-6261.1968.tb00315.x (archived at https://perma.cc/AMN6-8HVD)

Fabozzi, F J, Ma, K C and Oliphant, B J (2008) Sin stock returns, *The Journal of Portfolio Management*, 35(1), pp 82–94, doi.org/10.3905/JPM.2008.35.1.82 (archived at https://perma.cc/67EY-QBRQ)

Federated Hermes (2021) BP case study, www.hermes-investment.com/uki/eos-insight/case-study/bp-case-study-2021/ (archived at https://perma.cc/55QV-KLVS)

Fisher, L and Lorie, J H (1970) Some studies of variability of returns on investments in common stocks, *The Journal of Business*, 43(2), pp 99–134, www.jstor.org/stable/2352105 (archived at https://perma.cc/XV4Q-LR4D)

Friede, G, Busch, T and Bassen, A (2015) ESG and financial performance: aggregated evidence from more than 2000 empirical studies, *Journal of Sustainable Finance & Investment*, 5(4), pp 210–33, doi.org/10.1080/20430795.2015.1118917 (archived at https://perma.cc/5NJF-3XTG)

Gond, J P and Piani, V (2013) Enabling institutional investors' collective action: The role of the principles for responsible investment initiative, *Business & Society*, 52(1), pp 64–104, doi.org/10.1177/0007650312460012 (archived at https://perma.cc/U59J-FESM)

GSIA (2021) Global sustainable investment review 2020, www.gsi-alliance.org/trends-report-2020/ (archived at https://perma.cc/MN2M-44GD)

Hale, J (2021a) 4 things to keep in mind about sustainable investing in 2022, Morningstar, 21 December, www.morningstar.com/articles/1073065/4-things-to-keep-in-mind-about-sustainable-investing-in-2022 (archived at https://perma.cc/V58C-TVRN)

Hale, J (2021b) Sustainable equity funds outperform traditional peers in 2020, Morningstar, 8 January, www.morningstar.com/articles/1017056/sustainable-equity-funds-outperform-traditional-peers-in-2020 (archived at https://perma.cc/FQJ2-EXAX)

Heeb, F, Kellers, A and Kölbel, J (2022) Does ESG integration impact the real economy? A theory of change and review of current evidence, Center for Sustainable Finance and Private Wealth, University of Zurich, www.csp.uzh.ch/dam/jcr:ac4406e3-ae17-43c0-8fa1-f967cd5abacb/BAFU%20Report_DIGITAL_pages.pdf (archived at https://perma.cc/PU34-UKXJ)

Heinkel, R, Kraus, A and Zechner, J (2001) The effect of green investment on corporate behavior, *Journal of Financial and Quantitative Analysis*, 36(4), pp 431–49, doi.org/10.2307/2676219 (archived at https://perma.cc/KHS4-TTYE)

Herbst-Bayliss, S (2021) Little Engine No 1 beat Exxon with just $12.5 mln – sources, Reuters, 29 June, www.reuters.com/business/little-engine-no-1-beat-exxon-with-just-125-mln-sources-2021-06-29/ (archived at https://perma.cc/9LYF-WQN2)

Hermes Investment (no date) Hermes responsible ownership principles, www.hermes-investment.com/ukw/wp-content/uploads/sites/80/2018/03/final-responsible-ownership-principles-2018.pdf (archived at https://perma.cc/3RVW-DFL9)

Hoepner, A G F et al (2021) ESG Shareholder Engagement and Downside Risk, Finance Working Paper No 671/2020, European Corporate Governance Institute, doi.org/10.2139/ssrn.2874252 (archived at https://perma.cc/S77V-RWRE)

Hong, H and Kacperczyk, M (2009) The price of sin: The effects of social norms on markets, *Journal of Financial Economics*, 93(1), pp 15–36, doi.org/10.1016/j.jfineco.2008.09.001 (archived at https://perma.cc/KY4R-S5DL)

Howard-Grenville, J (2021) ESG impact is hard to measure – but it's not impossible, *Harvard Business Review*, 22 January, hbr.org/2021/01/esg-impact-is-hard-to-measure-but-its-not-impossible (archived at https://perma.cc/387N-W8M9)

ICCR (2017) A guide to filing resolutions, in *2017 Proxy Resolutions and Voting Guide*, www.iccr.org/sites/default/files/2017iccrguidetofilingproxyresolutions.pdf (archived at https://perma.cc/LM24-VNJV)

Impact Management Project (2018) Guide to classifying the impact of investments, impactmanagementproject.com/investor/new-guide-to-mapping-the-impact-of-investments/ (archived at https://perma.cc/V2UC-KNJW)

Investment Week (2020) Partner insight: Exclusion is a 'blunt tool' that ends engagement, www.investmentweek.co.uk/sponsored/4025134/partner-insight-exclusion-blunt-tool-engagement (archived at https://perma.cc/CT83-2RJH)

IPA (no date) BT: It's good to talk, ipa.co.uk/knowledge/case-studies/bt-it-s-good-to-talk (archived at https://perma.cc/3XGP-QFSG)

Johnson, K and Kerber, R (2021) Top US financial regulator reverses stance on social issues, Reuters, 3 November, www.reuters.com/business/us-sec-staff-outlines-how-companies-might-exclude-shareholder-proposal-corporate-2021-11-03/ (archived at https://perma.cc/9SH4-9JVY)

Kaul, A, Mehrotra, V and Morck, R (2000) Demand curves for stocks do slope down: New evidence from an index weights adjustment, *The Journal of Finance*, 55(2), pp 893–912, doi.org/10.1111/0022-1082.00230 (archived at https://perma.cc/TQ5C-XPRD)

Kennedy, E (2022) Double your ESG impact with funds tied to charities, Kiplinger, www.kiplinger.com/investing/esg/604114/double-your-esg-impact-with-funds-tied-to-charities (archived at https://perma.cc/7KPE-NQZF)

Khan, M, Serafeim, G and Yoon, A (2016) Corporate sustainability: First evidence on materiality, *The Accounting Review*, 91(6), pp 1697–1724, doi.org/10.2308/accr-51383 (archived at https://perma.cc/C9C9-2J2T)

Kölbel, J F et al (2020) Can sustainable investing save the world? Reviewing the mechanisms of investor impact, *Organization & Environment*, 33(4), pp 554–74, doi.org/10.1177/1086026620919202 (archived at https://perma.cc/Y3GQ-GXYF)

Konqui, M H, Millet, F and Darolles, S (2019) Why using ESG helps you build better portfolios, LYXOR Asset Management

La Torre, M et al (2020) Does the ESG index affect stock return? Evidence from the Eurostoxx50, *Sustainability*, 12(16), pp 1–12, econpapers.repec.org/article/gamjsusta/v_3a12_3ay_3a2020_3ai_3a16_3ap_3a6387-_3ad_3a396179.htm (archived at https://perma.cc/4V48-GRK3)

Lee, L-E, Nagy, Z and Eastman, M T (2017) Do corporate controversies help or hurt performance? A study of three portfolio strategies, *Journal of Environmental Investing*, 8(1), pp 222–51, https://cbey.yale.edu/sites/default/

files/Do%20Corporate%20Controversies%20Help%20or%20Hurt%20Performance%3F%20A%20Study%20of%20Three%20Portfolio%20Strategies.pdf (archived at https://perma.cc/X68Q-J2LN)

Madhavan, A, Sobczyk, A and Ang, A (2021) Toward ESG alpha: Analyzing ESG exposures through a factor lens, *Financial Analysts Journal*, 77(1), pp 69–88, doi.org/10.1080/0015198X.2020.1816366 (archived at https://perma.cc/5U7U-JKE4)

Markowitz, H (1952) Portfolio selection, *The Journal of Finance*, 7(1), pp 77–91, doi.org/10.1111/j.1540-6261.1952.tb01525.x (archived at https://perma.cc/AN7G-UYEX)

Morgan Stanley (2021) Sustainable funds outperform peers in 2020 during coronavirus, www.morganstanley.com/ideas/esg-funds-outperform-peers-coronavirus (archived at https://perma.cc/SG7H-KYJ5)

Morningstar Sustainalytics (no date) Morningstar Sustainalytics launches engagement 360 solution for investors, www.sustainalytics.com/esg-news/news-details/2022/02/23/morningstar-sustainalytics-launches-engagement-360-solution-for-investors (archived at https://perma.cc/KV7A-P2R7)

MSCI (2019) MSCI ESG business involvement screening research, www.msci.com/documents/1296102/1636401/MSCI_ESG_BIS_Research_Productsheet_April+2015.pdf/babff66f-d1d6-4308-b63d-57fb7c5ccfa9 (archived at https://perma.cc/38L9-LPKD)

MSCI (2020) MSCI ESG controversies, www.msci.com/documents/1296102/1636401/ESG_Controversies_Factsheet.pdf/4dfb3240-b5ed-0770-62c8-159c2ff785a0 (archived at https://perma.cc/3LCB-E392)

MSCI (2021) MSCI SRI indexes methodology, www.msci.com/eqb/methodology/meth_docs/MSCI_SRI_Methodology_Feb2021.pdf (archived at https://perma.cc/94DZ-NNCV)

MSCI (2022a) MSCI ACWI index (USD), www.msci.com/documents/10199/a71b65b5-d0ea-4b5c-a709-24b1213bc3c5 (archived at https://perma.cc/M54U-89RN)

MSCI (2022b) MSCI ACWI low carbon target index, www.msci.com/documents/10199/c64f0873-5818-4304-aaf2-df19d42ae47a (archived at https://perma.cc/7ETP-W2F5)

MSCI (2022c) MSCI world SRI index, www.msci.com/documents/10199/641712d5-6435-4b2d-9abb-84a53f6c00e4 (archived at https://perma.cc/F2NJ-MQ38)

Nellis, S (2021) US SEC rejects Apple bid to block shareholder proposal on forced labour-letter, Reuters, 23 December, www.reuters.com/technology/us-sec-rejects-apple-bid-block-shareholder-proposal-forced-labour-letter-2021-12-23/ (archived at https://perma.cc/ZXN6-KM9F)

Nobel Prize Organisation (no date) Richard H Thaler – Facts, NobelPrize.org, www.nobelprize.org/prizes/economic-sciences/2017/thaler/facts/ (archived at https://perma.cc/MU4T-V8TT)

OECD and FAO (2021) *OECD-FAO Agricultural Outlook 2021–2030* OECD Publishing, Paris, doi.org/10.1787/19428846-en (archived at https://perma.cc/JFT7-NHKM)

Orsagh, M, Sloggett, J and Georgieva, A (2018) ESG in equity analysis and credit analysis, UNPRI-CFA Institute, www.unpri.org/download?ac=4571 (archived at https://perma.cc/N4CH-9YV6)

Pastor, L, Stambaugh, R F and Taylor, L A (2021) Dissecting Green Returns, Working Paper No. 2021-70, University of Chicago, Becker Friedman Institute for Economics, doi.org/10.2139/ssrn.3869822 (archived at https://perma.cc/M4DH-X355)

Pástor, Ľ, Stambaugh, R F and Taylor, L A (2021) Sustainable investing in equilibrium, *Journal of Financial Economics*, 142(2), pp 550–71, doi.org/10.1016/j.jfineco.2020.12.011 (archived at https://perma.cc/764D-AUXM)

Patel, K (2018) ESG investing moves to the mainstream (summary), CFA Institute, www.cfainstitute.org/en/research/financial-analysts-journal/2018/ip-v3-n1-9-esg-investing-moves-mainstream (archived at https://perma.cc/QGZ4-BXK6)

Pedersen, L H, Fitzgibbons, S and Pomorski, L (2020) Responsible investing: The ESG-efficient frontier, *Journal of Financial Economics*, 142(2), pp 572–97, doi.org/10.1016/j.jfineco.2020.11.001 (archived at https://perma.cc/2QSK-SK9Y)

Perron, V B (2020) AXA IM to donate 5 per cent of management fees on impact fund range to charity, CityWire Selector, citywireselector.com/news/axa-im-to-donate-5-of-management-fees-on-impact-fund-range-to-charity/a1354053 (archived at https://perma.cc/C3ER-C598)

Pham, L and Marsh, A (2022) Hedge fund boss Chris Hohn rips into failed ESG strategies, Bloomberg, 5 May, www.bloomberg.com/news/articles/2022-05-05/hedge-fund-boss-chris-hohn-rips-into-failed-esg-strategies (archived at https://perma.cc/5HC7-KAZ6)

Phillipps, J (no date) A long engagement: why ESG influence may beat exclusion, CityWire Wealth Manager, citywire.com/wealth-manager/news/a-long-engagement-why-esg-influence-may-beat-exclusion/a1363875 (archived at https://perma.cc/LMM8-3YVS)

Pizzutilo, F (2017) Measuring the under-diversification of socially responsible investments, *Applied Economics Letters*, 24(14), pp 1005–18, doi.org/10.1080/13504851.2016.1248279 (archived at https://perma.cc/3HTF-AL99)

Proxy Pulse (2020) 2020 Proxy season review, www.broadridge.com/proxypulse/reports/2020/second-edition-2020.html (archived at https://perma.cc/HWK7-YU3S)

Quintet Private Bank (no date) The Quintet Earth Fund, www.quintet.com/en-gb/quintet-earth-fund (archived at https://perma.cc/2XEV-34KX)

RBC Global Asset Management (2021) Responsible investment: ESG in a pandemic world, Responsible Investment Survey 2021, www.rbcgam.com/en/ca/about-us/responsible-investment/our-latest-independent-research (archived at https://perma.cc/D7TL-XR94)

Reuters (2022) Anglo American completes exit from South African coal miner Thungela, Reuters, 25 March, www.reuters.com/business/sustainable-business/anglo-american-completes-exit-safrican-coal-miner-thungela-2022-03-25/ (archived at https://perma.cc/GRX4-E2XA)

Robeco (no date) Sustainable investing glossary: Exclusion, www.robeco.com/ch/en/key-strengths/sustainable-investing/glossary/exclusion.html (archived at https://perma.cc/7TUD-ZRAQ)

Rohleder, M, Wilkens, M and Zink, J (2022) The effects of mutual fund decarbonization on stock prices and carbon emissions, *Journal of Banking & Finance*, 134(C), ideas.repec.org/a/eee/jbfina/v134y2022ics0378426621003034.html (archived at https://perma.cc/XN24-5MTX)

Schroders (2017) Demystifying negative screens: The full implications of ESG exclusions, www.schroders.com/en/sysglobalassets/digital/insights/2018/thought-leadership/demystifying-negative-screens---the-full-implications-of-esg-exclusions.pdf (archived at https://perma.cc/59HB-VBA8)

Schroeder, J (2019) Candriam launches its first carbon-neutral investment fund, South Pole, www.southpole.com/news/candriam-launches-its-first-carbon-neutral-investment-fund (archived at https://perma.cc/U3PV-5WSA)

ShareAction (2022) HSBC scales up climate commitments following investor engagement, shareaction.org/news/hsbc-scales-up-climate-commitments-following-investor-engagement (archived at https://perma.cc/2EYV-AW4U)

Sharma, P (2021) Glass Lewis launches engagement solution, Glass Lewis, 13 September, www.glasslewis.com/press-release-engagement-solution/ (archived at https://perma.cc/F6AK-KDGB)

Shen, L et al (2019) Deep learning to improve breast cancer detection on screening mammography, *Scientific Reports*, 9(1), p 12495, doi.org/10.1038/s41598-019-48995-4 (archived at https://perma.cc/BP67-DS5U)

Statman, M (1987) How many stocks make a diversified portfolio? *The Journal of Financial and Quantitative Analysis*, 22(3), pp 353–63, doi.org/10.2307/2330969 (archived at https://perma.cc/E44K-Q339)

Statman, M and Glushkov, D (2009) The wages of social responsibility, *Financial Analysts Journal*, 65(4), pp 33–46, doi.org/10.2469/faj.v65.n4.5 (archived at https://perma.cc/8K4H-KTV2)

UBS (2019) UBS, Federated Investors, Inc and Hermes Investment Management launch innovative fixed income impact funds, www.ubs.com/global/en/media/display-page-ndp/en-20190926-ubs-federated-investors-hermes-investment.html (archived at https://perma.cc/4YWU-Q3LK)

Varley, S and Lewis, S (2021) How to realize the full potential of ESG-plus, EY, www.ey.com/en_gl/sustainability/realize-potential-esg-plus (archived at https://perma.cc/DK2W-KLZ5)

Wurgler, J and Zhuravskaya, E (2002) Does arbitrage flatten demand curves for stocks? *The Journal of Business*, 75(4), pp 583–608, doi.org/10.1086/341636 (archived at https://perma.cc/P4V6-D888)

Zerbib, O D (2019) A sustainable capital asset pricing model (S-CAPM): Evidence from green investing and sin stock exclusion, SSRN working paper no. 3455090

04

Sustainable public debt markets

Introduction

If you fish in a pond whose sole inhabitants are carp, whether you fish in an environmentally conscious way or not, you will end up with the same catch. You can exclude barbed hooks to minimize mouth wounds, integrate lead-weight release devices to ensure that no fish become tethered to snags, and engage with experts for sustainable fishing tips. Your methods may diverge from those of a conventional angler, but your results will be the same.

Traditional sustainable public debt market investors mimic our would-be sustainable angler. They too exclude, integrate and engage. While their methods may diverge from those of conventional investors, they wind up fishing in the same body of water, so to speak, assessing and buying the same bonds and loans as conventional investors. Fortunately, sustainable public debt market investors also have an alternative – dedicated assets – at their disposal. Unlike traditional public debt market instruments, dedicated assets contain unique sustainability features and the bonds and loans are rarely found in a conventional investor's portfolio. Dedicated assets provide sustainable investors with a different pond in which to fish.

Before we discuss dedicated assets, we open with a section that looks at 'How traditional sustainable public debt market processes operate'. We review exclusionary approaches that avoid or sell bonds issued by companies that pursue activities deemed unsavoury. We outline how integration works, with public debt market investors incorporating environmental, social and governance (ESG) information into their investment process. And we reflect on engagement, the deliberate and structured dialogues that take place between public debt market investors and the management of investee corporations.

With this review complete, we examine traditional sustainable public debt market approaches in theory and in practice to pose and answer three important questions:

- How popular are these processes? (Answer: Not very.)
- How much do they add to investment performance? (Answer: Almost none.)
- Do they help people and the planet? (Answer: No.)

In our second public debt market section, 'How sustainable dedicated assets operate', we discuss a range of public debt market investments that contain uniquely sustainable features. Starting with instruments where the issuers' stated mission is sustainability, we profile both multilateral development bank debt (such as bonds issued by the World Bank) and microcredit. After summarizing the workings of green bonds and other instruments whose proceeds are ring-fenced for sustainability, we dive deeper into the most innovative area of sustainable public debt markets. We look at instruments whose cost of debt depends on sustainability, such as sustainability-linked bonds.

Having described the key dedicated assets, we examine them in theory and in practice. Three key questions are raised:

- How much do they add to investment performance? (Answer: Almost zero.)
- Do they help people and the planet? (Answer: Yes.)
- Do investors purchasing them help people and the planet? (Answer: Not really. Perhaps only as a collective body.)

Before we tackle our final public debt section, we pause for an exclusive interview with Richard Curtis CBE. In addition to being a renowned screenwriter, producer and film director (whose credits include *Blackadder, Notting Hill* and *Love Actually*), Richard has had an outsized impact upon philanthropy and sustainable investments. Richard has leveraged his talents and network to move increasingly large sums of money into philanthropy, into partnering with politicians on various projects and now into engaging with institutional investors. His experience helps frame sustainable investing in practice and highlights some of the obstacles and opportunities discussed in the previous three equity sections.

Our final public debt market section delves into the future and considers the potential opportunities and how we might get there. We consider opportunities for investors, regulators and issuers of debt. These three stakeholders, when working in concert, have the potential to transform sustainable public debt markets.

- The first opportunity is investor focused and argues that mainstream investors should explicitly allocate to multilateral development bank debt as a near-perfect substitute for US treasuries or German bunds.
- The second concerns regulators. It asks for stronger rules across dedicated assets such as green bonds and sustainability-linked bonds with the goal of ensuring that this fast-growing market continues to prosper.
- The third highlights an opportunity for public debt market issuers. We argue for expanding the use-of-proceeds model to target waste – an annual multi-trillion $ global problem. Waste-reduction bonds eloquently align profit with people and planet and apply to almost all companies, sectors and governments.

How traditional sustainable public debt market processes operate

Exclusion: Can you tell me what you are doing?

Anyone seeking to cut out monounsaturated fats from their diet first needs to know which foods contain them. If food labels fail to disclose their presence, it's difficult to steer clear of them. To exclude something, you need to know where it's included.

A lack of corporate disclosure often leaves investors unclear about the activities that make up a company's operations. Schroders found that sustainable investing data providers struggled to agree whether an activity was occurring or not. For popular exclusions such as nuclear energy or fur, data providers only shared the same opinion in 40 per cent of cases (Schroders, 2017).

This problem, long an irritant for equity investors, is even more acute within the public debt market universe. Debt issued by companies whose equity is not listed comprises a significant minority of the almost $8 trillion non-financial corporate debt market (Kovner and Wei, 2014; Badertscher et al, 2019). Privately held firms typically have lower regulatory disclosure requirements than public companies. Exclusion is therefore even tougher to implement as a public debt market investor due to information scarcity.

In addition, an exclusionary public debt market strategy is unlikely to materially affect the demand–supply dynamics of the targeted bonds or affect the cost of capital for the corporation or sovereign. New bonds tend to be heavily oversubscribed. Sovereign issuance, as of 2021, can attract eight times more bids than available paper (Oliver, 2021). Any individual investor's refusal to purchase a bond becomes irrelevant. Another investor stands ready to take their place.

Integration: What means a whole lot to you...

The same action or event can have very different effects on different people. Consider a company that decides to offer a reasonably priced company car to every employee. This development has little direct impact on senior executives due to their large salaries. In contrast, for junior employees the impact on their personal finances is much larger.

Within a corporation, bonds are senior to equity in the capital structure. Bondholders have first claim on the cash flows of a company and only suffer losses after equity is depleted. As a result, small positive or negative developments in a corporation's fortunes have very little direct impact on the value of its senior bonds.

Sustainability factors intentionally overlooked by conventional investors are, almost by definition, unlikely to be the most financially significant ones. Consequently, when these 'overlooked' factors manifest, the magnitude of their impact is often not large enough to meaningfully affect senior bondholders.

Let's use a simplified example. Imagine a company with $50 of equity and $50 of debt, which gives the firm a total value of $100. An 'overlooked' sustainable factor leads to the value of the company increasing by 10 per cent to $110. Because equity is the residual value left after all company debts have been paid, the $10 increase will (largely) accrue to equity holders. The equity value might rise from $50 to $60, a sizeable 20 per cent increase, but because the likelihood of bond impairment has not significantly changed, the bonds' value will likely remain unchanged at $50.

Essentially, equity can be thought of as a geared play on the financial health and news flow of a corporation. As a result, integrating sustainable factors into financial analysis has fewer benefits for public debt market investors than for buyers of stock. It is no surprise then that, historically, public debt market investors adopting integration practices has lagged their equity counterparts (Palmer, 2021).

Engagement: More talk, less action

In corporate settings the CEO's personal assistant often wields considerable influence. Although unable to vote at executive meetings or exercise line-manager authority by dismissing employees, they regularly interact with the CEO, which gives them the ability to inform corporate decisions and steer policy.

Unlike their equity counterparts, public debt market investors do not get to vote at annual or extraordinary general meetings. They do not have the power to remove directors, reject executive compensation plans, or legally force the company to commit to environmental transparency or cultural change. Yet their regular interactions with company management afford them sizeable influence. Such interactions occur because public debt market investors are asked to provide capital far more frequently than their equity counterparts.

Typically, a company will raise equity via an initial public offering, a joyous event, rife with champagne and canapes, when privately held shares are listed on a stock exchange. For many companies this is the sole time when equity investors are asked for capital. In a minority of cases, particularly if things aren't going well, the company may execute a rights issue and request that existing shareholders provide additional cash.

Public debt markets are different. Unlike equity capital, which is permanent, public debt market instruments have a finite term as bonds are issued with a maturity date. The bonds that mature need to be refinanced, and public debt market investors are regularly approached for capital, either to replace existing bonds or to fund expansion. Because corporations regularly embark on roadshows to impress public debt market investors, the latter can pursue constructive dialogue and seek sustainability improvements in exchange for their continued financing.

Some commentators have questioned the ability of public debt market investors to pursue successful active ownership (UNPRI, 2014; Orsagh, 2019). And admittedly engagement by public debt market investors is less developed than it is in the equity arena, though a growing number of public debt market specialists are seeking to harness engagement's power by launching dedicated investment funds (Federated Hermes, 2021).

Having reviewed the basic tenets of traditional public debt market processes via exclusion, integration and engagement, let's now examine them in theory and in practice by asking and answering three key questions.

Traditional public debt market processes: How popular are these processes?

Short answer: Not very.

IN THEORY

Proponents of traditional sustainable public debt market processes theorize why exclusion, integration and engagement do not appeal to investors to the same degree that it does in the equity field. As mentioned above, this popularity shortfall can stem from three primary factors: the difficulty in obtaining meaningful ESG data to perform exclusionary screens; the reduced value, relative to equities, of uncovering 'overlooked' ESG information through ESG integration; and the absence of voting rights as part of an engagement strategy.

IN PRACTICE

The practice largely reflects the theory. Calculations from the International Monetary Fund, using Bloomberg data, found that, in 2010, sustainable public debt market funds comprised just 20 per cent of sustainable mutual fund assets under management. In seven of the nine subsequent years, sustainable equity assets grew faster than sustainable bond assets (Deese et al, 2019). Goldman Sachs confirms this relative lack of popularity. Their flow data reveals that sustainable public debt market funds received just 20–30 per cent of the inflows enjoyed by their equity counterparts (Goldman Sachs, n.d.).

Survey data of fund managers is also helpful for assessing the status of traditional sustainable public debt market processes. A survey of 800 asset owners conducted in both 2018 and 2019 by Canadian Bank Royal Bank of Canada found a stable 25 percentage point difference between managers claiming to perform ESG integration in equities compared with bonds (RBC Global Asset Management, 2019). The sizeable gap is remarkably consistent across other surveys, such as Schroder's questioning of 650 asset owners conducted yearly in 2017, 2018 and 2019 (Schroders, n.d.), and asset manager NN Investment Partners' 2019 queries of 290 institutional investors (NN Investment Partners, n.d.).

In summary, although traditional sustainable public debt market processes are implemented by many investors, they consistently find less favour than similar equity ones.

Traditional public debt market processes: How much do they add to investment performance?

Short answer: Almost zero.

IN THEORY

Proponents of traditional sustainable public debt market processes theorize as to why exclusion, integration and engagement should add to investment performance.

Their case centres on integration giving investors an informational edge. Financial markets are not fully efficient, according to this view, and not all public information is incorporated into a security's current price. Ergo, a superior understanding creates an opportunity for higher investment returns.

This line of argumentation may be complemented by a positive view on engagement. Investors, this view holds, can identify corporate deficiencies that materially affect corporate financial well-being. A company that listens to investor input and fixes its problems will improve its operations, financial health and the price of its issued securities.

There are also logical counter theories:

- First, due to debt's seniority in the capital structure, marginal benefits and detriments mechanically accrue to equity, not public debt market investors.
- Second, because bonds have a fixed maturity, the likelihood of sustainable risks or opportunities manifesting within the investment's lifetime is lower than for equities. Consequently, a public debt market investor could conceivably 'get the sustainability right' but see their investment mature prior to the benefits being realized.
- Third, sovereign bond issuance dwarfs corporate bond issuance (SIFMA, 2021). Few sovereign states are going to alter their sustainability-related policies based on pressure from a handful of external investors. So a large swathe of the public debt market is essentially immune to engagement as an investment strategy.

IN PRACTICE

Fewer studies have looked at the performance of sustainable public debt market investing than at sustainable equity investing. This discrepancy can be explained by the relative maturity of the respective fields, which may in itself be telling.

Studies that find traditional public debt market processes adding to investment performance often cite factors such as 'stronger cash flow metrics, lower levels of ex ante risk, and less-frequent severe incidents than lower-rated-ESG issuers' (Mendiratta, Varsani and Giese, 2021). Evidence points to such benefits persisting even after adjusting for credit ratings (Bahra and Thukral, 2020).

Other findings have suggested that improving sustainability ratings is consistent with tighter credit default swap (CDS) spreads (Barth, Hübel and Scholz, 2022) and that 'bonds with high ESG ratings have modestly outperformed their lower rated peers when controlling for various risk exposures' (Polbennikov et al, 2016). However, both the number of studies and the rigour of the analysis pale beside the body of work that supports sustainability increasing equity returns.

Traditional public debt market processes: Do they help people and the planet?

Short answer: No

IN THEORY

Proponents of traditional sustainable public debt market processes espouse theories as to why exclusion, integration and engagement should benefit people and the planet. The case for them doing so rests on the impacts stemming from two channels: the cost of capital and behaviour.

The cost-of-capital channel follows the same logic as equities. Through either exclusion or integration, investors may materially alter the pricing of securities and thus an entity's cost of capital. There is a difference between the assets, however. For traditional sustainable public debt market investors a change in the cost of capital would manifest through an explicit, rather than an implied, price. Because companies rarely issue equity, their cost of equity is implied from secondary markets. By contrast, a change in the cost of debt would be explicit via the coupon paid on regular bond issuance.

The impact on the behaviour channel also draws on equity theory, namely, that a provider of capital can exert notable influence and change the behaviour of a capital recipient (UNPRI, 2018).

IN PRACTICE

There is little to no evidence that the allocation decisions of traditional sustainable public debt market investors can lower the cost of the capital and thus affect the economic decision making of corporations and sovereigns.

Studies have demonstrated that companies which perform well on sustainability topics can enjoy a lower cost of capital than their peers. But it has not been proven that this effect resulted from investor flows. Instead, superior risk characteristics and differences in business models may explain it (Chava, 2014; Bolton and Kacperczyk, 2021).

Furthermore, in primary markets, new bonds tend to be heavily oversubscribed. Some sovereign issuance, as of 2021, attracts eight times more bids than available paper (Oliver, 2021). These unbalanced supply-and-demand dynamics mean that traditional sustainable public debt market investors' allocation decisions are unlikely either to increase or decrease the pricing of the issue and an entity's cost of capital.

Bondholder engagement has also not yet significantly altered company behaviour. While many practitioners share our view that regular corporate refinancing empowers sustainability-minded bondholders, practitioners often refer to bondholder engagement as undeveloped. For example, Aviva references bondholders 'untapped potential' (AIQ, 2022) and asset manager BlueBay discusses 'unlocking the bondholder's voice' (Byrne, 2021).

With practical evidence suggesting that traditional sustainable public debt market investors have virtually no impact on the cost of the capital and limited impact on company behaviour, it naturally follows that traditional sustainable public debt market investors are not meaningfully helping people and the planet through their actions.

How sustainable dedicated assets operate

Mission oriented: Born ready

Some things were created with a singular purpose. The weights you find at the gym were designed to be heavy. The stop sign on the street exists only to ask you to bring your car to a halt. Queen frontman Freddie Mercury was adamant that he 'was born to love you'.

There are also some issuers of bonds who operate with a single purpose: sustainability. It is incorporated into their mission and their ongoing existence is contingent upon delivering the sustainable goods. Two of the most prominent dedicated assets in this category are multilateral development bank bonds and microcredit. The market for the former, as of 2022, exceeds $400 billion (Spinoso, Purcell and Street, 2021) and the latter comprises an almost $200 billion ecosystem (Goswami, Borasi and Kumar, 2021).

MULTILATERAL DEVELOPMENT BANKS (MDBS)

MDBs trace their roots to 1945 and the creation of the World Bank. The World Bank's financing activity has a clear sustainable purpose – 'ending extreme poverty and boosting shared prosperity' (World Bank, n.d.). MDBs are created and backed via subscribed capital by member countries. They provide development financing through long-term loans as well as grants.

MDBs often issue publicly traded debt. A small number of them feature all G7 countries as capital-providing members. This level of support, coupled with relatively low leverage ratios and a history of zero defaults, accounts for their AAA credit ratings and leads to investment performance similar to US treasuries (in $) and German bunds (in EUR). As a result, Swiss Universal Bank, UBS, terms MDB bonds 'treasuries with a conscience' (UBS, 2019a).

As of 2022, there are seven MDBs fulfilling the G7 criteria. The World Bank has spawned three of them: the International Bank of Reconstruction and Development (IBRD), the International Finance Corporation (IFC) and the International Development Association (IDA). The other four are: the Inter-American Development Bank (IADB), the Asian Development Bank

(ADB), the European Bank for Reconstruction & Development (EBRD) and the African Development Bank (AfDB) (UBS, 2019b).

Despite their historical status as a safe haven, MDB bonds are not without their risks. They share many characteristics with conventional high-grade bonds. Their duration risk can cause mark-to-market losses for an investor. MDBs also theoretically carry the risk that their shareholder countries could withdraw their support. If a number of governments were to do so, an MDB's perceived credit quality could fall. Finally, MDB bonds are often 'tightly held' by existing investors. When coupled with the smaller pool of issuance relative to conventional high-grade bonds, this feature can constrain liquidity in certain market circumstances (Wacker, Lee and Howat, 2018).

A challenge associated with mission-oriented issuers is a potential lack of transparency. Because all proceeds are intended to benefit sustainable projects, it is not usually possible to track a single bond's proceeds.

The World Bank makes a credible attempt to compute annual figures for its collective operations. It aggregates common metrics from its activities to establish a series of numerical results. They include improving access to water sources for 1.2 million people, providing new or improved electricity services to 2.2 million people and reducing greenhouse gas emissions by 6.5 million tons of CO_2 equivalent annually (Keenan and Russo, 2021). Yet even the World Bank's approach lacks a denominator – a year's worth of bond issuance, for example – to adequately contextualize what investing a single dollar (or a million of them) ultimately achieves.

A further challenge arises from conflicting sustainability priorities. For example, the Asian Development Bank (ADB) financed coal-fired power plants throughout the 2010s. The ADB believed at the time that the role electricity generation played in economic development was of greater importance than its environmental impact (Asian Development Bank, 2021). Such involvements can prompt accusations of greenwashing if individuals project their own personal view of what is sustainable and what is not onto the complex discipline of economic development.

Another challenge faced by mission-oriented issuers is ensuring that the capital goes to the intended recipients. Operating in emerging and frontier markets, the threat of corruption always looms. The World Bank has undertaken extensive efforts to ensure that its funds are properly accounted for (Chanda, 2004), but, due to the sheer scale of its operations, losses do occur.

For example, it's estimated that in Indonesia in the early 1990s upwards of 30 per cent of World Bank funds were siphoned off through corruption (Winters, 2002). This risk is not limited to political elites and can occur at the community level as well. It is well documented that, through subsistence necessity, microcredit loans are often used for 'the immediate needs of the family' rather than for the intended entrepreneurial purposes (Sooryamoorthy, 2007).

MICROCREDIT

Microcredit is the practice of extending small-denomination loans to borrowers who typically lack collateral, employment or a verifiable credit history. Modern microfinance is typically traced to the 1980s and Bangladesh (Bateman, 2010).

While the microcredit ecosystem is said to be worth almost $200 billion in loans, what financial investors can invest in is just 10 per cent of the market (Mackinnon, Narayanan and Dominicé, 2020; Goswami, Borasi and Kumar, 2021). The investible portion typically involves a fund structure that, in turn, provides capital to microfinance institutions (MFIs) located in emerging and frontier markets. MFIs then make loans to the local populace.

Interest rates for local borrowers can be as high as 30 per cent annually in local currency, with the end investors in the fund structure receiving 2–4 per cent in US dollars. The vast discrepancy between the interest and return rates can be attributed to the labour intensity of running an MFI, whose operational costs are estimated to be approximately 10 times those of a conventional bank (Dominicé, 2012). Additional costs include default rates, currency translation effects and the ongoing charges associated with the aforementioned fund structure (typically in the range of 2.0 per cent) (Mackinnon, Narayanan and Dominicé, 2020).

Historically, microcredit has been highly decorrelated from public financial markets (Dahlberg and Dominicé, 2017). The ability of micro-entrepreneurs in frontier markets to repay loans has been largely independent of developed countries' stock and bond market gyrations. But microcredit is not without risks, which can cause financial losses throughout the value chain.

For example, at the end-borrower level, global events such as pandemics can shut down economic activity indiscriminate of company size and scale. Micro-entrepreneurs' ability to generate cash flows and repay debt can be severely affected in such scenarios. For MFIs this may lead to debt restructurings and/or bad loan provisioning.

The Microfinance Institutions Network, which operates as an industry association for Indian MFIs, noted that, during the Covid-19 pandemic, financing effectively dried up. Loan disbursements fell by over 90 per cent year over year in the second quarter of 2020. A significant liquidity squeeze hampered micro-entrepreneurs (Ghosh and Srivastava, 2021).

At the MFI level, sharp foreign exchange movements can impact MFIs that borrow in US $ but lend in local currency and pressure their solvency. At the microcredit fund level, the investment structures offered to end investors may have cash flow mismatches. The liquidity offered to end investors is reasonably frequent (often monthly), but the maturity and duration profile of the loans made to MFIs is much longer (Kruiff and Hartenstein, 2014).

Use of proceeds: An accidental trillion US $

When I (James) was young, my mother gave me 10 British pounds and told me I could only spend it on books. Had I treated myself to sweets or football stickers with the money I would have been in big trouble. She demanded that when I returned home I show her the books and the purchase receipts.

To be doubly sure of a return on her investment, she required me to write a book report later to prove that I had diligently done my reading. My mother didn't know it at the time, but she had inadvertently invented the premise for the use-of-proceeds bond market. This market, as of 2022, has cumulative issuance in excess of $2.5 trillion (BloombergNEF, n.d.).

Within dedicated assets, the use-of-proceeds model has arguably been the most commercially successful. The premise is straightforward. Unlike a conventional bond whose proceeds can be spent on anything from wages or factories or software upgrades, a use-of-proceeds bond has its proceeds earmarked and ring-fenced for sustainability purposes. The impacts are then reported upon and typically audited.

GREEN BONDS

The most widely recognized use-of-proceeds bond is the green bond. Originated in 2007 via the European Investment Bank (Climate Bonds Initiative, n.d.), green bonds now boast cumulative issuance that tops $1.5 trillion (BloombergNEF, n.d.). As of 2022, the market is predominantly self-regulating thanks to the International Capital Market Association (ICMA). Its Green Bond Principles (GBP) are a set of guidelines that 'seek to support issuers in financing environmentally sound and sustainable projects that foster a net-zero emissions economy and protect the environment' (ICMA, 2021).

Green bonds operating under the GBP subscribe to four key principles:

1. Use of proceeds
2. Process for project evaluation and selection
3. Management of proceeds
4. Reporting

The eligible categories for green projects include but are not limited to: renewable energy, pollution prevention and control, clean transportation, sustainable water and wastewater management, climate change adaptation and green buildings (ICMA, 2021)

The vast majority of green bonds operate with what the GBP refers to as 'standard green use of proceeds bond'. It is a standard recourse-to-the-issuer debt obligation which grants the green bond the same seniority as conventional bonds from the same issuer. Thus, while the proceeds are to be spent on a defined project(s), the repayment of the bond benefits from the entire operations and cash flows of the issuer.

Green bonds carry many of the same risks that conventional bonds do, including credit and duration risk. They can also be vulnerable to greenwashing, where a scandal related to the use and management of proceeds can trigger index ejection and/or investor flight. Green bonds are also typically 'tightly held'; this dynamic, coupled with the smaller pool of issuance relative to conventional bonds, can constrain liquidity under certain market circumstances.

Use-of-proceed bonds are not without challenges and complications. First, despite their growth, just 2 per cent of firms have outstanding green bonds, according to the Bank of International Settlements (BIS). And in any given year use-of-proceed bonds represent a low-single-digit percentage of all non-financial corporate bond issuance (Ehlers, Mojon and Packer, 2020). Adoption is still relatively nascent.

Second, the green bond market is sector skewed. In a typical corporate bond index financials and utilities make up slightly less than 50 per cent of issuance. With green bonds this figure exceeds 80 per cent (Wacker, Bolliger and Seimen, 2020). This sector skew can affect investors who are intent on replicating mainstream benchmarks and suggests that existing use-of-proceeds frameworks may not apply equally across the entire economy.

Third, while ICMA's Green Bond Principles are relatively well established, ambiguity about them remains. The 2021 ICMA update still referenced four different legal structures, though one is dominant (ICMA, 2021). Furthermore, the EU's emerging standards for green bonds only draws partial inspiration from ICMA and thus partly contradicts the established industry norms. MSCI estimates that less than 20 per cent of existing green bonds would comply with the EU taxonomy (MSCI, 2019).

Fourth, use-of-proceeds bonds have also come under fire when companies deemed unsustainable, such as oil multinationals, have sought to issue them despite the core of their business focusing on environmentally unfriendly activities (Viegas, n.d.). The BIS also questioned the impact of green bonds on companies as a whole, finding that those that issued them were not associated with falling or even comparatively low carbon emissions at the firm level (Ehlers, Mojon and Packer, 2020). The upshot is that some companies have used green bonds to signal supposed sustainable intentions while leaving the bulk of their business unchanged.

Sustainably linked: Pay for performance

We are all familiar with pay for performance. It is reflected in the system of bonuses (and clawbacks) that prevails for senior executives in the financial services industry; in the ambulance-chasing, no-win-no-fee lawyers who advertise on local daytime television; and in the promise of a reward to children who study hard for and pass a critical maths test.

There is an emerging field of pay-for-performance lending within dedicated assets. The cost of debt (the coupon) ratchets up or down in this case depending on whether sustainability targets are achieved or not. The metrics underpinning the ratchet are typically corporate social metrics such as carbon emissions, gender diversity or composite sustainability ratings. This pay-for-performance attribute is often called sustainability-linked.

Ahold Delhaize, a Dutch food retailer, has undertaken a textbook sustainability-linked transaction. It committed to reducing scope one and two carbon dioxide emissions (as classified by the Greenhouse Gas Protocol Corporate Standard) by 29 per cent from its 2018 baseline figures. The company also pledged to cut food waste by 32 per cent from a 2016 baseline. Failure to meet these targets by 2025 would result in a step-up in the coupon of 25 bps (GAM Investments, 2021).

The benefits of sustainability-linked instruments stem from their versatility. They can be structured as bonds, loans, repurchase agreements and a multitude of other debt structures. Unlike green bonds, which are biased toward a subset of sectors, any entity can issue a sustainability-linked instrument as the determinate metrics are sector agnostic. In short, sustainability-linked instruments are performance based while use-of-proceeds bonds are activity based.

Like anything else in this world, they are not perfect. First, they are currently driven by the issuer's desire to demonstrate sustainability credentials rather than investor demand. After all, a public debt market investor is unlikely to be able to accurately price a company's ability to hit or miss an internal corporate sustainability target. Thus, for buyers with a conventional financial motive, the sustainability-linked component is an inconvenient complication that requires additional resources to analyse. Consequently, the instruments often give off the flavour of a public relations exercise by the issuer with 'KPIs that are clearly readily achievable' (Sheng Ou Yong, 2021).

Second, the financing impacts are frequently immaterial. A 2021 analysis by UK asset manager Abrdn found that almost all sustainability-linked bonds include a ratchet of less than 10 per cent of the original interest rate and nearly half have a variation of less than 5 per cent of it (Lukaszewski, 2021). Such small interest rate changes create a very weak incentive for behavioural change.

Third, for sustainable investors, the incentives can be counterintuitive, practically perverse. Should the issuing company fail to implement the required sustainability initiatives, investors receive more money. In effect, because the desired impact has not occurred, sustainable investors get paid 'blood money' to compensate for the lack of real-world change (Sayer and Lai, 2021).

Sustainability-linked issuance is a fast-growing dedicated asset. In calendar year 2021, according to Bloomberg data, related bond and loan volumes topped $550 billion, compared with just $50 billion in 2018. However, just $100 billion of the 2021 figure came from publicly traded bonds (BloombergNEF, n.d.). For retail investors, partaking in the loan market is considerably more difficult than purchasing from the public bond market, meaning that many are unable to allocate their capital to this dedicated asset.

At the frontier of sustainable finance, sustainability-linked issuance is incredibly exciting and has huge potential, but multiple challenges must be addressed before it can go truly mainstream.

Having reviewed the innovative landscape that gave rise to them, we now examine sustainable dedicated assets in theory and in practice by asking and answering three important questions.

Dedicated assets: How much do they add to investment performance?

Short answer: Almost zero.

IN THEORY

Proponents argue that dedicated assets can add to risk-adjusted performance by expanding the universe of available assets and providing decorrelation benefits as per modern portfolio theory (Markowitz, 1952). This benefit, according to the theory, is likeliest to occur when assets are complex or somewhat illiquid, as is the case with microcredit (Ilmanen, Chandra and McQuinn, 2020).

Use-of-proceed debt creates greater economic frictions than conventional general-purpose debt does, however. Because segregating the proceeds of bonds reduces capital flexibility for issuers (Hachenberg and Schiereck, 2018), use-of-proceeds issuance requires firms to be incentivized either through paying lower rates of interest (detracting from investor performance) or through receiving a non-financial benefit such as an enhanced reputation or a more diversified investor base.

Sustainability-linked debt is also, theoretically, inefficient. The KPIs tied to coupon payments must be verified, which involves a cost not present with general purpose issuance. If this cost is to be borne by sustainable investors seeking positive impact, then investment performance would also, mechanically, suffer.

IN PRACTICE

Little evidence that dedicated assets add to investment performance has emerged. The risk-adjusted performance of MDB bonds mirrors that of conventional assets, with their correlation to US treasuries consistently close to one. Credit spreads of 5 to 30 basis points ensure higher returns in exchange for a consummate amount of risk and more volatility in times of market stress (Spinoso, Purcell and Street, 2021).

In the case of microcredit funds, long-run investment-return data illustrates that they have historically boosted the risk-adjusted return of a multi-asset portfolio (Spinoso, Purcell and Street, 2021). However, such empirical evidence comes with a caveat. There is a liquidity mismatch between what is offered to investors in microcredit funds (typically monthly) and the illiquid loans made by MFIs (which tend to range from 18 to 24 months). A 'hidden tail risk' may be buried within microcredit that has yet to materialize. Should such an event occur at some point, the investment losses could void the apparent attractiveness of the asset class.

Use-of-proceed debt appears to provide marginally lower risk-adjusted performance. Studies that seek to compare these specialized bonds to their conventional counterparts are hampered by the need to interpolate bond data to normalize for differences in maturity date and coupon. While they produce a range of results, two separate academic meta-studies published in 2020 and 2021 found a 'greenium' of one to 10 basis points across various methods (Cortellini and Panetta, 2021; MacAskill et al, 2021).

The 'greenium' discussion has been aided by so-called 'twin' issuance from the German sovereign. In 2020, Germany issued a pair of bonds identical in maturity and coupon. One was a conventional sovereign bund and the other a use-of-proceeds green bond backed by the sovereign's credit quality and with a fungibility clause to allow conversion into the conventional bund (Ravindirane, 2020). Since launch, these 'twins' have performed similarly, although the green bond has consistently offered yields one to five basis points lower than its conventional counterpart (Best Execution, 2021). This observable 'greenium' confirms that some sustainable investors consent to accept lower investment returns in exchange for perceived ESG benefits.

Sustainability-linked instruments do not have a long enough track record to come to meaningful conclusions about investment performance. Early signs suggest a small complexity risk premium of a couple of basis points as investors appear uneasy when pricing the sustainability-linked component. Those interested in marginally augmenting their returns may be able to do so by buying such idiosyncratic instruments.

Dedicated assets: Do they help people and the planet?

Short answer: Yes.

IN THEORY

Proponents contend that dedicated assets can benefit people and the planet. A clear, straightforward theory of change, they argue, explains how each sub-category of dedicated assets does so.

With MDB bonds and microcredit, the provision of capital is designed to produce impact across such measurable metrics as carbon emissions and access to education. Use-of-proceeds debt comes with an explicit statement that the money will be spent in a sustainable way and includes corresponding metrics, auditing and reporting. For instruments where the cost of debt depends on sustainability, the impact metrics that track the intended improvements are spelled out.

IN PRACTICE

The fact that MDBs and microcredit institutions exist at all is proof of their efficacy. If traditional market forces were able to fund sustainable outcomes, such entities would have no reason for being and mission-driven providers of capital would find themselves offering credit at a premium to market forces. Due to various market failures, multilateral development banks and the microcredit ecosystem sprang into existence and have channelled billions of dollars toward sustainable development and poverty alleviation.

Nonetheless, these institutions still prompt criticism – for three reasons. First, the credit that multilateral development banks offer often comes with conditions that reflect values-based judgements. These conditions and belief systems may not always be appropriate for the recipients and may inadvertently cause damage.

The World Bank's response to the 1979 energy crisis provides a telling example. It forced governments that received World Bank loans to cut social spending and adjust their exchange rates. By the late 1980s, with poverty on the rise, particularly in sub-Saharan Africa, recognition that its conditions were worsening the situation caused the World Bank to change its policy. In 1999, it abandoned the approach altogether (Graeber, 2009).

The existence of multilateral development banks is, according to critics, a double-edged sword and has led to accusations that they inadvertently retard local financial system development (Bird and Rowlands, 2007; Basílio, 2014). The low cost of funding they enjoy can squeeze out local market-based players, leaving an economy reliant on external funding and aid. Countries can struggle to develop their own systems of savings, loans and the economic efficiency brought about by competition and free markets.

Third, in the case of microcredit, accusations of 'debt traps' arise, especially when the starting point of borrowers is below the poverty line (Ghosh and Srivastava, 2021). Very bad outcomes, including suicide by borrowers, can occur (Polgreen and Bajaj, 2010). Some have accused microcredit proponents of romanticizing subsistence entrepreneurship at the expense of developing an economy of steady wage-based employment (Karnani, 2007). Borrowers are often not microentrepreneurs by choice. They typically have few specialized skills and must compete with all the other self-employed poor people in entry-level trades (Banerjee and Duflo, 2007). This observation is supported by the fact that, in the developed world, just 10 per cent of people opt for an entrepreneurial existence rather than wage-based or salaried jobs (International Labour Organization, n.d.). As a result, several studies have questioned the real-world effectiveness and extent of microcredit's positive impact (Banerjee, Karlan and Zinman, 2015; Meager, 2019).

Use-of-proceeds instruments are often accused of failing to generate additionality. In other words, the bonds fund activities that are already occurring and generate no incremental change in the world. In fact, researchers have suggested that most proceeds from green bond issuance refinance existing debt rather than fund new projects (Berensmann, Dafe and Lindenberg, 2018).

Furthermore, as already mentioned, firms that issue use-of-proceeds bonds achieve only marginal cost-of-capital improvements. This, in isolation, is unlikely to trigger a material change in otherwise sustainability-agnostic corporate or sovereign policies and result in projects beneficial to people and the planet.

The lack-of-additionality charge is also levelled at sustainability-linked instruments. As the issuing entity, not investors, determine the key performance indicators (KPIs) of most such instruments and as the KPIs tend to be readily achievable, the instruments are unlikely to provoke a wholesale policy change with a notably beneficial impact.

We'll go out on an aggregate limb and venture that, 'yes', dedicated assets do have a positive impact overall. However, as with much of sustainable investing, this conclusion is contentious and the data is varied.

Dedicated assets: Do investors purchasing them help people and the planet?

Short answer: Not really. Perhaps only as a collective body.

IN THEORY

This question differs subtly from the one above. Proponents of dedicated assets argue that the investors who purchase them bring about positive change, while our previous answer specified that the assets themselves are what produce desirable impact.

Within sustainable investing circles, theory increasingly differentiates between investor and investee impact (Kölbel et al, 2020). While an entity's operations and the debt instruments that fund them may create change for the good, an investor's decision to purchase a dedicated asset may not have actively contributed to that change. In other words, while the World Bank can offer categorical evidence about the effectiveness of its bonds, an investor who bought them may not be able to make the same claim.

Once we separate investor and investee impact, we can focus on the real-world changes wrought by investor actions. Theories of change suggest that sustainable investors, through their investment flows, can alter the cost of capital for targeted firms, making green projects more attractive to management. Theory also proposes that, through their purchases, sustainable investors signal the importance of sustainability topics and create a demand for, and encourage the development of, the dedicated asset marketplace. This, in turn, leads to greater issuance and more observable benefits.

IN PRACTICE

The evidence that dedicated assets result in differentiated investment returns is, as we suggested before, limited. The idea that investors can materially alter the cost of capital for investee entities is based on minimal proof as well.

It is very difficult for investors themselves to have a material impact by purchasing MDB debt. The volume of debt issued by MDBs is constrained by the amount of paid-in equity from its sovereign shareholders, not by investor demand (Landers and Aboneaaj, 2021). Investor demand therefore cannot directly lead to greater MDB issuance that effects real-world projects. At best, large-scale investor demand could help to initiate a political process to increase sovereign support and thus facilitate subsequent MDB issuance capacity.

The potential for investor-driven impact is slightly greater with microcredit because the amount of issuance is not constrained by external political factors. An increase in demand can lead to more loans and a corresponding rise in impact. But the investible portion of the microcredit market, to repeat, is only about 10 per cent (Mackinnon, Narayanan and Dominicé, 2020; Goswami, Borasi and Kumar, 2021). So, even a step change in investor demand would have a limited effect on the much larger overall market.

We see minor evidence of investor-driven impact for use-of-proceeds bonds. As discussed, significant investor demand may marginally reduce a corporate's or sovereign's cost of capital, which may incrementally increase the economic attractiveness of sustainable projects. However, the magnitude is small and the investor impact lessened by the high number of green bonds that refinance existing activities.

Although harder to systematically quantify, the existence of a fast-growing dedicated asset market offers hints, in its totality, that investors exert some practical influence through a collective signalling effect. After all, without willing buyers, MDB, microcredit, use-of-proceeds debt and sustainability-linked debt would not exist.

By providing a consistent bid for dedicated assets, investors have been able, in a relatively short time frame, to collectively generate a multi-trillion dollar marketplace of public debt market instruments designed to have a positive impact.

Isolating individual investor contributions to this effort is impossible, however. Furthermore, the elastic nature of financial markets is such that the participation or absence of any particular investor – or even a sizeable group of large investors – makes no discernible difference to the system and creates no additional benefits for people and the planet.

In this interview, James sat down with Richard Curtis CBE to discuss sustainable investing. Richard, in addition to being a renowned screenwriter, producer and film director (whose credits include *Blackadder, Notting Hill* and *Love Actually*) has had an outsized impact upon philanthropy and sustainable investments. He co-founded Comic Relief, which has raised more than £1.5 billion since its inception. He was also a co-founder of Make Poverty History, which pressured leaders of the leading economies to commit to tackling world poverty.

Most recently, he co-founded the Make My Money Matter campaign. It seeks public engagement and increased sustainable investment from pension providers. Richard has leveraged his talents and network to move increasingly large sums of money into philanthropy, into partnering with politicians on various projects and now into engaging with institutional investors. His experience helps frame sustainable investing in practice.

James: Thank you for taking the time Richard. I'd love to start by hearing how you became part of the sustainable investing ecosystem. Could we start with your philanthropic roots?

Richard: My journey to sustainable investment is quite long and strange. I never did anything for anyone until I was 31 and then I saw Live Aid. I ended up going to Ethiopia during the famine in the mid-1980s and that kind of branded me for life. I returned to England knowing that, in other places in the world, people's lives were absolutely intolerable, while I was just fooling around in Leicester Square. And I took advantage of the little thing that I had, which was that I was part of a powerful comedy community. And that started what's now been a

35-year journey of trying to take advantage of that in any way I can. And every new thing we try increases options for people wanting to help others – my experience is that if someone opens a door, which allows other people to easily do something that they think is the right thing, then millions of people leap through. I found over the years of Comic Relief through television, through merchandise, through corporate deals, through selling books or records, that if you look everywhere, you can find new ways of fundraising. And that's been the reason I've never given up because the result of my labours has been so out of proportion to my own earning power.

James: Incredible, and how did your philanthropic efforts migrate towards political action?

Richard: Things later started to change for me. I was inspired by the Jubilee Debt Campaign and then, in 2005, myself and Bono and Bob [Geldof] saw this opportunity to do Live 8 as a partner to the main Make Poverty History campaign. I sort of said, 'Well, we've raised one billion pounds from the public with Comic Relief, but politicians have billions'. And so, I became very interested in that and it became a relatively effective campaign, particularly in terms of the debt cancellation. Later, in 2013, I started to become very interested in the prospect of the UN Sustainable Development Goals (SDGs). I thought I would try and use my low-grade marketing talent to try and see if the SDGs can be presented as something interesting, lively and democratic – not just a dry document. I had the theory that you can't fight for your rights if you don't know what they are, and, therefore, I became very interested in working with the UN on that. Before then, I'd stuck very rigorously to 'I'm a poverty development person', aware that there were two other massive areas, climate and justice/equality. But now I embrace all of them. I think this has been a remarkable five years in terms of how issues of race, gender and climate are now in the DNA of the world – and in particular of the younger generation.

James: So, let's turn to investments. How did you transition again?

Richard: Sometime around 2018 or 2019 I was saying in the short films that I was producing for the UN, 'We need to turn the billions into trillions.' And I was asking the question: 'How can one alter the structure of money a little bit in order to try and get more money to work for the benefit of improving things for people and the planet?'

As I started to investigate, it triggered a whole sequence of events. First, there was this TED Talk by Bronwyn King, which I happened to come across. She is an Australian doctor who at 34 or something had her first meeting with a financial advisor. She's a cancer doctor and she found out, I think, that three of her top six investments were in cigarette companies and she thought, 'Oh, I've actually killed more people than I've saved. I've been working every day of my life to save them, but my money's been doing the opposite.' I found that really interesting and realized investments and pensions were this really big area which could work for the public good. It occurred to me that if changing your pension is one of the ways that we can move these trillions into sustainability, then that would be a genuinely worthwhile campaign. So, I then went into a period of about five months of finding out whether or not this was a real thing. The final thing which inspired me was meeting Bono's TPG Rise investment firm, and I thought, 'Oh, wow.' They were investing in real on-the-ground businesses that were making money, giving jobs, changing people's lives. And I thought, 'Well, that sounds like a new way of altering things, rather than just raising money and putting it into charities. This is planting seeds that are going to grow into trees.' I found that these were people who were funding businesses supplying sustainable food to schools, building affordable housing and facilitating affordable healthcare. As I got more and more examples of the kind of places money can go to, it became more and more intriguing. It was local, it was abroad, it was big, it was small. And so, I just threw myself into it.

James: And is that how the Make My Money Matter movement was conceived?

Richard: Yes, it really has been a gripping journey during the last few years. I think, in the last 18 months, we've now reached a trillion pounds in terms of pension providers in the UK who have committed to investing according to net zero. I thought the campaign was going to be conflictual. I thought it was going to be us versus the pension providers, but actually they were all thinking about it and a lot of them wanted to act on it. It was patently clear that with the UK law saying that everyone in a new job had to take out a pension that there'd be almost nobody under 25 who'd ever say, 'Oh no, I'll go for the non-sustainable pension option when I could have a sustainable one.' In some ways it's been the best thing I've ever been a part of because the figures are so huge – the UK pension pot alone is £2.7 trillion. And so that's my story, from charity, to government, to finance, then moving to business.

James: What I like about your narrative is it's about creating multiples of money, it's leveraging self-interest for good.

Richard: Yes, and unlocking the profit motive. I've heard many people now describe sustainability as the biggest investment opportunity since the Industrial Revolution. And it makes sense, doesn't it? If renewable energy is going to replace fossil fuel, there'll have to be a lot of new renewable energy companies. Otherwise we can't do it. So, it has an absolute logic to it.

James: As part of the Make My Money Matter movement I'm sure questions of engagement versus divestment have come up. Where do you stand?

Richard: Well, I come down listening to both sides. Some people say – if you divest, then new investment will come from people who don't give a damn about the planet and therefore you are better off investing and engaging. And, certainly, when you talk to the pension providers, they put a lot of emphasis on their influence and their ability to change a company's behaviour. However, for some individuals, divestment will be a major motivation, as they definitely don't want to be invested in things they don't approve of. So, I think there's good arguments on both sides and both arguments are helpful.

James: Understood. From your experience, what are the biggest challenges and opportunities for sustainable investing?

Richard: I'm particularly touched by the opportunity within pensions. It's so logical that you would want to be investing in a better future for the world in order to achieve a better future for yourself. However, we need progress on transparency. People say that if it was all their money being put into a single company, then they would be desperate to make sure that one company was absolutely sustainable in every way. But when you've got a broad portfolio, it becomes a lot less clear and we need to make it easier for people to get a proper overview of all their investments and the effect they have on the planet. I think another challenge is convincing the very rich that their philanthropic activities may be less important than their investment and financial activities. That's a generational thing as well. I think that's an interesting area where progress can and must be made.

James: Thank you Richard

The potential opportunities and how we might get there

Despite traditional sustainable public debt market processes struggling for traction, the rapid rise of dedicated assets has created new exposures for investors and mechanisms of change to benefit the world.

Much of the sustainable public debt market remains nascent, though. Investors still cling to traditional sub-asset class definitions such as high-grade and investment grade rather than embrace MDB and use-of-proceeds bonds as viable discrete allocations. Regulators have also been slow to respond to, and enable, the use-of-proceeds and sustainability-linked markets to blossom. Issuers, too, overwhelmingly continue to raise capital through conventional bonds.

To deal with these realities and seize the untapped opportunities, we believe that all sustainable public debt market stakeholders must be engaged. So here we focus explicitly on each of three main actors involved – investors, regulators and issuers.

The first opportunity argues that mainstream investors should explicitly allocate to multilateral development bank debt as a near-perfect substitute for US treasuries or German bunds. This step would evolve the conventional wisdom behind sub-asset class delineation within asset allocation.

The second opportunity concerns regulators. It asks for more stringent rules across dedicated assets such as green bonds and sustainability-linked bonds to ensure that this fast-growing market continues to prosper. As the market broadens and its economic impact on people and the planet widens, market participants need clear guidelines to minimize frictions and encourage high-quality issuance.

The third highlights an opportunity for public debt market issuers. We argue for expanding the use-of-proceeds model to target waste, a multi-trillion dollar annual problem worldwide. Waste-reduction bonds eloquently align profit with tangible benefits and are applicable to almost all companies, sectors and governments.

Investors

MDB debt should become mainstream and be allocated to in most conventional investor portfolios. With 70-years of issuance history, a correlation to US treasuries consistently close to one and half-a-trillion dollars of debt outstanding, these bonds are perhaps the most underappreciated and underutilized financial asset by average investors. They are frequently held as a liquidity instrument by central banks, commercial banks and other treasury departments. Yet they are rarely found in a strategic asset allocation alongside investment grade credit or global equities.

In 2018, the Swiss-domiciled bank UBS created the world's first exchange traded fund for multilateral development bank debt. It enables investors, retail and institutional alike, to access a diversified pool of dollar-denominated bonds (UBS, 2022). In 2020, Blackrock, the largest asset manager in the world, launched a competing product (UBS, 2020).

For traditional investors cautious about adopting sustainable practices and instruments, multilateral development bank debt represents a secure, straightforward substitution for an existing US treasury allocation.

OPPORTUNITIES

Mainstream investors should adopt multilateral development bank debt as a mainstream allocation within their multi-asset investment portfolios.

Regulators

Stronger, more consistent regulation across dedicated assets such as green bonds and sustainability-linked bonds is essential for further asset growth and high-quality issuance. It would boost investor confidence even more and accelerate dedicated asset adoption and development.

With EU, Chinese and industry (ICMA) leaders unable to agree on a consistent green bond framework (MSCI, 2019), a considerable degree of uncertainty clouds use-of-proceeds bonds. There are concerns about which activities are eligible and what the most consistent financial structures should be. This confusion is even greater in the fledgling sustainability-linked market. Despite recent ICMA attempts to create them, no standards for what constitutes suitable KPIs, appropriate ratchets in interest rates, verification or probability of success exist (ICMA, 2020).

It is a truism that investors abhor uncertainty. Resolving these ambiguities would likely go a long way to increasing investor and issuer adoption alike. Improving the per-dollar impact of use-of-proceeds and sustainability-linked issuance would constitute a happy bonus. By tightening the rules that govern bonds used to refinance pre-existing activity, regulators can nudge the dedicated asset market toward issuance that genuinely creates incremental, positive change. Stricter disclosure requirements would enable investors to seek greater evidence of the additionality generated by the bonds, making issuer greenwashing more difficult and leading to better real-world outcomes.

Which regulator should seize the mantel and act is beyond our scope to decide as mere authors. But we do note, with concern, increasing regulatory fragmentation. The EU chose not to directly adopt ICMA's green-bond standards (ICMA, 2022) and the UK does not fully follow the EU's green taxonomy (Caldecott, 2021).

OPPORTUNITIES

Establish globally consistent regulations and tighten the requirement for additionality across use-of-proceeds and sustainability-linked issuance.

Issuers

We argue for expanding the use-of-proceed models to target waste, a multi-trillion dollar per year global problem that affects almost all companies, sectors and governments. Waste-reduction bonds could target it and eloquently align profit with people and planet.

As 80 per cent of corporate green bond issuance originates from only two sectors, financials and utilities (Wacker, Bolliger, Seimen, 2020), a large number of potential sustainability-inclined corporate issuers struggle to match their operations to the current green bond model. The use-of-proceeds model has already proved adaptable. A number of so-called blue bonds concentrate on water and oceans. The Covid-19 pandemic and the fiscal response to it have also resulted in approximately $1 trillion of social/sustainability issuance (BloombergNEF, n.d.).

Waste in all forms is a natural fit for the use-of-proceeds model. Collectively, we throw away around 30 per cent of all food produced worldwide, at a cost of $1 trillion per year, despite 10 per cent of the global population going hungry. The volume of plastic packaging, a scourge of our beaches, could more than quadruple by 2050, and 95 per cent of the value of plastic is lost after a single use, at a cost of up to $120 billion annually. If our consumption habits don't change, plastics in the sea could outweigh fish by 2050 (Haefele et al, 2020). Yet the Climate Bond Initiative's review of 2021 green bond issuance estimates that just 5 per cent of the bonds fund projects relate to waste (Harrison, MacGeoch and Michetti, 2022).

This needn't be the case. In 2020, German chemical and consumer goods firm Henkel demonstrated the viability of dedicated waste-reduction bonds by issuing one solely intended to combat plastic waste (Henkel, 2020). The effort of cutting back on it is inherently profit enhancing as inefficiencies in operations and supply chains result in additional costs that would otherwise be profit. There is a natural alignment between investor, investee entity, and people and the planet.

Furthermore, waste is inherently measurable. Corporate sustainability reports frequently cite the tons of paper, food and solid waste that wind up in landfills, as well as the KWh of electricity needlessly consumed. Waste is also emotive and easily understood by retail investors, employees and the general population. For instance, while packaging hardly makes up McDonald's largest operating cost, the fast-food giant's pledge to remove plastic straws from its dispensers attracted outsized attention (BBC, 2018). These dynamics underpin the ease with which waste bonds could be scaled and highlight their potential impact in communicating a firm's sustainability credentials.

> OPPORTUNITIES
>
> Formalize a taxonomy for waste-reduction bonds within an existing use-of-proceeds framework – to expand the market to underrepresented economic sectors and increase the positive contribution to people and the planet.

References

AIQ (2022) Untapped potential: Harnessing the full power of bondholder engagement, Aviva Investors, 31 January, www.avivainvestors.com/en-gb/views/aiq-investment-thinking/2022/01/bondholder-engagement/ (archived at https://perma.cc/8FUW-ZWFP)

Asian Development Bank (2021) Draft Energy Policy: Supporting Low Carbon Transition in Asia and the Pacific, Asian Development Bank, www.adb.org/documents/draft-energy-policy-supporting-low-carbon-transition-asia-and-pacific (archived at https://perma.cc/SDJ6-52ZQ)

Badertscher, B A et al (2019) Private ownership and the cost of public debt: Evidence from the bond market, *Management Science*, 65(1), pp 301–26, doi.org/10.1287/mnsc.2017.2935 (archived at https://perma.cc/EG5E-VGVB)

Bahra, B and Thukral, L (2020) ESG in global corporate bonds: The analysis behind the hype, *The Journal of Portfolio Management*, 46(8), pp 133–47, doi.org/10.3905/jpm.2020.1.171 (archived at https://perma.cc/ANH5-JVNL)

Banerjee, A, Karlan, D and Zinman, J (2015) Six randomized evaluations of microcredit: Introduction and further steps, *American Economic Journal: Applied Economics*, 7(1), pp 1–21, doi.org/10.1257/app20140287 (archived at https://perma.cc/2EJP-C4FU)

Banerjee, A V and Duflo, E (2007) The economic lives of the poor, *Journal of Economic Perspectives*, 21(1), pp 141–168, doi.org/10.1257/jep.21.1.141 (archived at https://perma.cc/PP4J-WPXP)

Barth, F, Hübel, B and Scholz, H (2022) ESG and corporate credit spreads, *The Journal of Risk Finance*, 23(2), pp 169–90, doi.org/10.1108/JRF-03-2021-0045 (archived at https://perma.cc/J5C4-GTEA)

Basílio, M (2014) The determinants of multilateral development banks' participation in infrastructure projects, *Journal of Infrastructure Development*,

6(2), pp 83–110, journals.sagepub.com/doi/10.1177/0974930614564991 (archived at https://perma.cc/Q326-6UW7)

Bateman, M (2010) *Why Doesn't Microfinance Work? The destructive rise of local neoliberalism*, Zed Books, London

BBC (2018) McDonald's to ditch plastic straws, BBC News, 15 June, www.bbc.com/news/uk-44492352 (archived at https://perma.cc/WH7B-94ZJ)

Berensmann, K, Dafe, F and Lindenberg, N (2018) Demystifying green bonds, in Boubaker, S, Cumming, D and Nguyen, D K (eds) *Research Handbook of Investing in the Triple Bottom Line*, Edward Elgar Publishing, Cheltenham, pp 333–52, ideas.repec.org/h/elg/eechap/17813_15.html (archived at https://perma.cc/LBU9-J82X)

Best Execution (2021) Green bond oversubscription data, 6 April, www.bestexecution.net/green-bond-oversubscription-data/ (archived at https://perma.cc/B99N-93UV)

Bird, G and Rowlands, D (2007) The IMF and the mobilisation of foreign aid, *The Journal of Development Studies*, 43(5), pp 856–70, doi.org/10.1080/00220380701384521 (archived at https://perma.cc/UTE9-6AK2)

BloombergNEF (no date) about.bnef.com (archived at https://perma.cc/MPE4-U5XL)

Bolton, P and Kacperczyk, M (2021) Do investors care about carbon risk? *Journal of Financial Economics*, 142(2), pp 517–49, doi.org/10.1016/j.jfineco.2021.05.008 (archived at https://perma.cc/N3XD-BNHH)

Byrne, L (2021) ESG engagement: Unlocking the bondholder's voice, BlueBay Asset Management, institutional.rbcgam.com/documents/en/common/article/092121_Whitepaper_ESG_engagement.pdf (archived at https://perma.cc/3NRW-J7KR)

Caldecott, B (2021) UK green taxonomy: what we should learn from the EU taxonomy and how the UK can create a race to the top, *Responsible Investor*, 25 January, www.responsible-investor.com/uk-green-taxonomy-what-we-should-learn-from-the-eu-taxonomy-and-how-the-uk-can-create-a-race-to-the-top/ (archived at https://perma.cc/T356-ZCFZ)

Chanda, P (2004) The effectiveness of the World Bank's anti-corruption efforts: Current legal and structural obstacles and uncertainties, *Denver Journal of International Law & Policy*, 32(2), digitalcommons.du.edu/djilp/vol32/iss2/6 (archived at https://perma.cc/8AWZ-XQYY)

Chava, S (2014) Environmental externalities and cost of capital, *Management Science*, 60(9), pp 2223–47, doi.org/10.1287/mnsc.2013.1863 (archived at https://perma.cc/D2LX-V3Y2)

Climate Bonds Initiative (no date) Explaining green bonds, www.climatebonds.net/market/explaining-green-bonds (archived at https://perma.cc/6UAS-E54N)

Cortellini, G and Panetta, I C (2021) Green bond: A systematic literature review for future research agendas, *Journal of Risk and Financial Management*, 14(12), p 589, doi.org/10.3390/jrfm14120589 (archived at https://perma.cc/D35C-SVY2)

Dahlberg, C and Dominicé, R (2017) Why microfinance matters to investors, Symbiotics, symbioticsgroup.com/wp-content/uploads/2017/06/2017_05_Symbiotics_WhyMFmatters_web.pdf (archived at https://perma.cc/5VNP-P722)

Deese, B et al (2019) Sustainability: the bond that endures, BlackRock Investment Institute, www.blackrock.com/us/individual/literature/whitepaper/bii-sustainable-investing-bonds-november-2019.pdf (archived at https://perma.cc/6E4D-YYT5)

Dominicé, R (2012) *Microfinance investments: an investor's guide to financing the growth and wealth creation of small enterprises and low income households in emerging economies*, Symbiotics, Bellinzona, Switzerland

Ehlers, T, Mojon, B and Packer, F (2020) Green bonds and carbon emissions: exploring the case for a rating system at the firm level, *BIS Quarterly Review*, www.bis.org/publ/qtrpdf/r_qt2009c.htm (archived at https://perma.cc/766U-H49A)

Federated Hermes (2021) SDG Engagement High Yield Credit Annual Report 2020,

GAM Investments (2021) Sustainability-linked bonds – how can they benefit investors? www.gam.com/en/our-thinking/investment-opinions/sustainability-linked-bonds-how-can-they-benefit-investors (archived at https://perma.cc/7E6L-ZY5F)

Ghosh, S and Srivastava, S (2021) Millions of defaults threaten microfinance's future in India, Bloomberg, 4 February, www.bloomberg.com/news/articles/2021-02-04/microfinance-is-facing-a-crisis-with-one-in-20-indians-in-debt (archived at https://perma.cc/43SY-RVC4)

Goldman Sachs (no date) Marquee, marquee.gs.com/welcome/ (archived at https://perma.cc/Y2C8-Z3W7)

Goswami, A, Borasi, P and Kumar, V (2021) Microfinance market size, share and industry forecast 2021–2030, Allied Market Research, www.alliedmarketresearch.com/microfinance-market-A06004 (archived at https://perma.cc/BB37-44WN)

Graeber, D (2009) *Direct action: an ethnography,* AK Press, Edinburgh

Hachenberg, B and Schiereck, D (2018) Are green bonds priced differently from conventional bonds? *Journal of Asset Management*, 19(6), pp 371–83, doi.org/10.1057/s41260-018-0088-5 (archived at https://perma.cc/X4RB-UF8Q)

Haefele, M et al (2020) Future of waste: Finding opportunities in waste reduction, UBS, doi.org/10.1596/978-1-4648-1329-0 (archived at https://perma.cc/3P2G-SR4X)

Harrison, C, MacGeoch, M and Michetti, C (2022) Sustainable debt global state of the market 2021, Climate Bonds Initiative, www.climatebonds.net/files/reports/cbi_global_sotm_2021_02f.pdf (archived at https://perma.cc/P3H9-NYP3)

Henkel (2020) Henkel first company to conclude a plastic waste reduction bond, www.henkel.com/press-and-media/press-releases-and-kits/2020-07-03-henkel-first-company-to-conclude-a-plastic-waste-reduction-bond-1099796 (archived at https://perma.cc/ML4E-JXWD)

ICMA (2020) Sustainability-linked bond principles: Voluntary process guidelines, www.icmagroup.org/assets/documents/Regulatory/Green-Bonds/June-2020/Sustainability-Linked-Bond-Principles-June-2020-171120.pdf (archived at https://perma.cc/6ZQB-JHRS)

ICMA (2021) Green bond principles: Voluntary process guidelines for issuing green bonds, www.icmagroup.org/sustainable-finance/the-principles-guidelines-and-handbooks/green-bond-principles-gbp/ (archived at https://perma.cc/AV5P-ZHZZ)

ICMA (2022) Analysis of the amendments to the EuGB regulation proposed by the Rapporteur of the EU Parliament, www.icmagroup.org/assets/ICMA-update-to-its-analysis-of-the-EuGB-Regulation-05012022.pdf (archived at https://perma.cc/3BZD-SGUY)

Ilmanen, A, Chandra, S and McQuinn, N (2020) Demystifying illiquid assets: expected returns for private equity, *The Journal of Alternative Investments*, 22(3), pp 8–22, doi.org/10.3905/jai.2019.1.086 (archived at https://perma.cc/2XE2-Q99M)

International Labour Organization (no date) The leading source of labour statistics, ILOSTAT, ilostat.ilo.org/ (archived at https://perma.cc/VWZ6-9J73)

Karnani, A (2007) Microfinance misses its mark, SSIR, ssir.org/articles/entry/microfinance_misses_its_mark (archived at https://perma.cc/LY7R-SVL7)

Keenan, C and Russo, Z (2021) World Bank Sustainable Development Bonds & Green Bonds Impact Report 2020, World Bank, issuu.com/jlim5/docs/world-bank-ibrd-impact-report-2020/1 (archived at https://perma.cc/ZVB4-54X7)

Kölbel, J F et al (2020) Can sustainable investing save the world? Reviewing the mechanisms of investor impact, *Organization & Environment*, 33(4), pp 554–74, doi.org/10.1177/1086026620919202 (archived at https://perma.cc/Y3GQ-GXYF)

Kovner, A and Wei, C (2014) The private premium in public bonds, Federal Reserve Bank of New York, www.newyorkfed.org/medialibrary/media/research/staff_reports/sr553.html (archived at https://perma.cc/WE4Q-F2UF)

Kruiff, D and Hartenstein, S (2014) *Microfinance and the Global Financial Crisis: A Call for BASEL*, : International Finance Corporation, Washington, DC, openknowledge.worldbank.org/handle/10986/21722 (archived at https://perma.cc/V3CW-V75Y)

Landers, C and Aboneaaj, R (2021) Half a trillion in dry powder? The time for MDB financial reform is now, Center for Global Development, 1 September, www.cgdev.org/blog/half-trillion-dry-powder-time-mdb-financial-reform-now (archived at https://perma.cc/E29U-7Y7T)

Lukaszewski, P (2021) Sustainability-linked bonds: A new platform for greenwashing? Abrdn, 21 May, www.abrdn.com/en-gb/institutional/insights-thinking-aloud/article-page/fixed-income-esg-sustainability-linked-bond (archived at https://perma.cc/74XV-T7K8)

MacAskill, S et al (2021) Is there a green premium in the green bond market? Systematic literature review revealing premium determinants, *Journal of Cleaner Production*, 280 (Part 2), p 124491, doi.org/10.1016/j.jclepro.2020.124491 (archived at https://perma.cc/Y9FM-CVVZ)

Mackinnon, B, Narayanan, R and Dominicé, R (2020) Private Asset Impact Fund Report 2020, Symbiotics, symbioticsgroup.com/wp-content/uploads/2020/11/Symbiotics_PAIF-Report-2020-1.pdf (archived at https://perma.cc/4QCU-MGGV)

Markowitz, H (1952) Portfolio selection, *The Journal of Finance*, 7(1), pp 77–91, doi.org/10.1111/j.1540-6261.1952.tb01525.x (archived at https://perma.cc/AN7G-UYEX)

Meager, R (2019) Understanding the average impact of microcredit expansions: A Bayesian hierarchical analysis of seven randomized experiments, *American Economic Journal: Applied Economics*, 11(1), pp 57–91, doi.org/10.1257/app20170299 (archived at https://perma.cc/TB55-GQJG)

Mendiratta, R, Varsani, H D and Giese, G (2021) How ESG affected corporate credit risk and performance, *The Journal of Impact and ESG Investing*, 2(2), pp 101–116, doi.org/10.3905/jesg.2021.1.031 (archived at https://perma.cc/TZ6U-HHTF)

MSCI (2019) Bloomberg Barclays MSCI Green Bond Index Consultation, www.msci.com/documents/1296102/12275477/Bloomberg+Barclays+MSCI+Green+Bond+Index+Consultation.pdf/e887b067-1513-c94d-4441-e18b39f6170d?t=1561734332189 (archived at https://perma.cc/424L-WZE9)

NN Investment Partners (no date) Responsible Investing Report 2019, www.nnip.com/en-INT/professional/themes/responsible-investing-report-2019 (archived at https://perma.cc/ZBV3-4CLJ)

Oliver, J (2021) European bond sale order books grow to 'ridiculous' levels, *Financial Times*, 18 March, www.ft.com/content/56cd5018-2451-4800-be81-5b5975c5193b (archived at https://perma.cc/U6DW-PNZG)

Orsagh, M (2019) Equities versus fixed income: How ESG factors affect both asset classes, CFA Institute Market Integrity Insights, 3 June, blogs.cfainstitute.org/marketintegrity/2019/06/03/equities-versus-fixed-income-how-esg-factors-affect-both-asset-classes/ (archived at https://perma.cc/9LYA-6EQH)

Palmer, J (2021) An asset owner's guide to fixed-income ESG integration, Willis Towers Watson, 21 June, www.wtwco.com/en-GB/Insights/2021/06/an-asset-owners-guide-to-fixed-income-esg-integration (archived at https://perma.cc/9VFW-UYG6)

Polbennikov, S et al (2016) ESG ratings and performance of corporate bonds, *The Journal of Fixed Income*, 26(1), pp 21–41, doi.org/10.3905/jfi.2016.26.1.021 (archived at https://perma.cc/PB8Y-DUYZ)

Polgreen, L and Bajaj, V (2010) India microcredit faces collapse from defaults, *The New York Times*, 17 November, www.nytimes.com/2010/11/18/world/asia/18micro.html (archived at https://perma.cc/MNM9-JH8J)

Ravindirane, J (2020) German sovereign innovates with its Bund's inaugural green twins, Natixis, gsh.cib.natixis.com/our-center-of-expertise/articles/german-sovereign-innovates-with-its-bund-s-inaugural-green-twins (archived at https://perma.cc/5YZV-RD5G)

RBC Global Asset Management (2019) 2019 Responsible Investing Survey Key Findings, global.rbcgam.com/sitefiles/live/documents/pdf/rbc-gam-responsible-investing-survey-key-findings-2019.pdf (archived at https://perma.cc/8LVK-XVYE)

Sayer, J and Lai, I A (2021) Sustainability-linked finance: the unresolved dilemmas, Eco-Business, www.eco-business.com/opinion/sustainability-linked-finance-the-unresolved-dilemmas/ (archived at https://perma.cc/47RQ-X7Z4)

Schroders (2017) Demystifying negative screens: The full implications of ESG exclusions, www.schroders.com/en/sysglobalassets/digital/insights/2018/thought-leadership/demystifying-negative-screens---the-full-implications-of-esg-exclusions.pdf (archived at https://perma.cc/59HB-VBA8)

Schroders (no date) Institutional investor study 2019: Sustainability, www.schroders.com/en/hk/institutional-service/insights/institutional-investor-study-2019/sustainability/ (archived at https://perma.cc/5WPY-22QT)

Sheng Ou Yong, X (2021) Why investor appetite for sustainability-linked bonds is growing, Investors' Corner, 22 July, investors-corner.bnpparibas-am.com/investing/why-investor-appetite-for-sustainability-linked-bonds-is-growing/ (archived at https://perma.cc/82V2-JDDP)

SIFMA (2021) *2021 Capital Markets Fact Book*, www.sifma.org/wp-content/uploads/2021/07/CM-Fact-Book-2021-SIFMA.pdf (archived at https://perma.cc/Y5HM-2BRZ)

Sooryamoorthy, R (2007) Microcredit for microenterprises or for immediate consumption needs? *Sociological Bulletin*, 56(3), pp 401–13, www.jstor.org/stable/23620637 (archived at https://perma.cc/63AX-VDBW)

Spinoso, M, Purcell, J and Street, B (2021) Strategy primer: sustainable dedicated assets [Blog] Quintet Private Bank, www.quintet.com/en-gb/articles/strategy-primer-sustainable-dedicated-assets (archived at https://perma.cc/6ZFW-8P3G)

UBS (2019a) What are MDB bonds? 31 January, www.ubs.com/global/en/assetmanagement/insights/asset-class-perspectives/etf/articles/mdb-bonds.html (archived at https://perma.cc/WD8U-HL8T)

UBS (2019b) Impact investing through development banks, Available from: shorturl.at/avCN8 (archived at https://perma.cc/CQS5-3V8F)

UBS (2020) UBS and BlackRock partner on new development bank debt ETF, www.ubs.com/global/en/media/display-page-ndp/en-20200218-ubs-blackrock.html (archived at https://perma.cc/J39Q-ZKTF)

UBS (2022) UBS ETF (LU) Sustainable development bank bonds UCITS ETF (USD) A-dis, www.ubs.com/nl/en/asset-management/etf-private/etf-products/etf-product-detail.html (archived at https://perma.cc/7F6Q-YJC3)

UNPRI (2014) Fixed income investor guide, Principles for Responsible Investment, www.unpri.org/fixed-income/fixed-income-investor-guide/30.article (archived at https://perma.cc/4ZCN-H55K)

UNPRI (2018) How ESG engagement creates value for investors and companies, Principles for Responsible Investment, www.unpri.org/research/how-esg-engagement-creates-value-for-investors-and-companies/3054.article (archived at https://perma.cc/U4LA-5LLA)

Viegas, M (no date) Repsol's green bond: exploring the controversy, Environmental Finance, www.environmental-finance.com/content/analysis/repsols-green-bond-exploring-the-controversy.html (archived at https://perma.cc/P3TP-BLLC)

Wacker, T, Bolliger, M and Seimen, M (2020) Green bond slide pack: Introduction and issuer profiles, UBS

Wacker, T, Lee, A and Howat, M S (2018) Education primer: Global multilateral development bank bonds, UBS

Winters, J A (2002) Criminal Debt, in Pincus, J and Winters, J A (eds) *Reinventing the World Bank*, Cornell University Press, Ithaca

World Bank (no date) Who we are, www.worldbank.org/en/who-we-are (archived at https://perma.cc/N8S3-5897)

05

Sustainable private markets

Introduction

When Earth's mightiest superheroes assemble to save the world there are two things you come to notice. First, they are a heterogeneous and eclectic bunch. There's a god with a hammer, a big green angry man and a woman very good at kicking. Second, there is little ultimate point to the get-together. Even if they fail there are thousands of other identical planets scattered across the multiverse just waiting to reboot and resurrect crucial characters (such as the sulky one who shoots lots of arrows).

Like comic book heroes, private market sustainable investors are a heterogeneous group. And their vastly different investments and methodologies need to be channelled to a single essential goal – helping people and the planet. Unlike their superhero counterparts, however, there is no multiverse (that we know of!) and no second chances. As private market investors jostle for assets, profile and impact, their heterogeneity makes it difficult to understand what does and does not make a difference in the world.

This chapter kicks off with a look at the assets that comprise sustainable private markets. We examine the history of sustainable private markets before posing – and answering – critical questions about popularity, performance and people and the planet. We discuss the market's origins – the 'old world' – when investors were typically small scale and sought concessionary investment returns.

In the 2010s, the 'new world' dawned. Large-scale, market-rate return funds came to the fore, supported by leading private market investment firms. Our little history lesson concludes by examining how the 'old world' has sought to reinvent itself through blended finance and new forms of private debt whose return depends upon sustainable outcomes.

This review sets the stage for examining sustainable private markets in theory and in practice in light of three important questions. We ask and answer the following questions:

- How popular are sustainable private markets? (Answer: Their popularity is overstated.)
- Do they add to investment performance? (Answer: Only if there is no additionality.)
- Do they help people and the planet? (Answer: Yes, but the effect is often exaggerated.)

In the second section, we examine the standards that comprise sustainable private markets. Here we profile the ecosystem that has underpinned their development and the related field of impact investing. Before we consider how sustainable private standards have fared across sub-asset classes and regions, we delve into how the current tapestry of standards arose. We investigate the various industry bodies that establish indicators, frameworks and rankings. We look at the proprietary systems used by some of the world's largest sustainable private market investors to measure investment impact. And we consider legal structures and vehicles that facilitate investment.

Having profiled the standards, we then judge how successful they've been and consider three key questions:

- Do all private market sub-asset classes embrace sustainability standards? (Answer: No.)
- Do all private market geographies do so? (Answer: No.)
- Do private market firms deploy adequate resources to fulfil sustainability standards? (Answer: In most cases, no.)

Before we tackle the chapter's final section, we pause to include an exclusive interview with David Petraeus. As of 2022, David chairs Kohlberg Kravis Roberts & Co, LP's (KKR) Global Institute. It is the research arm of the $500 billion investment powerhouse arguably best known for its private market investments, although the firm also invests these days in public markets, all real assets, credit, capital markets and the ESG arena. Prior to assuming this chairmanship, David was the fourth Director of the US Central Intelligence Agency (CIA), serving under President Barack Obama. He also spent 37 years in the US Army. David thus brings a unique perspective to sustainable investing, having observed its rise not only within KKR but across the market and the wider economy.

Our final private market section looks to the future to consider the potential opportunities and how we might get there. We recognize that, of the asset classes we've considered, private markets feature the greatest potential to do good. Put simply, many private market strategies enable investors to purchase a controlling interest in a company and repurpose and retool it to create powerful effective change. Yet sustainable investing within private markets has lagged its public peers in terms of frameworks, standards and widespread investor adoption. To rectify this situation, we focus on three opportunities that we see and suggest how to achieve their promise.

- The first opportunity looks at private markets in the broadest sense. The basic practices honed in public equity markets, we believe, can – and should – be applied to private markets, too.
- The second builds from the bright spots we see within the sustainable private market ecosystem. We urge the industry to work to accelerate these initiatives for the wider good of the asset class.
- The third, in calling for innovation, takes inspiration from how public debt market created dedicated assets. The potential exists to expand the scope of impact investing beyond its growth equity heartland to areas such as venture capital and private debt.

The assets that comprise sustainable private markets

The old world: Little by little

Let's consider two ways in which you can make a difference for people and the planet as you approach retirement. You can plant a small garden, grow organic vegetables in it and feast several times a year on pesticide-free kale and stringy orange roots. You reduce your carbon footprint and become more self-sufficient.

The other way is to drive your car (*gasp*) to the offices of BigCompanyInc, earn a boatload of money and use it to invest in start-up technologies that will help rapidly decarbonize the global economy. The garden may make you feel like you are personally doing something good. The investing has greater real-world impact and scale.

Historically, sustainable investing within private markets has been mostly of the garden variety, figuratively speaking. On the private debt side, investors have concentrated on variants of philanthropy such as debt guarantees. On the private equity side, funds have routinely been small scale (under $100 million) and thematically oriented to passionate niches (ImpactAlpha, 2017).

A 2010 publication by investment bank JP Morgan and the Global Impact Investing Network (GIIN) surveyed the nascent sustainability-focused private market industry. It offers valuable insights into the operations of the 'old world'.

First, it found that return expectations varied markedly. In areas such as developed market venture capital, private market investors expected returns 10 percentage points lower from their sustainable investments relative to conventional benchmarks.

Second, many of the surveyed funds drew their capital from charities or foundations. These funds were often termed 'program-related investments' and invested grant capital – i.e., money normally donated with no expectation of a financial return – rather than funds from a return-seeking endowment. This arrangement characterizes many of the early sustainable private market investors as concessionary investors.

Third, most deals were small in scale. The dominant segment of surveyed investments was $1 million or less in notional value. Only three per cent of the reported deals exceeded $10 million. Small deal sizes led to higher costs relative to conventional investments as some costs were fixed (and sizeable). The cost challenge was compounded by regional factors, as many sustainable private market investments were located in emerging economies. In some cases, the high costs were subsidized by a charity or foundation. This was often termed a 'grant-sponsored technical assistance facility' and would improve returns for profit-seeking investors via a hybrid model of charity and investment (JP Morgan, 2010).

There were exceptions to the 'old world' rule. Actis is a notable one. The private market infrastructure-investment firm was spun out from CDC Group, the UK's development finance institution, in 2004. Armed with almost $1 billion of assets at inception and a mission to provide critical infrastructure to developing economies, Actis gathered more than $4.5 billion by 2012 and has since grown its assets to more than $15 billion (as of 2022) (Actis, n.d.).

The new world: Enter the big boys

At the 1948 Summer Olympics, Sweden, a country of just 7 million citizens, came in second in the medal table. The top 10 finishers also included Denmark, Finland and Switzerland, nations whose populations at the time numbered about 4 million each (IOC, n.d. a). Fast forward to the 2020 Summer Olympics and population and economic resources dominate. After 72 years of professionalization and billions of dollars of funding, four of the top five countries on the medal table can be found at the top of the equivalent GDP list. The medal table's top 10 is rounded out by the European Union's largest sovereigns, France, Germany and Italy (IOC, n.d. b).

The arrival of the private market 'big boys' started in the mid-2010s. In 2014, long-time impact investor Leapfrog Investments raised a record-breaking $400 million for a fund focused on financial inclusion throughout Africa and South Asia (Impact Investing Institute, n.d.). This was followed two years later by the world's largest wealth manager UBS teaming up with biotech specialist MPM Capital to construct a $470 million cancer-focused private equity vehicle called the UBS Oncology Impact Fund (MPM Capital, 2016).

Mainstream private equity firms took note. In 2017, Bain Capital raised $390 million for its Bain Capital Double Impact Fund (ImpactAlpha, 2017), while TPG Capital raised over $2 billion for its dedicated impact fund TPG Rise, with UBS anchoring the deal with a $325 million contribution (Joshua Franklin, 2017). Private market heavyweights KKR, Brookfield and Apollo have all since followed suit (New Private Markets, 2021) and both Bain and TPG Capital have created subsequent funds. Bain more than doubled its first impact raise (Schultz, 2021) and TPG added a further $2 billion for TPG Rise II (Falconer, 2020) before zeroing in on climate impact and bringing together in excess of $7 billion for TPG Rise Climate (The Rise Fund, 2022). The 'big boys' now dominate the asset private market impact fund-raising tables (New Private Markets, 2021).

Their arrival resulted in important positives. First, mainstream private market firms have considerable resources across the value chain and large-scale teams for deal sourcing and assessment. Their broad networks and expertise enable them to develop the firms they later invest in and create greater real-world impact through greater corporate success.

Second, their investment expertise attracts larger quantities of institutional capital from pension funds and insurers, which may otherwise have been reluctant to support 'untested' smaller impact funds. This influx of capital can support more impactful firms and encourage entrepreneurs to found new businesses, confident in the knowledge that a funding ecosystem exists.

Third, the profit-seeking focus of the 'big boys' can improve the efficiency of impactful technologies and services. Through objective decision-making, such as refusing to provide follow-on capital for an impactful but economically failing firm, the 'big boys' can enhance capital allocation efficiency and ensure that the most impactful ideas scale quickly while suboptimal practices are quickly discontinued.

However, their presence has also attracted criticism. That the wider portfolios of large private market firms may contain fossil fuel investments can discredit their efforts in the eyes of many. Critics have also questioned whether the 'big boys' create additionality – i.e., support impactful companies that otherwise would not have received mainstream funding. Some commentators have challenged the motivations of the mainstream firms and described their approach as 'impact washing' (Hurley, 2021).

The old world: Reinvention

In January 1999, Mike Tyson stepped into the ring to launch a boxing comeback and reinvent himself after his shocking disqualification 18 months previously for biting the ear of Evander Holyfield. Even as 'Iron Mike' sought reinvention, some signature elements, such as his unique aggression in the ring, remained. But controversial promoter Don King no longer promoted his fights. And Tyson stopped using his bob and weave defence. While the makeover of 'old world' Mike Tyson brought a few successes, ultimately, he could not escape his demons and encountered familiar problems, which led a few years later to his retirement.

In the late 2010s, the 'old world' approach of philanthropy and smaller-sized transactions made a comeback via two innovations. The first, development impact bonds (DIBs), sought to bring pay-for-performance to the private markets. The second, blended finance, promised to create significant impact and additionality by using charitable capital to make the uninvestible investible.

In 'Chapter 4 – Sustainable public debt markets', we outlined how sustainability-linked transactions decreased or increased the cost of debt depending upon whether sustainability targets were achieved or not. DIBs are effectively sustainably-linked instruments on steroids, as the investment return is fully dependent upon sustainability metrics – such as the number of girls in developing countries that continue on into secondary education.

DIBs trace their history to 2010 and a $8 million fund raise from Social Finance. It sought to reduce the number of short-sentenced offenders that leave a UK prison from returning to it (India Development Review, 2018). As of 2020, the Brookings Global Impact Bonds Database identified almost 200 DIBs worth over $400 million that had sprung up since (Gustafsson-Wright, n.d.). While DIBs have generated much fanfare, signature elements of the 'old world' remain. The market is small in scale and highly labour intensive – the final payout depends on difficult-to-obtain data, which leaves little room for error with data collection and quality (India Development Review, 2018). Furthermore, a DIB is very expensive to operate, typically incurring $1 to 8 million in measurement costs, which can, sadly, even dwarf the amount being channelled to sustainable projects (India Development Review, 2018; Starr, 2018).

Blended finance has attracted accolades since it was publicly championed at the Third International Conference on Financing for Development in Addis Ababa in 2015. Often cited as the financial innovation able to turn development finance 'billions into trillions' (Rosario, 2021), blended finance is based on a straightforward premise. Philanthropists, rather than simply donating capital, use their money to incentivize profit-seeking investors to join them in an impactful transaction. In simplified terms, imagine that profit-seeking investors are unwilling to fund the construction of new hospitals due to an unfavourable risk-return profile. Concurrently, a philanthropist can donate enough money to build and sustain a single hospital. If the philanthropist and the investor team up, however, the philanthropist's indifference to financial returns can augment the cash flows of the profit-seeking investors, which enables two or more hospitals to be built. The theoretical appeal is easy to understand. Investors enjoy market-rate returns and philanthropists catalyse impact on a larger scale than they otherwise could have.

Despite the potential, blended finance remains encumbered by many 'old world' obstacles, in particular, the difficulty of scaling. Exact definitions of blended finance vary, which, in turn, affects the estimated market size, but the OECD identifies only 15 or so new material funds or facilities being launched annually during the 2010s (Basile and Dutra, 2019). Blended finance ecosystem facilitator Convergence cites roughly $120 billion in total deal volume over a similar time frame (Convergence, n.d.). In practice, blended finance has yet to turn 'billions into trillions'. *The Economist* (2020) concluded that it is 'struggling to take off' while industry participant Blue Orchard admits that 'the potential of blended finance has yet to be fully attained'(Blue Orchard Academy, 2018).

Why has the old world's reinvention proved unable to shrug off familiar problems? The hurdles of cost, complexity and a lack of standardization simply refuse to go away. But perhaps the biggest, most glaring hindrance is the tension between philanthropic and investment capital. A philanthropist may be happy to give away money and receive no return to help those in need, but the thought of donating funds to aid profit-seeking investors (such as *gasp* hedge funds) is often deemed unpalatable. Despite the argument that the ends (more impact) justify the means (lining someone else's pockets), this tension appears to prevent philanthropists from moving en masse into blended finance and offering the sizeable incentives needed to bring mainstream investors with them.

Having reviewed the basic tenets of sustainable private markets, we now examine these markets in theory and in practice, asking and answering three key questions.

Sustainable private market investments: How popular are sustainable private markets?

Short answer: Their popularity is overstated.

IN THEORY

Proponents of sustainable private market investments put forward theories as to why sustainable private market investments should be highly popular.

The argumentation starts by considering private markets' substantial potential to do good. Put simply, many private market strategies enable investors to purchase a controlling interest in a company and repurpose and retool it to create powerful effective change.

This admirable intention has created a niche within private markets termed 'impact investing'. Theoretical frameworks define impact investing in numerous ways, but they often agree on it as 'investments into companies and organizations with the intent to contribute to measurable positive social or environmental impact alongside financial returns' (Operating Principles for Impact Management, n.d. a). The elements required to qualify as impact investing typically include:

- the investor's explicit intent to create impact through their investments (without resorting to claiming the company's impact as their own);
- the need to measure and verify the impact achieved; and
- a desire, in some cases, for additionality – i.e., creating impact that would not have occurred had it not been for the investor (GIIN, n.d. a).

When we consider the popularity of sustainable private markets in practice, we will focus predominantly on impact investing. While we do not deny the existence of a broader private market trend that considers sustainable factors, by narrowing of our view we create a defined universe to analyse.

IN PRACTICE

A long-running PwC survey of private market investment firms found that, between 2013 and 2021, the popularity of sustainability and its relative importance in their investment process appeared to rise dramatically. Interestingly, on the topic of investments, private equity firms claimed that the importance of considering sustainability throughout the deal cycle increased only mildly over the surveyed period (one-and-a-half points on a 1–10 scale). In contrast, when it came to communications, they reported a near six-point gain in the importance of sustainability when reporting to stakeholders (PwC, 2021). This suggests that sustainability's increase in popularity was somewhat superficial.

The 2021 survey also revealed that, while more than 75 per cent of private market investors claimed to be investing for impact to some extent, less than 40 per cent could confirm that they were actually measuring their impact (PwC, 2021). These data points imply that, in reality, private market firms overstate their adoption of sustainability.

The eagerness of firms to present sustainability credentials likely stems in part from investor pressure. Private equity firm clients, termed 'limited partners', also self-disclose a significant interest in sustainability. According to communication firm Edelman, 88 per cent of limited partners say they incorporate sustainability indicators when making investment decisions (Edelman, n.d.). However, once again, this figure may also be upwardly biased as it is self-disclosed.

Translating this self-declared interest in sustainability and impact into assets under management is fraught with difficulty. Since the early 2010s, GIIN has assessed the size of the impact investing market. It steadily raised its estimates from single-digit billions to more than $700 billion by 2020. Yet a survey of GIIN members shows that only about 60 per cent of impact investing comes from private markets, suggesting a private market figure closer to $400 billion (Hand et al, 2020).

This number broadly correlates to the one published in a study undertaken by the World Bank International Finance Corporation (IFC) in 2020. It estimates the size of the private impact investing market at about $300 billion. However, there could be another $300 billion of private assets where impact may be 'intended' but 'not measured', the IFC report says, as well as a further $2 trillion of assets if public markets are also included (Volk, 2021).

In summary, these metrics imply that the ecosystem overstates the true popularity of sustainability within private markets. Yet there is enough evidence to suggest that its popularity is indeed increasing.

Sustainable private market investments: Do they add to investment performance?

Short answer: Only if there is no additionality.

IN THEORY

Proponents of sustainable private market investments put forward theories as to why sustainable practices should add to investment performance. The case centres on integrating sustainable practices into acquired companies to enable them to reach a more comprehensive understanding of risk and opportunity. Proponents cite the business theory that, if employees are happier and more motivated, productivity will rise; if resources are managed accordingly, supply chains will remain intact; and if diversity is encouraged, superior ideas, innovations and, ultimately, profits will result.

There are also theoretical counterpoints. The most significant is that the presence of additionality implies mechanical investment underperformance. The Impact Management Project defines additionality as 'the extent to which desirable outcomes would have occurred without public intervention' (Impact Management Project, n.d. a). In other words, would the project or company be successful and receive funding if the sustainable private market investor did not invest in it?

For example, if a sustainable private market investor beats off competition from a conventional investor and backs a market-return private wind farm, there is no additionality. The equivalent investment would have happened regardless and the wind farm would have been able to invest and grow. Therefore, to achieve additionality one must invest in something that the market is not prepared to fund. Economic theory on demand and supply curves suggests that the market will only refuse to fund something if expected return is concessionary (Marshall, 2013). Theoretically, then, the quest for additionality must mechanically lead to investment underperformance.

IN PRACTICE

Ample academic evidence indicates that incorporating sustainable practices into private businesses can improve their operating performance. Academic studies are, typically, aggregated into meta studies that summarize findings from a range of countries and time periods and highlight metrics such as improvements in operating margins or return on capital. A 2014 meta study from researchers at the University of Oxford found that, in 88 per cent of the studies they surveyed, companies that adhered to social or environmental standards showed better operational performance (Clark, Feiner and Viehs, 2015), a finding documented in other credible meta studies as well (Friede, Busch and Bassen, 2015).

Explicitly for private market investment funds, research from $300 billion asset manager Carlyle validates the findings of academia (Carlyle, n.d.). Analysis of Carlyle's portfolio companies revealed that those with diverse boards grew earnings five times faster than those lacking such diversity. Adding employees and raising pay (as opposed to the stereotypical private equity action of cutting costs) also boosted earnings growth. Based on Carlyle's portfolio companies, every 10 per cent increase in payrolls led to additional returns in excess of 20 per cent, while decreasing payroll costs were associated with falling returns (Thomas and Starr, 2020).

Carlyle peer CVC asserts a similar focus on sustainability. A report on its approach states, 'When CVC buys a company, one of the first things it does is collect hard data on customer and employee satisfaction. It then helps management figure out how to target six key areas – customer focus, simplification, human capital, communities, environment and governance – to improve performance' (Bain & Company, 2021).

Yet a significant share of the current sustainable private market ecosystem, despite these findings, does deliver below-market rates. The likely cause is that firms deliberately seek maximum additionality and impact. The 2020 GIIN survey found that just two-thirds of respondents sought competitive investment returns, while 18 per cent accepted some underperformance and 15 per cent were merely seeking not to lose money on their investments (Hand et al, 2020).

Sustainable private market investments thus span the return spectrum, and whether sustainable techniques add or subtract from performance is predominantly a function of investor motivation and a desire to seek additionality.

Sustainable private market investments: Do they help people and the planet?

Short answer: Yes, but the effect is often overstated.

IN THEORY

Proponents of sustainable private market investments advance theories as to why investors who adhere to its principles can help people and the planet. Non-public companies typically comprise the vast majority of a country's economy as measured by GDP or employment (SBE Council, n.d.). Non-public companies that are owned by private equity investment firms make up a smaller, but still notable, portion of the economy. Eurostat, for instance, estimates that over 4 per cent of Europe's workforce is employed by a private equity-backed firm (Invest Europe, 2022). As a consequence, private market investors have the potential to influence the economy. They can reshape industries and supply chains and provide capital to the sustainable technologies and services of the future.

IN PRACTICE

The positive impact of private market investors is habitually overstated. A 2020 article from *Institutional Investor* found that 700 private market investing firms are signatories to the United Nations Principles of Responsible Investment, and that they control roughly two-thirds of all private market assets under management. Yet less than one-third of these firms performed systematic sustainability monitoring on their portfolio companies, and less than 10 per cent were methodically receiving sustainability data from these companies (Pucker and Kotsantonis, 2020).

Data aggregated by Bain & Company supports *Institutional Investor*'s findings. Its 2021, Global Private Equity Report stated that less than 30 per cent of private equity-owned portfolio companies reported carbon emissions, and in less than 10 per cent of cases did the reported emissions include Scope 3 (i.e., supply chain) or science-based targets for future emission reductions (Bain & Company, 2021).

While private market investors undoubtedly exert an array of positive and negative impacts on the world, these impacts are not being consistently monitored or targeted by most private market investors.

The standards that comprise sustainable private markets

Standards: Investor bodies

If you worked for a film studio in the early 1990s you had to choose whether to release your latest flick on VHS or Betamax or both. In the 2000s, you once again had to back a metaphorical technological horse in consumer home playback, this time in the form of either Blu-ray or HD DVD.

If sitting on the sofa eating popcorn isn't your thing and you box for a living instead, you currently have to choose a sanctioning body. You can win a recognized world title from the World Boxing Council, the World Boxing Association, the International Boxing Federation or the World Boxing Organization. In short, whether it's films or prize fighting, different standards and rules can fragment audiences, generate confusion and hinder development.

Sustainable private markets feature a number of investor groupings, principles and alliances that seek to define everything from what impact investing is to how the length of ocean coastline restored by conservationists should be measured. Standards have proliferated to such an extent that the problem has been satirized by the sustainable press. Editorial staff at *Responsible Investor* cheekily announced the formation of the 'Principles for Responsible Principles' with the tagline 'new principles seek to tackle risks around the proliferation of principles' (*Responsible Investor*, 2021).

Making sense of the investor bodies active in the field requires a categorization system (and a great deal of free time). What follows is our best attempt.

Broadly speaking, there are two popular investor bodies that set frameworks for indicator level data at the project or portfolio company level, including the aforementioned measurement of restored coastline. GIIN created the IRIS and IRIS+ frameworks. There is also the Harmonized Indicators for Private Sector Operations (HIPSO), which has historically been favoured by development finance institutions. In 2021, the World Bank announced an attempt to harmonize IRIS and HIPSO by means of a project called the Joint Impact Indicators. As of 2022, it remains to be seen whether this harmonization will create greater cohesion and certainty among investors (International Finance Corporation, 2021).

The next level of sustainable private market investor bodies consists of organizations that take the indicators and create standards and rankings. Somewhat worryingly, IRIS+ proudly states that its metrics are valid for over 50 standard bodies (GIIN, n.d. b), while other standards, such as the Sustainability Accounting Standards Board (SASB) or the UN General Reporting Initiative (GRI), may also recommend specific indicators in addition to their own standards.

The final level of bodies tends to focus on high-level principles and frameworks. Examples include the Impact Management Project and the World Bank-sponsored Operating Principles for Impact Management. The former operates a range of simple templates and considers, for instance, an investment's impact via a *What, Who, How Much, Contribution and Risk* framework. The latter views an investment value chain by starting at *Intent* and working through *Origination, Structuring, Portfolio Management* and finally *Impact Upon Exit* (Impact Management Project, n.d. b; Operating Principles for Impact Management, n.d. a).

A GIIN survey of the use of tools, frameworks and systems discovered no consensus among investors. The UN Sustainable Development goals were popular with around 50 per cent of respondents, who reported using them either for objectives, performance measurement or performance reporting. IRIS and IRIS+ meanwhile found favour with approximately one-third of respondents. Other frameworks cited by more than 10 per cent of the private market firms surveyed include the Impact Management Project, UN PRI, B Analytics and its GIIRS framework and the Operating Principles for Impact Management (Hand et al, 2020).

In short, the impact measurement and reporting ecosystems developed by investor bodies are numerous and heterogeneous and they create confusion throughout the private market investment industry.

Standards: Proprietary systems

When I (Simon) ask my daughter how well she did on her latest school test she responds with an enthusiastic double thumbs up. I'm delighted for her as a student and for me as a parent. Of course, her proprietary analytics system has its drawbacks. Since she is both candidate and assessor, I'm inclined to believe that the evaluations she gives herself have an upward bias, with a conflict of interest hiding behind those raised appendages.

Within the sustainable private market ecosystem, the use of proprietary systems is common. The GIIN surveys found that almost 90 per cent of investors use one to measure impact, a response level that has remained consistent across a decade of surveys (Hand et al, 2020). This lack of standardization and harmonization within the industry creates ample opportunities for selective reporting. Many leading investors have sought to address this shortcoming by creating their own, 'better' methodologies to measure the impact of their investments.

TPG, with its sizeable impact funds TPG Rise and TPG Rise Climate, founded Y Analytics, a two-dozen person strong team dedicated to measuring and reporting impact. Y Analytics and TPG created the concept of impact multiple of money (IMM), which seeks to place a dollar value on both positive and negative externalities to aggregate diverse impacts ranging from access to education, improved healthcare and carbon avoidance into a single number (Y Analytics, n.d.). The approach has parallels with the work of a number of Harvard University professors who created impact-weighted accounting (Harvard Business School, n.d.).

Y Analytics estimated, for example, that the portfolio companies of TPG Rise avoided releasing into the environment 48 million tonnes of carbon in a calendar year, which translated into a monetary value of $1.3 billion. The companies provided 4.2 million lower-income households with access to the banking system which, through the channel of poverty alleviation, was calculated to deliver around $200 million of impact. Their healthcare services saved over 30,000 lives and created an impact value of $30 million as positive social impacts were partially offset by greater consumption as a result of longer life spans (The Rise Fund, n.d.).

TPG peer KKR takes a different approach. Its framework draws on four key criteria and seeks to align impact metrics to pre-existing indicators and standards frameworks. The frameworks that the indicators are drawn from may differ from investment to investment.

KKR considers investments based on whether:

- they can achieve attractive, risk-adjusted returns;
- they measurably improve ESG performance during KKR's ownership;
- the core product or service contributes locally relevant solutions to the SDGs; and
- the impacts generated are measurable using metrics sourced from third-party frameworks wherever possible.

TPG's and KKR's approaches each have their merits. The challenge is that it is not currently possible to meaningfully compare TPG's impact with KKR's. For a private market investor focused on sustainability and impact, it is difficult to ascertain which fund has provided greater impact, or even which firm has the more credible impact-measurement process.

The lack of comparability between sustainability-focused private market firms concerns many within the industry. The 2020 GIIN survey found that 66 per cent of investors expressed anxiety about 'impact washing', and 35 per cent were worried about an 'inability to demonstrate impact results'. A full 34 per cent of respondents were frustrated by 'an inability to compare impact results with peers' (Hand et al, 2020).

In summary, while some sustainable private market investors have devoted time and money to measuring, reporting and increasing their impact, significant challenges remain. Because comparing private market firms is difficult, end investors cannot always make informed investment decisions.

Standards: Legal structures

If you want to travel to Paris from London for the weekend you have plenty of options. You can fly, take a train or perhaps sail over from Dover; even drive your car (most of the way). Every option comes with its positives and negatives and each has a unique price. One choice is not categorically better than the other. Whatever difficulty you have in deciding results from the diversity of choices available.

Investors have a wide array of investment structures that they can invest in within private markets. The structures range from traditional limited partner/general partner arrangements (which typically include a 10-year holding period and annual fees in the range of 2 per cent, plus 20 per cent of all profits) to open-ended trust structures that trade on stock exchanges. Many come with significant regulatory-imposed restrictions that prevent retail investors from partaking, typically for their own protection.

In Europe in the late 2010s, a new structure joined the catalogue of options. Called a European Long-term Investment Fund (ELTIF), it was designed to increase the amount of non-bank finance available for companies investing in the real economy of the EU. ELTIFs can be 'passported' across EU member states to enable widespread distribution and, crucially, they can be distributed to retail investors (European Commission, 2015).

ELTIFs have encountered some criticism because of such issues as the return drag caused by calling capital upfront and the relatively few issuers of eligible assets. Revised legislation in 2022 aimed to increase ELTIF appeal and the first dedicated sustainable and energy transition funds have since emerged (Ogier, 2022; ESMA, n.d.). Mirova, an affiliate of universal bank Natixis, has sought to raise an impact-focused ELTIF while ThomasLloyd has sought to create one predicated on investing in decarbonization and energy transition (Bucak, 2021; ThomasLloyd, 2021).

Having reviewed the structures behind sustainable private markets, we now turn our attention to how they function in theory and in practice by asking and answering three important questions.

Investors: Do all private market sub asset classes embrace sustainability standards?

Short answer: No.

IN THEORY

Proponents of sustainability in private markets suggest that sustainable practices can be integrated into all sub-asset classes, from real estate to venture capital to private debt. These sub-asset classes, after all, share many features and represent investment in corporations that have employees, consume resources and operate supply chains.

IN PRACTICE

In practice, the adoption of sustainable practices by sub-asset classes in private markets varies considerably. Some of the classes, venture capital being a prime example, have lagged behind.

Consulting firm PwC surveyed 70 venture capital firms in 2021. While 75 per cent claimed to 'have integrated ESG into their investment process' to 'some extent' or to a 'great extent', the firms cited a laundry list of challenges they faced. This suggests that their embrace of sustainability standards was actually more aspirational than their original responses suggested. The most common concerns were:

- a lack of dedicated resources within investable early-stage companies;
- a paucity of data and resources at fund level;
- insufficient influence over early-stage companies to effect change;
- an incompatibility between sustainability and the high growth/dynamic nature of successful startup organizations; and
- a difficulty in identifying the risks and mitigation approaches in early-stage companies where frameworks are inadequate (PwC, 2021).

Other areas of private markets are much more advanced. Real estate, for instance, has greater homogeneity among funds and several well-established sustainability considerations, such as carbon emissions. It has therefore been able to align to a real-estate-specific set of standards, known as GRESB (GRESB, n.d.). Most sustainable real-estate funds are now measured against these standards.

In summary, the diversity of private market sub-asset classes can lead to a variety of sustainability standards. In addition, private market sub-asset classes have each reached a different level of maturity in terms of sustainable standards and frameworks.

Investors: Do all private market geographies embrace sustainability standards?

Short answer: No.

IN THEORY

Proponents of sustainability in private markets theorize that sustainable practices could be integrated worldwide. The location of an investment will expose the investor to differing sustainable factors and societal norms, on topics such as employee working conditions, resource consumption and supply chains. However, all these elements will, regardless of where the company is located, still impact the investment case. Data-measurement systems and data integrity will also differ by geography. But this too should not negate the ability of companies to embrace sustainability standards.

IN PRACTICE

The adoption of sustainable practices varies considerably by region, according to Bain & Capital. The discrepancies in practices are also vast. Typically, Europe embraces sustainability to a greater extent. For example, 80 per cent of leading European private equity firms are committed to at least one of the UN Principles for Responsible Investment, the Net-Zero Asset Owner Alliance or the Task Force on Climate-related Financial Disclosures. This figure falls to 55 per cent in Asia and just 45 per cent in the US (Bain & Company, 2021).

This lack of willingness by US private market investors to adopt sustainable standards and frameworks is reflected in the actions of their portfolio companies. The share of these companies that report carbon emissions or utilize science-based targets is notably lower than their European-backed counterparts. On some metrics, such as the adoption of renewable energy, the gap between US and European portfolio companies exceeds 10 percentage points (Bain & Company, 2021).

In summary, culture and regional nuances matter. Although sustainability standards are theoretically applicable to investment firms worldwide, there are material differences in how readily they are adopted.

Investors: Do private market firms deploy adequate resources to fulfil sustainability standards?

Short answer: No, in most cases.

IN THEORY

Proponents of sustainability in private markets suggest that private market firms comprehensively integrate sustainability into their operations and thus fulfil sustainability standards. They point to survey data that cites enthusiastic support for sustainability from the management of private market investment firms. A 2021 PwC survey found that over 70 per cent of these firms said that they integrate environmental, social and governance concerns into their analysis. The same survey found that over 90 per cent of respondents regard diversity and inclusion as a critical issue when investing (PwC, 2021).

IN PRACTICE

The actual data on the actions of private market firms contradicts the theory. In most cases, the firms do not deploy the resources required to adhere to, and make full use of, the various sustainability standards and frameworks.

Ardian, a large fund of funds provider, has investments in over 170 general partners. It has found that only 20 per cent of private market investors employ at least one full-time staff member in the area of sustainability. A full 56 per cent of general partners consider work in the field a part-time role. With such limited resources devoted to it, many companies are unlikely to be engaging deeply with sustainability and its standards and frameworks.

Furthermore, despite their headline statements about diversity and inclusion, only 40 per cent of private market investment firms had a formal diversity and inclusion strategy and only 10 per cent employed 30 per cent or more women at the executive level. Discussions with portfolio companies on sustainability topics were not typically structured, with 72 per cent of general partners describing their interactions with company management teams on sustainability matters as 'informal' (Ardian, 2020).

In summary, despite strong statements of self-identified enthusiasm for sustainability, few firms have the resources, expertise or current practices to fully utilize their potential value.

In this interview, Simon sat down with retired US Army General David Petraeus to discuss sustainable investing, with an emphasis on private market investing. As of 2022, David is currently the Chairman of Kohlberg Kravis Roberts & Co, LP's (KKR) Global Institute. It is the research arm of the $500 billion investment powerhouse arguably best known for its private market investments, although the firm also invests these days in public markets, all real assets, credit, capital markets and the ESG arena. Prior to assuming this chairmanship, David was the fourth Director of the US Central Intelligence Agency (CIA), serving under President Barack Obama. He also served 37 years in the US Army. David thus brings a unique perspective to sustainable investing, having observed its rise, not only within KKR, but across the market and wider economy.

Simon: Thank you for taking the time. David, you've come to sustainable investing following a career in public service – it's a great perspective. You've thus seen it grow, without operating within its confines day-to-day. Can you tell us a little more?

David: Yes, Henry Kravis and George Roberts asked me to establish what is the KKR Global Institute, that does geopolitical risk analysis during the diligence phase of investing and also integrates macro and ESG risk analyses. Only recently has KKR established an Impact Fund, which seeks to invest in companies that pursue the UN Sustainable Development Goals. And, while KKR has been very active in its ESG efforts and now is well established in impact investing, my perspective for this interview is as a private venture capitalist with investments in some 20 startups, one of which happens to be one of the leading vertical farming firms.

Simon: I'd love to hear about vertical farming. In particular, the business opportunity from an investment perspective and also from a societal perspective.

David: The firm started out in an old paintball warehouse in New Jersey, and they have built impressively since then. Originally, they just made a limited number of leafy greens but now they have developed a whole variety of different products. What I find interesting is that it has become a real technology platform in all elements of vertical farming. They've collected a huge amount of data over time and can now understand and plan with unprecedented accuracy. Now, from a sustainability perspective, what's really interesting about this is that you can establish these vertical farms inside cities. It is often in such locations where you can find either unused or under-used warehouses. One of the key determinants for a site is that the electricity doesn't cost too much, because obviously they have to use electricity to provide synthetic sunlight. Additionally, from a social perspective, in some cases these farms can be located in neighbourhoods that cannot access conventional leafy greens easily, and so local grocery stores can benefit considerably.

Simon: That's impressive. How do the sustainable and financial elements interact?

David: Firstly, there's a huge water savings compared to conventional farming, in excess of 95 per cent. There's also zero pesticide use. And, depending on the location, in many cases, vertical farms have much lower supply chain and transportation costs. They can also achieve a very consistent product, as they control all aspects of the product via the nutrients that are provided as well as other elements in the actual production. Another interesting angle linked to population and demographics is that it's likely that vertical farming costs will go down as the process gets more efficient and cheap renewable energy becomes more prevalent. In contrast, conventional farming costs may go up due to climate change and land shortages. There's a huge market out there, and while it's very difficult to estimate future trends, the vertical farming market could experience a substantial compound annual growth rate of well over 20 per cent over the next five years.

Simon: Through the lens of your vertical farming investment, what makes a good private market or venture investment?

David: Technology and experimentation are important. In the case of vertical framing there is still an enormous amount of experimentation. They are undertaking research to develop blueberry production, strawberries and so forth. They are moving up the value chain. Again, it is really a technology platform, not just an agricultural endeavour, and that is really quite extraordinary. They continue to refine the cloth upon which the produce grows, there's various aspects of the genetics of the actual plants, and other factors such as the optimal amount of nutrients, water, oxygen etcetera. Automation often unlocks a lot of value – in this case automated nutrient delivery systems, the unloading of seed, the growing, the harvesting, the packaging. Increasingly the controls are digitized with algorithms that are constantly refined for every stage of the growth cycle. There is even experimentation in various 'vision capabilities' – ways to monitor all this. One experimentation is with artificial intelligence-enabled drones. Keep in mind these farming units are stacked one on top of the other in huge warehouses, so they are very high. For me, it really has been a pleasure to be one of their investors and to follow this progress over the last seven years.

Simon: Thank you David.

The potential opportunities and how we might get there

Among the asset classes we consider in this book, private markets have the greatest potential to do good for people and the planet. Put simply, many private market strategies enable investors to purchase a controlling interest in a company and repurpose and retool it to create powerful effective change. This power dwarfs that of a public equity investor, who typically purchases a miniscule fraction of company ownership.

Nonetheless, sustainable investing within private markets has greatly lagged its public peers in terms of frameworks, standards and widespread investor adoption. Limited data, extreme heterogeneity and immature standards have conspired to hold the sub-asset class back. To rectify this situation, we focus on three opportunities that hold out considerable promise for closing the sustainability gap.

The first looks at private markets in the broadest sense, not from the cutting edge of impact investing. The basic practices developed within public equity markets can – and should – be applied to private markets, too, we contend. The second recognizes the bright spots that light up the ecosystem from a sustainable standpoint and urges the industry to accelerate these initiatives for the wider good of the asset class.

Our final path to sustainable improvement calls for innovation. We take inspiration from how public debt markets have created dedicated assets. We also highlight the potential to expand the scope of impact investing beyond its growth equity heartland to areas such as venture capital and private debt to increase its positive impact.

Public market practices

The heterogeneous world of private markets can take inspiration from their public cousins. Investors in public markets have integrated sustainable factors into the investment process to such an extent that it is often considered mainstream. The rationale for private markets to adopt public market practices is straightforward: integrating material information can incrementally improve the investment process and ensure that all relevant stakeholders are aware of how sustainability affects investment returns. While there is debate as to whether adopting these processes will significantly enhance investment returns, it will undoubtedly ensure that the private market ecosystem is aware and actively considering the most material sustainability factors.

Public market investors have gone to great lengths to seek (relatively) consistent data from the corporations they invest in. They have gone to even greater lengths to categorize and assess that data according to the principles of financial materiality – i.e., according to its relevance to the financial performance of their investment – by using frameworks such as those derived by the Sustainability Accounting Standards Board (SASB).

Private companies are not routinely subject to the same regulatory-enforced mandatory disclosures as public ones are. But private market investors can exert their considerable influence and demand similar transparency to better inform their investment decisions. These fundamental processes and actions long practised in public markets would materially enhance sustainable private market investment.

> OPPORTUNITIES
>
> Adopt SASB's sector-specific disclosure frameworks to increase data availability and standardization. Use the information to integrate ESG factors into the investment process and corporate strategy in proportion to their financial materiality.

Bright spots

Among the multiple heterogeneous investor bodies that seek to govern, score and rank sustainable private markets, the World Bank stands out as the most credible participant seeking market alignment. We believe that the opportunity for sustainable private markets requires the industry to align behind the world's leading multilateral development bank, which counts nearly 200 countries as shareholders (World Bank, n.d.).

The World Bank is arguably the world's original impact investor and has already demonstrated its power in the area of standards. It convened the Operating Principles for Impact Management which, since its launch in 2019, has acquired over 150 high-profile signatories (Operating Principles for Impact Management, n.d. b). This framework is fast becoming the dominant holistic methodology for impact investing and sets itself apart by demanding third-party verification of signatories' disclosures and reports.

At the other end of the investor body spectrum, the World Bank also acts as a convener of common measurement metrics. Its Joint Impact Indicators seek to harmonize the popular private sector IRIS+

framework with the multilateral development-bank-favoured HIPSO framework (International Finance Corporation, 2021). In an environment of fragmented standards and limited regulation, the World Bank occupies a unique industry position of credibility and impartiality. This empowers the nearly 80-year-old organization to establish market norms and drive convergence as well as real-world impact.

> OPPORTUNITIES
>
> The sustainable private market industry needs to rally behind the World Bank's attempts to standardize sustainable private markets. Investor disclosure should align with the Operating Principles of Impact Management and measurement should draw on the Joint Impact Indicators.

Innovation

Inspired by public debt market's creation of dedicated assets, we highlight the potential to expand impact investing within private markets beyond its growth equity heartland to areas such as venture capital and private debt. While 'impact investing' has succeeded in moving from its concessionary small-scale roots to mainstream growth-stage equity private market investment, its broader reach remains limited.

To truly benefit the real world, sustainable private markets must build a stronger presence in areas such as venture capital and distressed debt. Public debt markets have innovated repeatedly by creating dedicated assets – from green bonds to sustainability-linked debt. Given the breadth of strategies available to private market investors, ample opportunity exists to create instruments and sub-asset class strategies that place people and the planet at the heart of the investment strategy.

History has shown that 'old world' approaches have struggled to scale up. The path to adopting more innovative approaches more widely will likely rely on a subset of mainstream multi-disciplinary private market investors who have already embraced impact investing in part of their business. In many cases, this will mean firms with strong growth private equity franchises deploying their skills and learnings across a wider set of sub-asset classes.

OPPORTUNITIES

Knowledge transfers within multi-disciplinary private market firms can expand private market impact investing beyond its growth-stage private equity heartland. Impact-focused venture capital is the most logical candidate – by funding the innovative technologies and services that can transform the world.

References

Actis (no date) About us, www.act.is/about-us/ (archived at https://perma.cc/V6ZY-32P2)

Ardian (2020) Sustainability in the private fund of funds market: Key insights from Ardian's GP engagement program, www.ardian.com/sites/default/files/2021-07/Ardian-Sustainability-in-the-FoF-market.pdf (archived at https://perma.cc/A7WH-G8D7)

Bain & Company (2021) Global Private Equity Report 2021, www.bain.com/globalassets/noindex/2021/bain_report_2021-global-private-equity-report.pdf (archived at https://perma.cc/7365-DYSA)

Basile, I and Dutra, J (2019) *Blended Finance Funds and Facilities: 2018 Survey Results*, OECD, Paris, doi.org/10.1787/806991a2-en (archived at https://perma.cc/Y9PU-AFQ3)

BlueOrchard Academy (2018) Blended finance 2.0: Giving voice to the private sector, www.blueorchard.com/wp-content/uploads/181016_BlueOrchard_Blended_Finance-2.0.pdf (archived at https://perma.cc/PC2G-RM3C)

Bucak, S (2021) Mirova seeks €300m for impact private equity Eltif, CityWire Selector, 29 September, citywireselector.com/news/mirova-seeks-300m-for-impact-private-equity-eltif/a1560860 (archived at https://perma.cc/KS5C-GBXX)

Carlyle (no date) Our firm, www.carlyle.com/our-firm (archived at https://perma.cc/L9RM-NVZB)

Clark, G L, Feiner, A and Viehs, M (2015) From the stockholder to the stakeholder: How sustainability can drive financial outperformance', Oxford University Smith School of Enterprise and the Environment and Arabesque Partners, arabesque.com/research/From_the_stockholder_to_the_stakeholder_web.pdf (archived at https://perma.cc/UN48-SNDG)

Convergence (no date) Blended finance, www.convergence.finance/blended-finance (archived at https://perma.cc/E9TT-JT8M)

Edelman (no date) '2020 Trust Barometer Special Report: Institutional Investors', www.edelman.com/research/2020-edelman-trust-barometer-special-report-institutional-investors (archived at https://perma.cc/4SVJ-F4YE)

ESMA (no date) Register of authorised European long-term investment funds (ELTIFs), www.esma.europa.eu/document/register-authorised-european-long-term-investment-funds-eltifs (archived at https://perma.cc/B3ZW-E8EG)

European Commission (2015) European long-term investment funds – Frequently asked questions, ec.europa.eu/commission/presscorner/detail/fr/MEMO_15_4423 (archived at https://perma.cc/M8A5-L72L)

Falconer, K (2020) TPG's Rise Fund II charts course for final close after passing $2bn mark, Buyouts, 22 October, www.buyoutsinsider.com/tpgs-rise-fund-ii-charts-course-for-final-close-after-passing-2bn-mark/ (archived at https://perma.cc/WPF6-GQ4X)

Franklin, J (2017) UBS raises $325 million for Bono-backed impact investment fund, Reuters, 10 July, www.reuters.com/article/us-ubs-group-ag-philanthropy-wealth-idUSKBN19V0Z7 (archived at https://perma.cc/M5QS-5BPN)

Friede, G, Busch, T and Bassen, A (2015) ESG and financial performance: Aggregated evidence from more than 2000 empirical studies, *Journal of Sustainable Finance & Investment*, 5(4), pp 210–33, doi.org/10.1080/20430795.2015.1118917 (archived at https://perma.cc/5NJF-3XTG)

GIIN (no date a) What you need to know about impact investing, Global Impact Investing Network, thegiin.org/impact-investing/need-to-know/ (archived at https://perma.cc/GEK2-97HM)

GIIN (no date b) Aligned standards, Global Impact Investing Network, iris.thegiin.org/aligned-standards/ (archived at https://perma.cc/E4TE-N5HE)

GRESB (no date) GRESB | Global ESG benchmark for real assets, www.gresb.com/nl-en/ (archived at https://perma.cc/FF4J-VU6S)

Gustafsson-Wright, E (no date) What is the size and scope of the impact bonds market?, Brookings, www.brookings.edu/wp-content/uploads/2020/09/Impact_Bonds-Brief_1-FINAL.pdf (archived at https://perma.cc/XXN2-UGD9)

Hand, D et al (2020) 2020 Annual impact investor durvey, GIIN, thegiin.org/research/publication/impinv-survey-2020 (archived at https://perma.cc/L4SU-UNHY)

Harvard Business School (no date) Impact-weighted accounts, www.hbs.edu/impact-weighted-accounts/Pages/default.aspx (archived at https://perma.cc/VG9U-AV7K)

Hurley, M (2021) The billion-dollar funds that have changed impact investing, Environmental Finance, www.environmental-finance.com/content/analysis/the-billion-dollar-funds-that-have-changed-impact-investing.html (archived at https://perma.cc/3FQ3-JXFD)

Impact Investing Institute (no date) Case study: Financial Inclusion Fund II LeapFrog Investments, www.impactinvest.org.uk/wp-content/uploads/2021/04/Financial-Inclusion-Fund-II.pdf (archived at https://perma.cc/B2DG-XMEW)

Impact Management Project (no date a) Glossary, impactmanagementproject.com/glossary/ (archived at https://perma.cc/DQP8-UWTV)

Impact Management Project (no date b) Mainstreaming the practice of impact management, impactmanagementproject.com/ (archived at https://perma.cc/GMQ6-HAD7)

ImpactAlpha (2017) What we know about Bain Capital's $390 million double impact fund, impactalpha.com/what-we-know-about-bain-capitals-390-million-double-impact-fund-8dd4e0c90571/ (archived at https://perma.cc/W2TB-M2B4)

India Development Review (2018) What are development and social impact bonds and do they work? idronline.org/idr-explains-development-impact-bonds/ (archived at https://perma.cc/NR8T-2NEC)

International Finance Corporation (2021) Leading impact investors make progress toward harmonized impact measurement with release of joint indicators, pressroom.ifc.org/all/pages/PressDetail.aspx?ID=26260 (archived at https://perma.cc/M63N-D375)

Invest Europe (2022) Private equity at work: Employment & job creation across Europe, www.investeurope.eu (archived at https://perma.cc/DSS7-LVUG) https://www.investeurope.eu/research/private-equity-at-work/ (archived at https://perma.cc/4CUU-UXQP)

IOC (no date a) London 1948 Olympic medal table – gold, silver & bronze, Olympics.com, olympics.com/en/olympic-games/london-1948/medals (archived at https://perma.cc/W8SK-V8Z3)

IOC (no date b) Tokyo 2020 Olympic medal table – gold, silver & bronze. Olympics.com, olympics.com/en/olympic-games/tokyo-2020/medals (archived at https://perma.cc/74MT-7PBJ)

JP Morgan (2010) Impact investments: An emerging asset class, thegiin.org/assets/documents/Impact%20Investments%20an%20Emerging%20Asset%20Class2.pdf (archived at https://perma.cc/5J7P-4KXY)

Marshall, A (2013) *Principles of Economics*, Palgrave Macmillan, London, doi.org/10.1057/9781137375261 (archived at https://perma.cc/BG5Q-JP4E)

MPM Capital (2016) UBS raises record $471 million for oncology impact fund, www.mpmcapital.com/press/ubs-raises-record-471-million-oncology-impact-fund/ (archived at https://perma.cc/6BDL-BCXS)

New Private Markets (2021) Impact 20: Ranking the largest private markets impact managers, 29 June, www.newprivatemarkets.com/impact-20-ranking-the-largest-private-markets-impact-managers/ (archived at https://perma.cc/23FF-3WCP)

Ogier (2022) 2021 Capital Markets Union package: Review of the ELTIF regulation, www.ogier.com/publications/2021-capital-markets-union-package-review-of-the-eltif-regulation (archived at https://perma.cc/UV6S-DQ3Z)

Operating Principles for Impact Management (no date a) What is impact investing? www.impactprinciples.org/ (archived at https://perma.cc/WA5N-AJVY)

Operating Principles for Impact Management (no date b) Signatories & reporting, www.impactprinciples.org/signatories-reporting (archived at https://perma.cc/M4GU-TG3S)

Pucker, K and Kotsantonis, S (2020) Private equity makes ESG promises, but their impact is often superficial, *Institutional Investor*, www.institutionalinvestor.com/article/b1m8spzx5bp6g7/Private-Equity-Makes-ESG-Promises-But-Their-Impact-Is-Often-Superficial (archived at https://perma.cc/YEB2-HHDY)

PwC (2021) Private equity's ESG journey: From compliance to value creation – Global Private Equity Responsible Investment Survey 2021, www.pwc.com/gx/en/services/sustainability/publications/private-equity-and-the-responsible-investment-survey.html (archived at https://perma.cc/UWK6-67TE)

Responsible Investor (2021) Principles for responsible principles launches, 1 April, www.responsible-investor.com/principles-for-responsible-principles-launches/ (archived at https://perma.cc/3RHH-T2GY)

Rosario, K (2021) What is holding blended finance back? Uxolo, 26 October, www.uxolo.com/articles/7070/what-is-holding-blended-finance-back (archived at https://perma.cc/EU5Z-TRZ4)

SBE Council (no date) Facts & data on small business and entrepreneurship, Small Business & Entrepreneurship Council, sbecouncil.org/about-us/facts-and-data/ (archived at https://perma.cc/4GCK-5XBE)

Schultz, A (2021) Future returns: Bain Capital double impact's approach to the market, Barrons, www.barrons.com/articles/future-returns-bain-capital-double-impacts-approach-to-the-market-01617741561 (archived at https://perma.cc/PQC2-4XM3)

Starr, K (2018) Development impact bonds: There's still no free lunch, Stanford Social Innovation Review, 13 December, ssir.org/articles/entry/development_impact_bonds_theres_still_no_free_lunch (archived at https://perma.cc/F22W-N6GV)

The Economist (2020) Blended finance is struggling to take off, 13 August, www.economist.com/finance-and-economics/2020/08/13/blended-finance-is-struggling-to-take-off (archived at https://perma.cc/GE9V-FHC4)
The Rise Fund (2022) TPG closes rise climate fund at $7.3 billion, 27 April, therisefund.com/news/tpg-closes-rise-climate-fund-73-billion (archived at https://perma.cc/5YTW-ZYY7)
The Rise Fund (no date) Impact report highlights, therisefund.com/impact-report-highlights (archived at https://perma.cc/WN76-YD52)
Thomas, J and Starr, M (2020) From impact investing to investing with impact, Carlyle, www.carlyle.com/global-insights/invest-with-impact-whitepaper-thomas-starr (archived at https://perma.cc/WY2R-PT9C)
ThomasLloyd (2021) ThomasLloyd unveils ELTIF to support long terms investors seeking dedicated impact solutions, 4 October, www.thomas-lloyd.com/en/thomaslloyd-unveils-eltif-to-support-long-terms-investors-seeking-dedicated-impact-solutions/ (archived at https://perma.cc/9SRV-HKAL)
Volk, A (2021) *Investing for Impact*, International Finance Corporation, Washington, DC, www.ifc.org/wps/wcm/connect/365d09e3-e8d6-4da4-badb-741933e76f3b/2021-Investing+for+Impact_FIN2.pdf?MOD=AJPERES&CVID=nL5SF6G (archived at https://perma.cc/G3NU-AS4X)
World Bank (no date) Member countries, www.worldbank.org/en/about/leadership/members (archived at https://perma.cc/DH2L-X2PU)
Y Analytics (no date) Where research and capital converge for good, yanalytics.org/ (archived at https://perma.cc/L6YZ-FYGW)

06

Themes and the United Nations Sustainable Development Goals

Introduction

Science fiction franchise *Star Trek* has predicted the future on numerous occasions. In the original television series (1966–69) Lieutenant Uhura wears what looks like a Bluetooth headset. In *Star Trek: The Next Generation* (1987–94) the crew use a device nearly identical to an iPad, and in the series *Star Trek: Deep Space 9* (1993–99) a virtual display device presages Google Glass. Other prescient examples include augmented reality, universal translators, voice activated control and 3D printing (Pierce-Bohen, 2019). Throughout the second half of the 20th century, a budding investor could have done far worse than investing in companies aiming to mimic the products and services used aboard the USS Enterprise and other iconic Starfleet starships.

Sustainable thematic investing entails envisioning the future and investing in it. The emphasis is on what companies do – the products and the services they create. Fittingly, given our *Star Trek* reference, thematic investing traces its roots to 1948 and the Chicago-based Television Shares Management Corp. It launched The Television Fund, which sought (unsurprisingly) to profit from the burgeoning television industry at a time when there were about one million TV sets in the US. Thematic investing has since grown into a thriving industry with $800 billion of assets under management (Morningstar, 2022).

We start the action in this chapter with a section called 'How sustainable themes operate'. A brief history lesson leads to a description of, and a nod to, some of the challenges thematic investors face. The plot moves on to the core premise of thematic investing, that human beings struggle to comprehend exponential growth and often overlook paradigm-shifting technologies and services. We close this section by noting that the potential for exponential growth is not the only desirable thematic trait: network effects, blank slate design, ecosystem development and decentralized technologies all occupy a list of 'what makes a good theme' (Das, 2021).

With our review complete, we examine thematic investing in theory and in practice to pose and answer three important questions:

- How popular are sustainable themes? (Answer: Increasingly.)
- Do they add to investment performance? (Answer: Rarely.)
- Should thematic investing be active or passive? (Answer: Active.)

Our second section dives deep into the United Nations Sustainable Development Goals (SDGs). Launched in 2015, the SDGs were designed as a 'blueprint to achieve a better and more sustainable future for all. They address the global challenges we face, including poverty, inequality, climate change, environmental degradation, peace and justice' (UN, n.d. a). Their long-term nature and sustainable focus make them a potential framework for sustainable thematic investors. We review the basics of the SDGs before considering the extent to which investment capital can help to achieve them. The section concludes with a double click on SDG 13 – Climate Action, a highly popular one among sustainable thematic investors.

Having profiled the UN SDGs, we examine them in theory and in practice and address three key questions:

- Will the SDGs be achieved by 2030? (Answer: Almost certainly not.)
- Do public companies significantly contribute to them? (Answer: They align with them more than work to achieve them.)

- Do thematic investors use the SDGs as an investment framework? (Answer: Rarely.)

Before we tackle the final section we pause to include an exclusive interview with Paul Polman. Paul is a sustainability pioneer. He served for ten years as Chief Executive Officer of consumer giant Unilever and instigated the highly impactful Unilever Sustainable Living Plan. Today he works to accelerate private sector action to deliver the 2030 United Nations Sustainable Development Goals (SDGs). He helped develop the SDGs through roles at the UN, the International Chamber of Commerce, as an advisor to governments and as a convener of leading CEOs. He is the author of *Net Positive: How Courageous Companies Thrive by Giving More Than They Take.*

In our final thematic section, we gaze into the crystal ball and consider the potential opportunities and how we might get there. Of all the investment approaches, thematic investing is, arguably, the most intuitive to a retail investor. The focus on what companies *do*, the potential to capture transformative growth and the feeling it sparks in investors (rightly or wrongly) of contributing to a better future enhance its appeal.

Yet thematic investing is not without its pitfalls. Its historical investment performance has been poor, its real-world impacts have been limited and the SDGs tend to be used more as a set of stickers than as a genuine investment framework. Given this reality, we suggest concrete actions to exploit three more opportunities that we see and provide suggestions on how we might get there.

- The first centres on retail investors. We call for them to critically assess their actual impact on people and the planet and not to assuage their consciences by claiming the impact of their investee companies as their own.
- The second seeks to support institutional investors. We suggest increasing thematic exposure to the most impactful asset class private markets.
- The third makes a recommendation for companies and highlights the benefits of taking action and contributing to the SDGs rather than merely aligning with them.

How sustainable themes operate

Investing: Imagine the future

In 1932, British author HG Wells made a visionary plea via the British Broadcasting Corporation (BBC) for a 'Professor of Foresight'. Wells lamented that there were thousands of professors of history but 'not a single person anywhere who makes a whole-time job of estimating the future consequences of new inventions and new devices' (Wells, 1932).

Wells would be pleased to know that forecasting how the latest inventions and devices will transform our lives and help us tread more lightly on Earth has become a multi-billion-dollar industry. If, as with sustainable investing in general, there is no single accepted definition of what constitutes thematic investing, BlackRock has made a good attempt to provide one:

'Thematic investing is an approach which focuses on predicted long-term trends rather than specific companies or sectors, enabling investors to access structural, one-off shifts that can change an entire industry' (BlackRock, n.d.).

Less concerned with how companies *act* than with what they *do*, thematic investing concentrates on the products and services that can help to create a sustainable future for people and the planet.

The discipline traces its roots to 1948, when the Chicago-based Television Shares Management Corp. launched The Television Fund. As the baby-boom era dawned, only one million TV sets glowed in US living rooms, but the fund's managers could see the bright future and sought to profit from the burgeoning television industry. The stage was set for other, similar funds to try to read the postwar technological, demographic and sociological tea leaves and turn thematic investing into an approach that, as of 2022, claims $800 billion in invested assets (Morningstar, 2022).

In imagining the decades ahead, a thematic investor may look at the intersection of predictable long-term trends such as population growth, technological progress, urbanization and social and regulatory change in order to identify the beneficiaries. Unlike many of their conventional counterparts, thematic investors don't often focus on singling out a 'winning' company. Instead they look for diversified exposure, betting that 'the pie' will grow for all market players. They remain relatively agnostic about market darlings and tend to ignore the ebbs and flows in companies' relative market share.

Their indifference toward stock picking doesn't shield them from critiques about trend hopping or herd behaviour. Asset manager Lazard warns that thematic strategies are vulnerable to 'slick, but ultimately empty, marketing narratives rather than genuine return opportunities' (Lazard Asset Management, 2021). Themes can rise and fall in popularity as enthusiastic retail investors adopt and dump them. This gives rise to unfortunate traits such as low quality, residual volatility and momentum (Rao and Doole, 2021). The thematic industry also continues to debate the merits of 'purity' – selecting pure-play companies that depend totally on the theme as opposed to purchasing larger firms that may have only partial exposure (Banz, 2019; Lazard Asset Management, 2021).

Investing: To infinity and beyond

In the 13th century, the Islamic scholar Ibn Khallikan recorded the story of a man who requested a reward. He wanted a volume of rice equivalent to one grain of the foodstuff placed on the first square of a chessboard, two grains on the second square, four on the third, eight on the fourth and so on. At first assessment the request appears fair, amounting to a reasonable quantity of rice. However, due to geometric progression, the volume across the 64 chessboard squares skyrockets until the sum exceeds 18 quintillion (18 followed by 18 zeros) grains of rice. When his mathematical trickery was revealed, the man, depending on the variant of the story, was either killed or promoted to high office (a lesson worthy of a fable in itself) (Pickover, 2009).

The chessboard story illuminates a deficiency in the human psyche. People think linearly and struggle to understand geometric or exponential growth patterns. Anyone who has started a journey a mere five minutes late only to find themselves stuck in unmoving rush-hour traffic can relate, as can almost every government health official confronted with the COVID-19 pandemic.

Our linear bias is rooted in hundreds of thousands of years of evolution. Three caves offered shelter to triple the number of hominids as one cave did, and our hunter-gatherer actions fitted into days that became incrementally longer then progressively shorter during seasons that followed cyclical patterns.

A failure to consider exponential growth is a regular occurrence in business settings. Perhaps the most famous example took place in 1980 when AT&T and McKinsey forecast a mere 900,000 cell phone subscribers by the end of the century, only to discover that the figure turned out to be in excess of 100 million (*The Economist*, 1999).

Sustainable thematic investing seeks to counter this human deficiency. Investors try to look past the quarterly earnings calls and the linear analyst estimates to discover the transformative products and services that target the largest addressable market. In doing so they pursue a form of time-horizon arbitrage that exploits the market's short-term obsession by means of their long-term and exponential thinking.

Concepts such as Roger's bell curve are drawn on for matters such as technology adoption. Roger's bell curve envisages a small number of 'innovators' first using a new product or service. They are soon joined by the 'early adopters' before the floodgates eventually open, the mass public arrives and nonlinear growth ensues (Rogers, 1962).

Such frameworks lead thematic investors to value the long-term potential of companies and far-dated cash flows. Because the difference between a linear and an exponential progression increases over time, the greatest differential between a thematic investor's forecasts and consensus will likely occur over a long horizon. The stocks of companies with a large proportion of their cash flows and value projected into the future also react more to changes in prevailing interest or discount rates, as these values determine the present value of the future cash flows.

It is no surprise then that thematic funds tilt markedly to growth stocks. A Morningstar analysis found that 72 per cent of their thematic equity fund universe exhibited growth traits rather than value or blend characteristics (Morningstar, 2022). The nonlinear dynamics also explain the paucity of thematic debt funds. When investing for the long term to capture an exponential change unpriced by the market, one shuns bonds whose maximum return is capped at the value of their coupon in favour of the infinite upside of equities. Morningstar refers to thematic debt funds as being 'largely non-existent' (Morningstar, 2022).

Investing: Common attributes

Long before Deliveroo, DoorDash and Uber Eats took a huge bite out of the food delivery market, we had a similar idea while trying to find takeaway delivered to James' neighbourhood. We envisioned a centralized platform where we could order all the Swiss–German delights – Rösti, Birchermüesli and Züri Geschnetzeltes – in one carbohydrate-intensive place.

Knowing the power of network effects and how hard it was to establish a two-sided network, Simon suggested that we kick-start our platform by faking one side of the network (he didn't use those exact words). We planned to create a call centre that would simply relay the hungry customer's order to the correct restaurant, and thus enable us to build a loyal customer base that we could later use to lure restaurants onto our platform. It was genius. We didn't do it.

Network effects are a powerful driver of successful thematic investments (think Airbnb, eBay, Facebook). As more users join, the platform soars in value as more content is created and more services are provided. Network effects often exhibit exponential growth. It takes time to build that critical user base, but once achieved the famous 'second half of the chessboard' takes over and users rush to join en masse.

Network effects aren't the only concept underpinning thematic investing. Learning effects, first codified by Theodore Paul Wright in 1936 (Wright, 1936), are often cited as well, as first movers gain efficiencies through accumulated knowledge. Moore's law, the forecast that computer processing power grows exponentially (Moore, 1965), is another common feature of tech-focused themes, its relevance only increasing in recent decades given its implications across neural networks, machine learning and artificial intelligence. And let's not forget blank slate design, ecosystem development and decentralized technologies – all of which feature high on a list of 'what makes a good theme' (Das, 2021).

In short, thematic investors look for structural drivers that can create a persistent economic moat and facilitate the rapid scaling of a product or service into a large targetable market in a way that conventional, linear-minded investors fail to foresee.

Interestingly, while sustainability is considered part and parcel of successful thematic investment by major practitioners such as Ark, Pictet and Robeco (ARK Invest, n.d.; Pictet Asset Management, n.d.; Robeco, n.d.), not all themes are inherently sustainable. Funds exist for several digital economy themes that raise sustainability questions about the way portfolio companies treat their distribution centre workers, package and recycle and promote excessive consumption. A number of consumer-targeted thematic funds invest in areas such as cannabis that can trigger traditional sustainable exclusionary policies, while blockchain-themed products, which require enormous processing power to perform complex proof-of-work calculations, court criticism for the huge energy consumption and carbon footprint of the firms that make up the underlying investments (Morningstar, 2022).

The investment appeal of some highly intuitive sustainable themes is also questionable. Themes such as water, waste and clean energy offer relatively low growth and a utility-like profile as a large portion of their value comes from tangible rather than intangible assets (Das, 2021). Set within a wider thematic universe, sustainable characteristics alone do not ensure a good theme. This is a lesson investors in solar energy will remember only too well from the swathe of industry bankruptcies in the late 2000s and early 2010s (BBC News, 2012).

Having explored the key tenets of thematic investing, let's now examine them in theory and in practice by asking and answering three key questions.

How popular are they?

Short answer: Increasingly.

IN THEORY

Proponents of thematic investing put forth ideas about why it should be particularly popular. Central to their thinking is that the approach is highly intuitive and accessible to retail investors because it focuses on what companies do.

Inherently narrative led, thematic investing offers a theory of change and generates excitement by discussing the potential of new products and services. Retail investors tend to be far more engaged by investment stories than by a technical discussion of margins and capital structure.

IN PRACTICE

According to data provider Morningstar, public market thematic fund assets hovered around $100 billion for most of the 2010s, until the strategy's popularity exploded in 2020 and the figure leaped to $800 billion. Over half of these assets are domiciled in, and originate from, Europe.

Investment managers have been quick to jump on the bandwagon. The number of annual thematic fund launches surpassed 100 in 2017 and 200 in 2018. By 2021, more than 550 new thematic funds had sprung into existence that year (Morningstar, 2022). Demand has remained robust. A 2021 survey by Swiss asset and wealth manager Vontobel of 300 professional investors found that 49 per cent were planning to increase their thematic allocations over the following three years (Vontobel, 2021).

This soaring popularity has many roots and causes. An extended period of ultra-low interest rates that made long-dated cash flows incrementally more attractive is chief among them, along with sluggish global GDP growth that pushed investors to hunt for pockets of innovation and, not least, the COVID-19 pandemic, which accelerated a host of structural drivers such as remote working and video streaming.

While thematic investing has, in aggregate, boomed, not all themes are equally favoured. When ranked by assets under management, energy transition and resource management themes top the leaderboard (Morningstar, 2022), while survey data routinely places variants of climate change as the theme that most appeals to retail investors (UBS, 2018; Morgan Stanley, 2019).

Do they add to investment performance?

Short answer: Rarely.

IN THEORY

Proponents of thematic investing hypothesize that it should contribute to investment performance. This theory derives from the long-run composition of stock market returns, which exhibit significant positive skew.

In other words, a small fraction of stocks account for the vast majority of long-term market gains. The logic here is clear. A single stock's maximum downside is 100 per cent while its maximum upside is infinite, which all but guarantees that the mean return of the stock market will be greater than its median.

A seminal study by Hendrik Bessembinder fleshed out this phenomenon and found that only 4 per cent of stocks in the period from 1926 to 2015 produced returns superior to cash. Stunningly, less than 0.33 per cent of all stocks were responsible for half of the entire US dollar wealth creation (Bessembinder, 2018).

It follows that if one buys the shares of those long-lived companies that can prosper in a future economic state, one will outperform the broader stock market. Thematic investing's basic premise, that investors with a long-term mindset should seek out and exploit structural shifts, fits with this hypothesis.

Which raises the question: Do investors have the ability to identify these trends? Therein lies the theoretical rub. Mathematically, a randomly selected portfolio of, say, 40 stocks is likelier to underperform than outperform the benchmark. Furthermore, given that thematic portfolios are relatively concentrated (a fund's top

10 positions typically make up 50 per cent of it, compared with about 15 per cent for a conventional global index fund) (Sotiroff, 2021; MSCI, 2022) the probability of holding the small number of 'winners' is theoretically low. Bessembinder succinctly explains, 'Poorly diversified portfolios may underperform because they omit the relatively few stocks that generate large positive returns' (Bessembinder, 2018).

IN PRACTICE

The optimism about the approach appears misplaced. Although themes are ill suited to quantitative backtesting (since by nature they are forward looking), we can analyse the live track records of funds that invest accordingly.

The analysis is sobering. In the 15 years to the end of 2021, more than 75 per cent of thematic funds closed due to a decline in investor interest or poor performance. Paradoxically, given that such funds hope to harness long-term trends, their typical lifespan is often shorter than the themes they seek exposure to. Just one in 10 thematic funds that existed 15 years ago managed to survive and outperform a conventional benchmark.

The data is little better when looking at thematic cohorts present for 10 years. And even for those in existence only five years, barely 39 per cent have survived and/or outperformed the market: the majority have either closed or underperformed (Morningstar, 2022).

Of course, it would be neglectful not to note that future returns may differ from past ones. After all, the notion of dramatic change is at the heart of thematic investing. Support for this view can be found in the shifting composition of equity markets from tangible to intangible assets. In 1975, just 17 per cent of the US S&P 500's market capitalization was attributable to intangible assets. Railroads and factories still held sway. The Big Three automakers ruled the road. By 2020, the S&P 500s' market cap had reversed to the point that 90 per cent of its valuation originated from intangible assets. Today, intellectual property dominates physical resources (Ocean Tomo, 2020).

The good news for thematic investors is that, while tangible assets tend to grow linearly – a firm that has five factories may open a sixth

– intangible assets can grow rapidly. And intellectual property yields network effects, learning curves and open-source decentralized innovation. The bad news is that recent thematic fund performance has not benefited from them and, in fact, offers a buzzkill reality check.

Should thematic investing be active or passive?

Short answer: Active.

IN THEORY

Proponents of thematic investing contend that it is the preserve of active investors. Envisioning the future and investing accordingly is, theoretically, an intellectual undertaking that requires fundamental research and evidence-based analytics.

By the time a theme is sufficiently established with objective data points that allow for passive tracking by a predetermined index, the theme likely has come to at least partial fruition, with big initial gains already realized. And once objective data points come into being, the metrics needed to facilitate a rules-based passive index still need to be selected, which is an active decision.

IN PRACTICE

Roughly 75 per cent of thematic fund assets are actively managed. However, the split varies dramatically by region. In Europe, active funds make up around 90 per cent of thematic fund assets while in the US they comprise just 30 per cent (Morningstar, 2022).

Interestingly, thematic investing has helped spawn an active–passive hybrid known as the active exchange traded fund (ETF). Historically, ETFs, with their intraday liquidity, have served as vehicles for passive index replication funds that rebalanced to market capitalization-derived weightings on a regular basis. Cathie Wood's Ark Invest, whose flagship active ETF at one point managed $28 billion, has led the repositioning and repurposing of the humble ETF from its passive roots (Agnew, 2022).

United Nations Sustainable Development Goals

SDGs: Best picture

In 1929, the Academy of Motion Picture Arts and Sciences handed the first Oscar (for Best Actor) to the German Emil Jannings to honour his performances in *The Last Command* and *The Way of All Flesh* (Oscars.org, n.d.). Aided by clever branding and iconic statuettes, the Oscars quickly became the dominant Hollywood yardstick for what counts as a good role or film. While by no means definitive (the 1998 award for Best Film going to *Shakespeare in Love* rather than *Saving Private Ryan* proves the fallibility of the academy), the Oscars are an integral part of film history.

In 2015, the UN, aided by filmmaker Richard Curtis, who provides an exclusive interview in 'Chapter 4 – Sustainable public debt markets', launched its Sustainable Development Goals (SDGs). Complete with brilliant multicoloured branding, the iconic SDGs serve as a 'blueprint to achieve a better and more sustainable future for all. They address the global challenges we face, including poverty, inequality, climate change, environmental degradation, peace and justice' (UN, n.d. a). While the SDGs are by no means definitive, they are an integral part of sustainable development.

As mentioned above, thematic investing need not explicitly or exclusively emphasize sustainability. With the advent of the SDGs though, sustainable investors were gifted a thematic taxonomy that covered all elements of the economy, put sustainability in its crosshairs and had the backing and credibility of the UN.

THE UN SDGS

The SDGs were launched in 2015 by the UN General Assembly and adopted by over 190 countries worldwide. The UN SDGs comprise 17 goals. They are (by number):

1 No Poverty

2 Zero Hunger

3 Good Health and Wellbeing

4 Quality Education

5 Gender Equality

6 Clean Water and Sanitation

7 Affordable and Clean Energy

8 Decent Work and Economic Growth

9 Industry, Innovation and Infrastructure

10 Reduced Inequality

11 Sustainable Cities and Communities

12 Responsible Consumption and Production

13 Climate Action

14 Life Below Water

15 Life on Land

16 Peace, Justice and Strong Institutions

17 Partnerships for the Goals

Each goal contains specific targets; in total there are more than 200 measurement indicators. For example, SDG number 5 Gender Equality contains a pledge to 'eliminate child marriage' and a separate ambition to 'ensure women's full participation and equal opportunities in national parliaments'. The SDGs are monitored under the auspices of the UN Economic and Social Council and reviewed annually at the UN High-Level Political Forum on Sustainable Development (UN, 2022, n.d. b).

SDGs: Investment challenges

If you want to pound a nail into a piece of wood, a hammer is your best choice. It will also serve you well for bending and shaping metal and, in a pinch, for warding off would-be attackers. But if you need to cut wood or metal a hammer isn't much help. You need a saw. This doesn't make the hammer a bad tool. It's just appropriate for some tasks and not suited to others.

Countries originally signed on to the UN SDGs. Corporates and investors may find a number of them ill-suited to private sector participation and profit-seeking investment. Certain SDGs require government policy or charitable aid to achieve progress on them. This doesn't make investment a bad tool for realizing the SDGs. It just means that it is appropriate for some of them and not suited to others.

The challenges facing profit-seeking investors were aptly highlighted by a 2018 survey conducted by French bank Natixtis, in which 42 professional investors representing $43 trillion of assets were queried. It found that only five of the 17 SDGs were considered 'highly investible' by more than 40 per cent of the respondents: Affordable and Clean Energy (SDG No. 7), Climate Action (13), Good Health and Wellbeing (3), Industry, Innovation and Infrastructure (9) and Clean Water and Sanitation (6) (Merle and Nguyen, 2018).

Several SDGs were only tangentially applicable to the investment universe of this representative group of money managers. Indeed, it is difficult to envision how Zero Hunger (2) would be reflected in a profit-seeking public-market investment portfolio. It is a cognitive and ethical stretch to claim that investing in food and beverage companies and agriculture fertilizer firms contributes credibly to meeting the goals.

BlackRock, viewing the challenge through the other end of the telescope, tried to identify which sectors were materially impacted by the SDGs. For each of the 11 super sectors that make up financial markets, the firm mapped the SDG indicators to the data points deemed financially material by the Sustainability Accounting Standards Board (SASB). The SDGs were found to be financially material for only three sectors: Extractives and Minerals Processing, Infrastructure and Food and Beverage (Hildebrand et al, 2021).

The upshot is that, while many persons working in sustainable development regard the SDGs as essential, for thematic investors they are, unfortunately, an imperfect tool.

SDGs: Climate change

In the early 2000s, the group Destiny's Child lit up the airwaves with dance-pop hits such as 'Say My Name', 'Survivor' and 'Bootylicious'. For most fans the star of the group was Beyoncé Knowles, now known to the world as one of the best-selling musical solo artists of all time and to my (James') son as the voice of Nala in the remake of *The Lion King* (Biography.com Editors, 2021). When it came to Destiny's Child, Beyoncé Knowles was first among equals.

As far as the SDGs are concerned, among retail and institutional investors alike, Climate Action (13) routinely tops the charts of the most cared about or most investible of the group (Merle and Nguyen, 2018; Morgan Stanley, 2019). It is fair to say that it is first among equals. As such, we'll undertake a deep dive into it through the lens of thematic investing.

At a headline level, investors seem highly motivated to contribute to Climate Action (13). The Glasgow Financial Alliance for Net Zero (GFANZ) is an investor group that oversees an impressive $130 trillion of assets. Its members commit some or all of their assets to being invested according to a net-zero carbon emission objective by 2050. Yet healthy scepticism should attach to these commitments.

The GFANZ is not the only financial grouping that prioritizes Climate Action (13). The Task Force on Climate-related Financial Disclosures (TCFD), which has established a taxonomy for 'climate-related financial disclosures that would be useful to investors and others in understanding material risks', counts over 1000 financial firm members (TCFD, 2021).

Yet, despite all the good investor intentions and notable efforts, carbon emissions continue to rise. Energy-related CO_2 output increased by 6 per cent in 2021 to 36.3 billion tonnes worldwide, a record (IEA, 2022). Climate Action (13) thematic investors have yet to reverse this ongoing global trend and catalyse an overdue transformation that materially benefits people and the planet.

One reason why they have failed to make a serious Climate Action (13) dent is that liquid secondary markets are a low-impact asset class. In 'Chapter 3 – Sustainable public equity markets', we illustrated how buying or selling liquid secondary-market securities creates little to no incremental positive real-world impact because a company's behaviour and capital structure remain unchanged (Berk and van Binsbergen, 2021). This limits the effectiveness of groups such as GFANZ.

Furthermore, public investor agitation concerning Climate Action (13) may even have the opposite of the intended effect and breed negative consequences. Pressured by investors, many public firms have divested their most carbon-intensive assets. These coal mining and oil and gas operations have not disappeared from the global economy, however. They have merely migrated into private hands, which receive much less scrutiny of their actions. Research by the *Economist* underlined the scale of the potential problem. In the years 2020–22, $60 billion worth of oil, gas and coal assets moved from public to private firms through approximately 500 transactions (*The Economist*, 2022).

Some thematic investors, squarely focused on what companies *do*, have turned to the private markets to fund the next generation of carbon solutions and opportunities. Private equity giant TPG raised $7 billion for a flagship climate fund centred on activities such as direct carbon removal and alternative proteins (The Rise Fund, 2022). Billionaire venture capitalist Chris Sacca was lured out of retirement to launch Lowercarbon Capital, whose mission statement is unapologetically brash. His firm seeks to back 'kickass companies that make real money slashing CO_2 emissions, sucking carbon out of the sky and buying us time to unf**k the planet' (Lowercarbon Capital, n.d.).

Unlike their public market counterparts, these private equity investors *can* alter a company's capital stock and cost of capital. By providing incremental funding, they enable impactful companies to grow and scale their innovative technologies at a speed that may not have been possible had the thematic investors' capital not been present.

In summary, while Climate Action (13) may be first among equals in the SDG lineup, the investment community's contribution to it has thus far only been limited.

Now that we've considered the SDGs in the context of thematic investing, let's turn our attention to three key questions concerning the goals.

Will the SDGs be achieved by 2030?

Short answer: Almost certainly not.

IN THEORY

Proponents of the SDGs believe that each can be met by the 2030 target date. At their launch in 2015, the goals were termed ambitious but the intention to realize them was not mere feel-good PR. The signatory text reads: 'We commit ourselves to working tirelessly for the full implementation of this Agenda by 2030' (UN, n.d. b).

IN PRACTICE

The SDGs are lagging well behind target. The UN's *Sustainable Development Goals Progress Chart 2021* shows that, of the 35 sub-goals, none is 'at target or almost met' and only five are judged to have made 'Substantial progress/on track'. Perhaps more worryingly, five are said to be deteriorating from their pre-SDG baseline, including the poster child of thematic SDG investing: Climate Action (13).

The data contained in the 2021 report comes, in many cases, from 2019 and 2020 and leads the authors to conclude: 'The world was already off track in realizing the ambitions and fulfilling the commitments of the 2030 Agenda, even before COVID-19' (UN, 2021).

Although thematic investing has failed at this point to drive SDG attainment, we should (as we've learned in this chapter!) be wary of linearly extending the past into the future. An optimist would point to the growing popularity of sustainable thematic investing as a sign that progress could accelerate exponentially. Pragmatists, however, may favour the more pessimistic consensus of third-party experts and conclude almost certainly not.

Do public companies significantly contribute to the SDGs?

Short answer: They align with them more than work to achieve them.

IN THEORY

Proponents of the SDGs have theorized how public companies can advance the goals. Although nation states originally signed on to them, a substantial literature has arisen about how companies can also contribute.

UN Secretary-General Ban Ki-moon referred to the corporate sector as a 'vital partner' in achieving the SDGs. He asked 'companies everywhere to assess their impact, set ambitious goals and communicate transparently about the results' (GRI, UN Global Compact and WBCSD, n.d.).

A number of expert groups have stepped into the void and designed theoretical frameworks and roadmaps to assist in doing so. A highly prominent one is the World Business Council for Sustainable Development (WBCSD), a CEO-led grouping of more than 200 multinational companies. The SDGs help companies 'better manage their risks, anticipate consumer demand, build positions in growth markets, secure access to needed resources and strengthen their supply chains', according to the WBCSD (n.d.). To guide management teams, it developed *SDG Sector Roadmaps*, which assess the materiality of the goals on an industry-by-industry level.

For its part, the UN Global Reporting Initiative (GRI) has estimated that achieving the SDGs could 'be worth at least $12 trillion a year in market opportunities and generate up to 380 million new jobs by 2030' in the private sector. To unlock this potential, it spearheaded the development of the *SDG Compass* so 'companies can use the SDGs as an overarching framework to shape, steer, communicate and report their strategies, goals and activities' (GRI, UN Global Compact and WBCSD, n.d.).

IN PRACTICE

Despite widespread corporate alignment with and use of the splashy SDG paraphernalia, public companies have not made a significant aggregate contribution.

A 2019 study summarized in the *Harvard Business Review* concluded that 'the commitment of almost every company we studied appears to be merely cosmetic' and that existing corporate sustainability practices 'were simply relabelled with the relevant goals'. The authors noted disappointingly that 'We found very few companies doing anything new or different to advance the goals' (Kramer, Agarwal and Srinivas, 2019).

This downbeat assessment is echoed by other credible sources. In the UN GRI's 2021 survey of companies, 83 per cent of them stated that they sought to align their activities with the SDGs but just 20 per cent provided evidence of doing so (GRI and Support the Goals, n.d.). This finding mirrors PwC's 2019 examination of over 1,000 companies. PwC discovered that 72 per cent of firms mentioned the SDGs in their reporting but just 25 per cent did so in their business strategy, with a mere 14 per cent issuing SDG-related targets (Scott and McGill, 2019).

MSCI has also amassed valuable data about public companies' contributions, or lack thereof. In ranking 8500 public companies from 'strongly aligned' to 'strongly misaligned' with the SDGs overall, MSCI concluded that just 0.2 per cent of the firms earned the 'strongly aligned' heading. When each SDG was considered separately, no company was deemed 'strongly aligned' with nine of the 17 SDGs (Neufeld, 2021).

A separate MSCI study examined the number of public companies that had aligned themselves with the SDGs in their communications. The most popular SDG (Climate Action 13) had attracted just over 350 public pledges (as of March 2020) from the universe of 3000 companies MSCI studied. Six SDGs had received fewer than 200 commitments. Interestingly, in the case of almost 300 companies, MSCI found 'rainbow washing', the practice of committing to an SDG and then subsequently being involved in a serious controversy that might discredit the declared support (MSCI, n.d.).

It appears that many companies treat the SDGs in a business-as-usual manner. Their behaviour provides further evidence of the difficulty sustainable thematic investors have in adopting the UN SDGs as a primary investment framework.

Do thematic investors use the SDGs as an investment framework?

Short answer: Rarely.

IN THEORY

Proponents of thematic investing advance credible reasons why the SDGs should prove popular with investors. The broad scope of the goals, their focus on sustainability and the UN's credible backing should all theoretically entice investors into using them as an investment framework.

IN REALITY

As mentioned above, many of the goals have limited investibility (Merle and Nguyen, 2018) and are financially material for only a small number of sectors (Hildebrand et al, 2021). The result is that when investment firms reported about their activities to the UN PRI, only 31 per cent mentioned the SDGs in their submissions (UN PRI, n.d.).

This muted response finds echoes in a 2018 survey conducted by the US Forum for Sustainable and Responsible Investment (US SIF). Forty per cent of asset managers told US SIF that they considered the SDGs a motivating factor in pursuing sustainable investing strategies, while just 23 per cent of asset owners said the same (Phalen, n.d.).

Both the UN PRI reporting and the US SIF survey prompt investment managers to say whether they take the SDGs into account or not. This prompting alone can inflate the number of affirmative responses. A review of fund descriptions, the 50 words of text that fund managers use to describe their strategies and communicate other purposes, offers a potentially better measure of genuine SDG sentiment.

According to the Bloomberg database, 4500 funds include the word 'sustainable' in their description and 3000 categorize themselves as thematic. Just 75 use the words 'SDG' or 'Sustainable Development Goals' in their description, however. This figure is markedly less than 'water' (approximately 200 uses) and barely more than 'tobacco' (roughly 50) (Bloomberg, 2022).

In short, very few funds proactively describe their investment framework with reference to the SDGs when they are not prompted to do so.

The nuances of terminology notwithstanding, whether thematic investors use the SDGs as a genuine investment framework ultimately reveals itself in private sector investment flows. To determine this we turned to the UN Conference on Trade and Development (UN CTAD), which has been publishing the World Investment Report since 1991.

In 2014, the UN CTAD identified an annual $2.5 trillion 'investment gap' between what was needed to achieve the proposed SDGs and what was being spent on them. The 2020 edition updated the data and included the trend in private sector investment flows. Of the 10 sectors monitored, which together encompass all 17 SDGs, not a single sector showed a positive trend for private sector investment flows and only three sectors maintained a flat trajectory. The data strongly suggests that there is a failure in the transmission mechanism between well-intentioned thematic investors and actual incremental capital flows that have meaningful impact (UN CTAD, 2020).

Faced with this reality, one must conclude that the SDGs serve many thematic investors as marketing or investment alignment tools and not as a framework for channelling significant capital flows to benefit people and the planet.

In this interview, James sat down with Paul Polman to discuss sustainable investing across business and finance. Paul is a sustainability pioneer. He served for ten years as the chief executive officer of consumer giant Unilever and instigated the highly impactful Unilever Sustainable Living Plan. Today he works to accelerate private sector action to deliver the 2030 UN Sustainable Development Goals (SDGs). He helped develop the SDGs in roles at the UN, the International Chamber of Commerce, as an advisor to governments and as a convener of leading CEOs. He is the author of *Net Positive: How Courageous Companies Thrive by Giving More Than They Take.*

James: Thank you for taking the time, Paul. Could we start by hearing about your big-picture view of sustainability?

Paul: For me, sustainability is all about human development and inclusion. Ultimately, sustainability is about the future of our children and their children being more important than our own greed. So, at the end of the day, it has to serve a broader purpose. This broader promise is to ensure that we don't leave anybody behind and strive for universal values such as dignity and respect, inclusion, equity and compassion. Climate change, conflict, food insecurity, inequality, these crises are actually the symptoms of a deeper crisis of apathy, selfishness and greed. Above all, we have a moral challenge here.

I've always felt that the role of business is to solve the world's problems, not to create them. And that you have to ask a simple question as a business leader: Is the world a better place with your business in it, or not? A lot of companies need to move fast to find themselves on the right side of this question, because if they do not, society will increasingly isolate them.

What is very clear is that most of our current global challenges have been visible for some time, including during the 2008 financial crisis, which should have been an opportunity for deep systemic change but which was ultimately an opportunity squandered. And, as a result of moving too slowly, our social, economic and environmental problems, from climate to inequality, are now incurring higher costs for business and government than if we had dealt with them sooner.

The financial markets are, at least, beginning to pay attention, driven by these higher costs and we're finally moving in a better direction, but not at the speed and scale needed. We're up against a human bias or mindset that thinks linear, that doesn't think exponential, that thinks short term instead of long term, that thinks 'my world' instead of 'our world'. So, long story short, this is above all a human or leadership problem that we need to address.

James: And how would you connect these dynamics to the financial industry?

Paul: If we look at climate specifically, the biggest challenge we have with the financial community is that most will say climate change is an issue and a risk, but then they won't act with the urgency it deserves. Now, since the COVID pandemic things have truly started to improve and move. We're seeing more ambitious targets and bigger commitments from countries, companies and financial institutions. However, while we are finally making progress, we're not moving fast enough or with the needed partnerships across key industries, and between industry, government and civil society. Too many carbon targets are set for 2050 and too few for 2030, which is the critical deadline for keeping a global temperature increase below 1.5 degrees. This decade alone we need to drive emissions down by 45 per cent, but the numbers unfortunately still project an absolute increase. Kicking the can down the road is not an option anymore.

Fortunately, more players in business and finance are starting to understand the opportunities inherent in moving to a greener, more inclusive economy. More see the value of the United Nations Sustainable Development Goals (SDGs) as a framework to guide them, and it is a great, moral framework. And more stakeholders increasingly understand that this is not an issue of risk mitigation, but actually an enormous economic opportunity. But, unfortunately, we are not at a tipping point yet and the global geopolitical situation risks pushing us backwards. We don't yet know which way things will fall. Many finance leaders made commitments to decarbonize their portfolios at COP26. How many just wanted to be part of the photo opportunity with politicians is an open question. Will they, for instance, continue actively supporting the fossil fuel industry? Or will they stand by their words, with these commitments speaking to real, genuine change? This remains to be seen, but the future will tell us, and it will tell us soon.

James: There are undoubtedly many challenges. Could you articulate the ones you see as most significant?

Paul: The overriding challenge is one of courage and leadership. We have never been so forewarned about what is going to happen to our species and planet, and we have never been so forearmed with tools to do something about it. Climate change, poverty and inequality are symptoms of greed, apathy and selfishness. We are as short of leaders as we are of trees. And, beneath this, we face a range of specific, more technical obstacles and policy issues that we need to innovate through. For example, and one that is especially problematic at the moment, is the lack of transparency in financial reporting. The majority of corporate leaders claim no visibility on Scope 3 emissions, which is actually where we find most of the emissions for many industries. There are challenges on comparability, materiality and transparency with the multitude of reporting standards out there. Because ESG covers everything from child labour to investing in coal, from firearms and toxic leaks to unsustainable sourcing it's hard to boil it down to simple measures.

Furthermore, how do you make that data forward-looking? We haven't quite figured it out yet. There are some good things like the Task Force on Climate-related Financial Disclosures (TCFD) and the European taxonomy and now early efforts by the Securities Exchange Commission in the United States. But we're still frankly falling far short of what is needed. The recent establishment of the International Sustainability Standards Board is a good step forward and deserves our full support. Ultimately, we need to define success differently. GDP alone, or simply seeking return on financial capital, only brings you so far. We now also need to start measuring the return on financial, social and human capital. After all, we treasure what we measure.

James: So, what do you think are the best solutions?

Paul: We will not be able to move faster without stronger government action, delivered by individual nations and, collectively, through effective multilateralism. We need legislation that sets clear, transparent, measurable and comparable standards, that requires action within the limited time frame we have and that, more importantly, encourages and incentivizes the transition rather than discourages it. We still have today, for example, more than $1.8 trillion in perverse subsidies that drive use of fossil fuels and encourage deforestation and land degradation. We need the right legislative and regulatory frameworks, which are as simple and consistent as possible across countries.

Voluntary action without consequence simply does not get us there. The gap between what people say, and sign up to, and commit to and what they actually do is simply still too wide. That's why we very quickly need standards that whole industries can adhere to. Just like we have nutritional standards or labelling standards. It starts with simple actions, like the way we report on gender, salary differences, or carbon emissions across the value chain. We clearly see that standards can help. The companies that are reporting on climate are actually making more progress. They're also more resilient in general and all these factors translate ultimately into business success.

And, of course, we need to make sure that any transition is a just transition and ensures that the people most affected are fully included.

If we close a coal mine we need to retrain the coal miners, or invest in digital skills for our workforce to adapt to a fast-changing environment and equally we just need to ensure that the green jobs are well-paid jobs and respect human rights.

James: Can we dig a little deeper on the financial system and its role in avoiding failure?

Paul: The financial system is crucial. If the finance community doesn't get actively involved to make the money flow in a sustainable direction, or to hold companies in which they invest to a higher standard, then it's not going to work. We need to get beyond celebrating a few good anecdotes, such as an oil major getting a few new board members, or the occasional request to a company invested in to show progress on diversity. We need a bigger, deeper shift, in which more of the key players in finance move faster and move together.

Often the financial industry is the catalyst for change, but they cannot do it alone. Institutions, whether commercial banks or multilateral development banks, can be very slow to change, and they don't tend to drive the bigger conversations we need to be having about the transition to a new, clean, just global economy. It will help to bring the sector together, giving leaders the greater courage and ambition that comes with working with your peers. It will also help to position finance in wider partnerships that put it alongside business, policymakers and civil society, partnerships that help reattach the financial world to the real world. In doing so we can help drive the systems change the world needs and we can work towards making the financial sector again subservient to the real economy.

James: You of course led a highly progressive corporation, Unilever. What were some of the positive surprises you found when you took Unilever in a sustainability direction?

Paul: Well, the positive surprise didn't come from the financial market. There was pushback when we stopped quarterly reporting, scepticism when we launched the Unilever Sustainable Living Plan (USLP), and reluctance to invest in longer-term sustainable projects. It took a 300 per cent shareholder return over 10 years to show that, increasingly, pursuing a longer-term, multi-stakeholder business model, with purpose at its core, also serves the long-term shareholders well. However, even after COVID, we still see too many companies chasing short-term performance and CEOs resorting to share buybacks and other financial tools to shore up share prices without strengthening underlying business fundamentals.

We tried to use Unilever to drive more transformative changes in society, well beyond Unilever. The reason we started green bonds and we were the first consumer goods firm in the world to do that was because banks were keen to deal with Unilever. And one requirement for dealing with Unilever was not to fund deforestation and to respect human rights in the value chain. And I can tell you that still too many banks withdrew from participating in issuing Unilever's green bonds for that reason. They simply did not want to make that commitment. It was amazing to me.

My biggest positive surprise was how much energy the USLP unlocked for our employees and partners in the value chain. How it became increasingly relevant for the citizens we were serving and how it clearly accelerated results well beyond the competitive set. We became the third-most looked-up company on LinkedIn. We saw our engagement scores go to the top tercile. Another surprise was how strong the stakeholder alliances became. When we dealt with the Kraft Heinz attempted takeover bid, and there were plenty in the financial market that wanted to pocket the 17 per cent premium, we received amazing support from our stakeholders. We have shown that when you stand by the world, which we did with our multi-stakeholder model, the world stands by you. And, yes, the ones that stuck with us got generously rewarded while the Kraft Heinz financial manipulation scheme quickly ran out of steam.

The other surprise was how many things you can achieve by thinking about things differently. By including sustainability in the design stage, by setting absolute goals, by being systematic thinkers. For example, many said it was impossible to run our factories at zero waste. We achieved it within three years. And we did it because we thought in systems. People were more motivated, the quality of our products was going up and we saved hundreds of millions of dollars by not having that waste. Change often seems impossible until it's getting done. The challenge was often partnerships. We couldn't do all this alone. It is very challenging in a society with levels of trust so low to form these bigger partnerships. And even Unilever needed governments to be supportive to get to fully green energy and sustainable supply chains. If governments continue to fund the fossil fuel industry rather than green energy, it's really difficult to make that transition.

Finally, I saw the power of purpose in action. An aligned and motivated organization can move mountains. Our most powerful brands growing twice as fast and also being more profitable was a great proof point that converted many sceptics. It takes effort to change cultures, even in Unilever. It took us five to six years before we really saw the culture change in a way that made me say, 'Okay, it's getting ingrained in the company, we're really doing it.' As Stephen Covey rightfully said, 'You cannot talk yourself out of a problem you have behaved yourself into.' Changing behaviour takes time but that's time well spent. After all, the future of humanity depends on it.

James: Thank you, Paul.

The potential opportunities and how we might get there

Of all the investment approaches, thematic investing can be billed without much controversy as the most intuitive to retail investors. The emphasis on what companies *do*, the potential to capture transformative growth, and the (justified or unjustified) feeling of those engaged in it that they are contributing to a better future all speak to its appeal.

Thematic investing, however, has other hurdles to overcome. Historically, its investment performance has been poor, its real-world impacts have been limited and the SDGs have more frequently been used as a set of promotional stickers than as a genuine investment framework. Faced with this dichotomy we suggest concrete actions to exploit three more opportunities that we see and provide suggestions as to how we might get there.

The first concerns retail investors. We call for them to critically assess their own impact on people and the planet and not to assuage their consciences by claiming the impact of their investee companies as their own. The second seeks to support institutional investors. We suggest increasing thematic exposure to the most impactful sub-asset class: private markets. The third makes a recommendation for companies and highlights the benefits of seeking SDG action and contribution rather than mere alignment.

Retail investors

Earlier in the chapter we established that most thematic investing results in limited incremental impact, as publicly traded shares are merely exchanged among investors without consequences for the underlying company. We therefore note that even the best sustainable investing approaches and ideas can only do so much and advance the SDGs only so far. Investment action must be accompanied with other practical, even more systematic efforts in the fight against climate change and other ESG issues. We implore individuals not to lose sight of personal responsibility nor underestimate the positive impact that their collective action can have.

Our view runs counter to some investment firms' narratives. In 2021, Germany's Deka Bank claimed that a €10,000 investment in one of its funds would lower carbon emissions by 575 kilograms, the rough equivalent of driving a diesel car 3,500 kilometres. The claim was later retracted when a consumer watchdog voiced the view that real-world carbon emissions would not actually be lowered in the slightest as a result of a person's investment (Verney, 2021).

Nordic bank Nordea faced a similar backlash when it claimed that moving one's pension to sustainable funds would have 27 times the carbon-footprint impact that making a host of lifestyle changes would (Mair, 2021).

We are therefore compelled to take the other side of this debate and implore individuals not to lose sight of personal responsibility, nor underestimate the positive impact their collective lifestyle actions can have.

OPPORTUNITIES

Retail investors may find it tempting to invest thematically and ease their conscience. Unfortunately, there is no substitute for personal action such as reducing the number of airline flights and the amount of meat consumption or lending one's voice to stimulate political change.

Institutional investors

As detailed in 'Chapter 5 – Sustainable private markets', investing in private markets has the greatest potential to do good for people and the planet. Many private market strategies investors have the wherewithal to purchase a controlling interest in a company, repurposing and retooling it to advance powerful effective change. As a result, we argue that sustainably conscious institutional investors should, to the extent possible, concentrate their thematic investing efforts on the private sector and fund the sustainable products and services of the future.

While some of the world's largest private market investors such as TPG and KKR operate sustainable thematic funds, or at least general impact funds, the majority of the largest private market players are yet to meaningfully enter the fray (New Private Markets, 2021; Private Equity International, n.d.). Furthermore, the largest public market thematic investment houses, such as Ark, Pictet and Robeco, have limited to no exposure to private markets (Morningstar, 2022).

As we look for opportunities, we see TPG's commercially successful $7 billion raise for a flagship climate fund as a potential trigger for a new wave of private market thematic investment (The Rise Fund, 2022). TPG's success coincides with a period of industry consolidation as investment manager merger and acquisition volume reached record levels in 2021 (Kozlowski, 2022). Consequently, the path to getting there may involve public market thematic firms combining with their private market counterparts.

OPPORTUNITIES

Increasing thematic exposure to the most impactful sub-asset class – private markets – can generate the greatest positive impact. Opportunities may arise by facilitating a knowledge transfer between leading public market thematic investors and private market managers.

Corporations

Research has shown that corporations tend to align their reporting to the SDGs without markedly altering their behaviour in a way likely to advance the SDGs (Kramer, Agarwal and Srinivas, 2019). Stakeholder incentives must be better matched, we believe, to resolve this situation. We argue that catalysing business model changes that help the SDGs will necessitate opportunities that also support corporate profitability.

Development economists, we concede, are far more knowledgeable than we are in this regard. The World Bank, for one, summarizes dozens of credible research studies that estimate the amount of money required to meet the SDGs (Vorisek and Yu, 2020). We will therefore stay in our lane and focus on a topic with sizeable real-world impact that is well suited to the corporate environment. That topic is waste.

Waste is an immense problem that affects almost all companies, sectors, countries and governments. While 10 per cent of the global population goes hungry, 30 per cent of all food produced around the world is thrown away – at a cost of $1 trillion per year. The volume of plastic packaging, a scourge of our beaches, could more than quadruple by 2050, and 95 per cent of the value of plastic is lost after a single use, at a cost of up to $120 billion annually. If our consumption habits don't change, plastics in the sea could outweigh fish by 2050 (Haefele et al, 2020).

Waste is specifically referred to throughout the official indicators used to track the SDGs. It's there in 6.3.1 'Proportion of wastewater successfully treated'; in 11.6.1 'Proportion of urban solid waste regularly collected'; and in 12.3.1 'Global food loss index'. Reducing waste can also help to achieve dozens of other indicators, even those where waste is not explicitly mentioned. For example, 2.1.1 'Prevalence of undernourishment' and 7.1.1 'Proportion of population with access to electricity' would both be furthered by waste reduction (UN General Assembly, 2017).

Corporations serious about generating an incremental, and material, benefit to the SDGs should consider a deep dive into the waste they generate, we contend. Cutting back on it is inherently profit-enhancing, as inefficiencies in operations and supply chains result in additional costs that would otherwise be profit. This creates a natural alignment between corporations and the UN SDGs.

OPPORTUNITIES

Corporations seeking SDG action and contribution rather than mere alignment should take action on waste – an annual multi-trillion US dollar global problem/opportunity and a key enabler of the UN SDGs.

References

Agnew, H (2022) Cathie Wood's flagship Ark fund suffers fresh blow in early 2022, *Financial Times*, 6 January, www.ft.com/content/208f8669-de4b-444a-89d0-a6ba6af076e9 (archived at https://perma.cc/F8YL-HWKP)

ARK Invest (no date) Sustainable investing by ARK Invest, ark-invest.com/sustainable-investing/ (archived at https://perma.cc/N2QL-L5L2)

Banz, R (2019) Thematic stocks – an alternative to mainstream global equities, Pictet Asset Management, am.pictet/en/switzerland/global-articles/2016/insights/equities/in-depth/thematicstocks-jun2016 (archived at https://perma.cc/BMQ9-U3VJ)

BBC News (2012) Solar panel maker Q-Cells to file for bankruptcy, 2 April, www.bbc.com/news/business-17587830 (archived at https://perma.cc/PSV9-D64T)

Berk, J B and van Binsbergen, J H (2021) The Impact of Impact Investing, Working Paper No 3981, Stanford Graduate School of Business, www.gsb.stanford.edu/faculty-research/working-papers/impact-impact-investing (archived at https://perma.cc/JQX7-GB9A)

Bessembinder, H (2018) Do stocks outperform Treasury bills? *Journal of Financial Economics*, 129(3), pp 440–457, doi.org/10.1016/j.jfineco.2018.06.004 (archived at https://perma.cc/PPN2-2T3K)

Biography.com Editors (2021) Beyoncé Knowles, The Biography.com website, 15 March, www.biography.com/musician/beyonce-knowles (archived at https://perma.cc/43X9-4F28)

BlackRock (no date) Thematic investing with BlackRock and iShares, www.blackrock.com/lu/individual/themes/thematic-investing/why-invest-thematically (archived at https://perma.cc/UM2Q-SPZZ)

Bloomberg (2022) Bloomberg terminal fund screener (Version 93.7.8), www.bloomberg.com/professional/support/software-updates/ (archived at https://perma.cc/3VUQ-6XZX)

Das, P (2021) Thematic investing: The Quintet approach, www.quintet.com/getmedia/b7fa1ad5-226f-4ad4-a760-5ece98044fce/thematic-investing-framework-2021-final.pdf (archived at https://perma.cc/Q9YJ-Z4RR)

GRI and Support the Goals (no date) State of progress: Business contributions to the SDGs – a 2020-2021 study in support of the Sustainable Development Goals, www.globalreporting.org/media/ab5lun0h/stg-gri-report-final.pdf (archived at https://perma.cc/P2HN-24X7)

GRI, UN Global Compact, and WBCSD (no date) SDG Compass: The guide for business action on the SDGs, sdgcompass.org/wp-content/uploads/2015/12/019104_SDG_Compass_Guide_2015.pdf (archived at https://perma.cc/9TMS-D7WL)

Haefele, M et al (2020) Future of waste: Finding opportunities in waste reduction, UBS, doi.org/10.1596/978-1-4648-1329-0 (archived at https://perma.cc/3P2G-SR4X)

Hildebrand, P et al (2021) Sustainable investing: Integrating the UN SDGs in investments, BlackRock, www.blackrock.com/institutions/en-ch/literature/whitepaper/integrating-un-sdgs-investments.pdf (archived at https://perma.cc/9FVH-FNJC)

IEA (2022) Global CO_2 emissions rebounded to their highest level in history in 2021, 8 March, www.iea.org/news/global-co2-emissions-rebounded-to-their-highest-level-in-history-in-2021 (archived at https://perma.cc/9BZ4-Z2LR)

Kozlowski, R (2022) Money manager M&A hits record 392 transactions in 2021 – Piper Sandler, Pensions & Investments, www.pionline.com/money-management/money-manager-ma-hits-record-392-transactions-2021-piper-sandler (archived at https://perma.cc/Q6FD-LJVW)

Kramer, M R, Agarwal, R and Srinivas, A (2019) Business as usual will not save the planet, *Harvard Business Review*, 12 June, hbr.org/2019/06/business-as-usual-will-not-save-the-planet (archived at https://perma.cc/FQW4-WMEZ)

Lazard Asset Management (2021) The seven sins of thematic investing: Common implementation mistakes in long-term equity strategies, www.lazardassetmanagement.com/docs/product/-s32-/121642/TheSevenSinsOfThematicInvesting_LazardPerspectives_en.pdf (archived at https://perma.cc/7UZY-H378)
Lowercarbon Capital (no date) Home, lowercarboncapital.com/ (archived at https://perma.cc/BQH9-FDAP)
Mair, V (2021) UK green pensions campaign branded 'misleading' and 'unethical', Responsible Investor, 13 July, www.responsible-investor.com/uk-green-pensions-campaign-branded-misleading-and-unethical/ (archived at https://perma.cc/6QVW-H3XZ)
Merle, C and Nguyen, H-M (2018) Solving the Sustainable Development Goals Rubik's cube: An impact based toolkit for issuers and investors, Natixis, gsh.cib.natixis.com/our-center-of-expertise/articles/solving-the-sustainable-development-goals-rubik-s-cube (archived at https://perma.cc/B6QX-C48B)
Moore, G E (1965) Cramming more components onto integrated circuits, *Electronics*, 38(8), p 4, newsroom.intel.com/wp-content/uploads/sites/11/2018/05/moores-law-electronics.pdf (archived at https://perma.cc/S2UC-WT2Q)
Morgan Stanley (2019) Sustainable signals: Individual investor interest driven by impact, conviction and choice, www.morganstanley.com/pub/content/dam/msdotcom/infographics/sustainable-investing/Sustainable_Signals_Individual_Investor_White_Paper_Final.pdf (archived at https://perma.cc/4YXV-W5B6)
Morningstar (2022) 'Morningstar global thematic funds landscape 2022', www.morningstar.com/lp/global-thematic-fund-landscape (archived at https://perma.cc/V2KY-TUFN)
MSCI (2022) MSCI ACWI index (USD), www.msci.com/documents/10199/a71b65b5-d0ea-4b5c-a709-24b1213bc3c5 (archived at https://perma.cc/M54U-89RN)
MSCI (no date) Who cares about the UN Sustainable Development Goals? www.msci.com/who-cares-about-the-un-sustainable-development-goals (archived at https://perma.cc/N9GD-6QV9)
Neufeld, D (2021) UN Sustainable Development Goals: How companies stack up, World Economic Forum, 18 March, www.weforum.org/agenda/2021/03/how-aligned-are-un-companies-with-their-sustainable-development-goals/ (archived at https://perma.cc/8XBA-V2US)
New Private Markets (2021) Impact 20: Ranking the largest private markets impact managers, 29 June, www.newprivatemarkets.com/impact-20-ranking-the-largest-private-markets-impact-managers/ (archived at https://perma.cc/23FF-3WCP)

Ocean Tomo (2020) Intangible asset market value study www.oceantomo.com/intangible-asset-market-value-study/ (archived at https://perma.cc/ZP66-LFX8)

Oscars.org (no date) Experience over nine decades of the Oscars from 1927 to 2022, www.oscars.org/oscars/ceremonies/1929 (archived at https://perma.cc/8D7K-543N)

Phalen, C (no date) Investing to achieve the UN Sustainable Development Goals: A report for the US investor community, US SIF Foundation, www.ussif.org/files/Publications/USSIF_Investing%20to%20Achieve%20the%20UN%20SDGs_FINAL.pdf (archived at https://perma.cc/U6EV-ALZ4)

Pickover, C A (2009) *The math book: From Pythagoras to the 57th Dimension, 250 milestones in the history of mathematics*, Sterling, New York

Pictet Asset Management (no date) Thematics, am.pictet/en/switzerland/institutional/capabilities/thematics/tab/ThematicHeritage (archived at https://perma.cc/M8FB-NNKL)

Pierce-Bohen, K (2019) Star Trek: 10 times the show predicted the future, ScreenRant, 11 October, screenrant.com/star-trek-show-predicted-future/ (archived at https://perma.cc/KN37-GARE)

Private Equity International (no date) PEI 300 2022 full ranking, www.privateequityinternational.com/pei-300-2022-ranking/ (archived at https://perma.cc/KX55-NB46)

Rao, A and Doole, S (2021) The pace of fast change: Growth vs. thematic investing, MSCI, www.msci.com/www/blog-posts/the-pace-of-fast-change-growth/02386088177 (archived at https://perma.cc/T92L-QLUD)

Robeco (no date) Thematic investing, www.robeco.com/ch/en/key-strengths/trends-investing/ (archived at https://perma.cc/N2PF-N3UY)

Rogers, E M (1962) *Diffusion of innovations*, Free Press of Glencoe, New York

Scott, L and McGill, A (2019) Creating a strategy for a better world, PwC, www.pwc.com/gx/en/sustainability/SDG/sdg-2019.pdf (archived at https://perma.cc/5SA6-PBRM)

Sotiroff, D (2021) High burnout rate for thematic funds, Morningstar, www.morningstar.com/articles/1015842/high-burnout-rate-for-thematic-funds (archived at https://perma.cc/XV8V-6HBV)

TCFD (2021) Task Force on Climate-related Financial Disclosures: 2021 Status Report, www.fsb.org/2021/10/2021-status-report-task-force-on-climate-related-financial-disclosures/ (archived at https://perma.cc/Z2SY-MSAR)

The Economist (1999) Cutting the cord, 7 October, www.economist.com/special-report/1999/10/07/cutting-the-cord (archived at https://perma.cc/5BDG-25HT)

The Economist (2022) Who buys the dirty energy assets public companies no longer want? 12 February, www.economist.com/finance-and-economics/who-buys-the-dirty-energy-assets-public-companies-no-longer-want/21807594 (archived at https://perma.cc/ZB2K-PKDG)

The Rise Fund (2022) TPG closes rise climate fund at $7.3 billion, 27 April, therisefund.com/news/tpg-closes-rise-climate-fund-73-billion (archived at https://perma.cc/5YTW-ZYY7)

UBS (2018) UBS Investor Watch: Return on Values, www.ubs.com/content/dam/ubs/microsites/ubs-investor-watch/IW-09-2018/return-on-value-global-report-final.pdf (archived at https://perma.cc/W2Z9-SNGT)

UN (2021) Sustainable Development Goals progress chart 2021, Statistics Division, Department of Economic and Social Affairs, doi.org/10.1891/9780826190123.0013 (archived at https://perma.cc/4TGZ-796B)

UN (2022) *IAEG-SDGs:* Tier classification for global SDG indicators, United Nations Statistics Division, unstats.un.org/sdgs/iaeg-sdgs/tier-classification/ (archived at https://perma.cc/Q59S-HPFQ)

UN (no date a) Take action for the Sustainable Development Goals, United Nations Sustainable Development, www.un.org/sustainabledevelopment/sustainable-development-goals/ (archived at https://perma.cc/9R2U-D5BN)

UN (no date b) Transforming our world: The 2030 Agenda for Sustainable Development, Department of Economic and Social Affairs, sdgs.un.org/2030agenda (archived at https://perma.cc/3AE8-HXRU)

UN CTAD (2020) Investing in the SDGs, in *World Investment Report: International Production Beyond the Pandemic*, United Nations, Geneva unctad.org/system/files/official-document/WIR2020_CH5.pdf (archived at https://perma.cc/C479-6QDA)

UN General Assembly (2017) *Resolution Adopted by the General Assembly on 6 July 2017: Work of the Statistical Commission Pertaining to the 2030 Agenda for Sustainable Development*, A/RES/71/313, documents-dds-ny.un.org/doc/UNDOC/GEN/N17/207/63/PDF/N1720763.pdf?OpenElement (archived at https://perma.cc/6XAQ-PLWZ)

UN PRI (no date) Investing with SDG outcomes: A five-part framework, www.unpri.org/download?ac=10795 (archived at https://perma.cc/547T-6582)

Verney, P (2021) DekaBank drops impact calculator for sustainability funds to avoid lawsuit over greenwashing claims, Responsible Investor, 19 April, www.responsible-investor.com/dekabank-drops-impact-calculator-for-sustainability-funds-to-avoid-lawsuit-over-greenwashing-claims/ (archived at https://perma.cc/M4GH-4PKF)

Vontobel (2021) Thematic investment shows rapid growth, am.vontobel.com/en/insights/thematic-investment-shows-rapid-growth (archived at https://perma.cc/P5SL-2MQK)

Vorisek, D and Yu, S (2020) Understanding the cost of achieving the Sustainable Development Goals, Policy Research Working Paper 9146, World Bank, Washington, DC, doi.org/10.1596/1813-9450-9164 (archived at https://perma.cc/VYR2-DWQH)

WBCSD (no date) CEO guide to the Sustainable Development Goals, docs.wbcsd.org/2017/03/CEO_Guide_to_the_SDGs/English.pdf (archived at https://perma.cc/KJ7C-EUG5)

Wells, H G (1932) Communications 1922–1932 – HG Wells, BBC Archive, www.bbc.co.uk/archive/communications-1922-1932--hg-wells/z4f6kmn (archived at https://perma.cc/Z7AZ-3D4U)

Wright, T P (1936) Factors affecting the cost of airplanes, *Journal of the Aeronautical Sciences*, 3(4), pp 122–28, doi.org/10.2514/8.155 (archived at https://perma.cc/U7S5-E3UL)

07

Sustainable multi-asset portfolios

Introduction

A typical supermarket might contain 50,000 products (Rooks, 2022). Their display is far from random and highly curated to produce maximum consumer spend. 'Essentials' such as eggs and bread sit far from the entrance, forcing the unsuspecting shopper to walk the isles of temptation. Colourful fruit and vegetables adorn the entrance to brighten the mood – an utterly impractical arrangement as those plump peaches will soon be crushed in your trolley under a six pack of beer. And the highest-margin products are placed at eye level to maximize the chance of you plucking and wheeling them toward checkout (BBC Food, n.d.).

Sustainable investment products come in similar abundance. Data-firm Morningstar estimated in early 2022 that there were almost 6500 sustainable funds worldwide (Morningstar, 2022). And in our previous chapters we've discussed a multitude of sustainable investing approaches that exist across the asset classes. But how are they curated in a retail investor's or institutional investor's overall, multi-asset portfolio? Is such effective cohesion even possible?

This chapter opens with a look at how traditional approaches to sustainable multi-asset portfolios operate. We consider three approaches before posing – and answering – critical questions about popularity, performance and impact upon people and the planet.

The section starts with an approach we term screening. This method involves comparing a traditional portfolio against one or more sustainable metrics to determine the validity of the investment instrument components. Next, we consider an exclusion approach, which takes a traditional portfolio and removes certain undesirable elements from it. Finally, we review a core-satellite approach in which a traditional portfolio is augmented by specific sustainable assets.

With this review complete, we examine traditional sustainable multi-asset portfolios in theory and in practice, and we asking and answering three key questions about them:

- How popular are they? (Answer: Not very.)
- Do they add to investment performance? (Answer: No.)
- Do they help people and the planet? (Answer: No.)

With the past – and those uninspiring answers – behind us, we move on to how modern approaches to sustainable multi-asset portfolios operate. In this section, we outline the leaps forward that sustainable multi-asset investing has made, predominantly in the late 2010s.

We start by considering the entire investment value chain and the role that sustainability can play both in macro forecasting and in creating capital market assumptions. We discuss sub-asset class substitutions, such as replacing high-quality government bond exposure with multilateral development bank bonds, to enhance portfolio sustainability. We then evaluate the advantages of deploying different sustainable techniques in combination to obtain desired factor and risk-premia exposures.

Having profiled the modern approaches, we judge how successful they've been, and again pose and answer three important questions about what is projected in theory and what occurs in practice:

- How popular are they? (Answer: Their popularity is growing.)
- Do they add to investment performance? (Answer: A little.)
- Do they help people and the planet? (Answer: Only as much as the underlying investments do.)

Before tackling our final multi-asset section, we pause to include an exclusive interview with Rick Lacaille. As of 2022, Rick serves as executive vice president and global head of environmental, social and governance (ESG) initiatives at investment juggernaut State Street. For more than a decade before this, he was the global chief investment officer (CIO) at State Street Global Advisors. He witnessed at first hand sustainable investing's growth, as well as the challenges posed and the opportunities presented by multi-asset investing. His experience helps to frame sustainable multi-asset investing in practice and the intricacies discussed in the previous two private market sections.

Our final multi-asset section looks to the future and assesses the potential opportunities and how we might get there. Multi-asset class sustainable portfolios could conceivably represent the entirety of an individual's liquid financial wealth. But, as we discuss, they often fall short in several areas. To rectify this situation, we go beyond a call to adopt current solutions and focus on three potential improvements, with suggestions on how they can be implemented.

- The first calls for new sub-asset class solutions to enhance the opportunity set, typically utilizing what we termed 'dedicated assets' in 'Chapter 4 – Sustainable public debt markets'.
- The second requests regulatory change to aid in incorporating alternatives into sustainable multi-asset portfolios. For individual investors without sizeable wealth or the regulatory-defined sophistication to make large-scale alternative investments, this is essential.
- The third urges personalization. As the bench of sub-asset class solutions grows, so does the opportunity to tailor sustainable multi-asset portfolios to individuals. As of 2022, a lower carbon and carbon solution multi-asset portfolio is already possible for investors who prefer one.

How traditional approaches to sustainable multi-asset portfolios operate

Screening: Passing the test

In my youth, I (James) misspent three years attempting to body build. My approach to nutrition left much to be desired. I took my standard diet, based on bacon sandwiches, scrambled eggs and Kentucky Fried Chicken, and performed a quick screen: Did the meal contain more protein than saturated fat? If so, it passed my bodybuilding test. This screening process led to me to substitute more nutritious foods for certain favourites, but for the most part my diet remained unchanged. It certainly wasn't designed optimally for my muscular objectives.

Within traditional approaches to sustainable multi-asset portfolios, screening approaches are common. Essentially, an asset allocation process is run for a standard portfolio. It starts with economic assumptions, which lead to capital market assumptions and, ultimately, asset class weightings populated by an array of investment instruments.

As a final step, the investment instruments are screened for their sustainability credentials. This screening could be as simple as applying a third-party sustainability rating from the likes of MSCI or Sustainalytics to the holdings of invested funds or directly held equities and bonds. Any such equities or bonds, as well as aggregated fund holdings, that score above a threshold are deemed sustainable (Conde-Herman, 2014).

Screening approaches suffer from many of the failings and biases that we highlighted in 'Chapter 2 – Sustainable data and ESG ratings'. A major one is that headline sustainability ratings favour larger companies and lead to conventional passive funds such as the US's S&P 500 or the Eurozone's EuroStoxx 50 being deemed sustainable (Akgun, Mudge and Townsend, 2021). Conventional active funds may also, by chance, hold stocks that screen as sustainable despite the fund manager having no intention of managing assets sustainably and no method for incorporating sustainability in the investment process.

Another weakness of screened multi-asset portfolios is that they may rely on sustainability ratings expressed as portfolio averages. Glaringly unsustainable instruments can find a way into the portfolio provided they are 'offset' by more sustainable instruments elsewhere.

Screening-based portfolios appeal to product manufacturers, who can extract considerable operational leverage from existing conventional operations. Typically, a single data source and approach, such as a third-party sustainability rating, is used indiscriminately across the portfolio. When averages are employed, either at sub-asset, asset or even portfolio level, the required adaptations to a conventional portfolio can be minimal.

A sustainable multi-asset portfolio derived from screening is, frequently, not a very sophisticated creature. It may incorporate sustainability considerations only as the final step in the investment process and may look nearly identical to a conventional portfolio in its composition.

Exclusion: An inferior version

Many vegetarians will be familiar with a variant of the following story. What is touted on a restaurant menu as a vegetable caesar salad is ordered. When it arrives it contains strips of chicken and chunks of crunchy bacon. A complaint is aired. The 'solution' consists of the plate being whisked away and the sous chef removing the offending animal flesh with a fork. The dish is then returned – without a hint of embarrassment – to the diner. While the resulting salad does not (technically) contain meat, it was not designed to be vegetarian. The flavour and texture combinations were not created for a vegetarian consumer and the end product is simply an inferior version of the standard menu item.

Within traditional approaches to sustainable multi-asset portfolios, exclusion approaches take their place beside screening ones. Essentially, an asset allocation process is run for a conventional portfolio. It starts, again, with economic assumptions and leads to capital market assumptions and, ultimately, asset class weightings. At this stage, a series of asset, sub-asset and instrument exclusions may be applied, a process that removes securities otherwise found in the corresponding conventional portfolio. These securities might belong to 'non-compliant' asset classes such as commodities, sub-asset classes such as certain emerging markets and sectors that derive a major portion of revenue from activities involving tobacco or thermal coal.

Exclusion-driven portfolios also appeal to product manufacturers, who can extract considerable operational leverage from existing conventional operations. Relatively rudimentary adaptations ensure compliance with the desired sustainability metrics. In this traditional approach, sustainability is treated as a constraint – a deviation from the desired optimal. Therefore, assuming that the investment manager has the ability to generate alpha, then, mechanically, the exclusion-driven sustainable portfolio will be inferior to the unconstrained, best-ideas, conventional multi-asset portfolio.

As a result, a sustainable multi-asset portfolio derived from exclusionary approaches may incorporate sustainability considerations only as a final step and resemble a classic portfolio in composition, only with fewer components.

Core-Satellite: Bolting on

In 1987, burger monolith McDonald's introduced salads to its menu in a bid to combat its unhealthy fast food image (Walsh, 1986). In Europe, the chain's background logo switched in 2009 from red to eco-friendly green (NBC News, 2009). These shifts did not change the core McDonald's proposition – burgers and fries. In the mid-2010s, the company confirmed that salads were very much a niche offering. They made up less than 4 per cent of sales (Patton, 2013) and in the 2020s disappeared, in some geographies, from the menu altogether (Taylor, 2020). Essentially, while healthier and greener options were bolted on as satellite elements, the tried-and-true offering remained unchanged.

Within traditional approaches to sustainable multi-asset portfolios, core-satellite approaches are another common tack taken. A typical process relies upon a successful conventional multi-asset portfolio and bolts on sustainable assets without materially changing the fundamental approach. An illustrative process might include taglines such as 'X per cent in sustainable or impact investing' (McGachey, 2019).

Core-satellite portfolios are yet another approach that appeals to product manufacturers because, again, they can extract considerable operational leverage from existing conventional operations. The chosen satellites commonly provide a compelling narrative to end clients while not materially affecting portfolio risk-adjusted return. Their advantage is that they keep investment and risk professionals comfortable with the portfolio's investment characteristics and fulfilment of the firm's fiduciary duty, while not requiring major re-engineering of the value chain. But core-satellite approaches have obvious faults from a sustainability standpoint. The most pertinent is that the bulk of the multi-asset portfolio is often subject to limited, or even no, meaningful sustainability criteria or process.

As a result, a sustainable multi-asset portfolio derived from a core-satellite approach may incorporate sustainability considerations in only a minority of the investment solution and closely resemble a conventional portfolio in composition.

With a review of the basic tenets of sustainable multi-asset portfolios under our belts, let's turn to theory and practice by asking and answering three key questions:

Traditional multi-asset sustainable portfolios: How popular are they?

Short answer: Not very.

IN THEORY

Proponents of traditional multi-asset portfolios theorize that an end investor's preference for investing sustainably through equities or bonds should translate into a demand for sustainable multi-asset portfolios. After all, such portfolios typically are a combination of composite equity and bond parts. Naively, one might expect the share of sustainable multi-asset funds vis-à-vis conventional multi-asset funds to compare with the percentage of sustainable equity funds relative to conventional equity funds.

IN PRACTICE

Traditional sustainable multi-asset funds have, historically, not proved popular. Calculations from the International Monetary Fund, using Bloomberg data, found that, in 2010, sustainable-multi-asset funds comprised just 10 per cent of sustainable mutual fund assets-under-management (Deese et al, 2019). As described above, they became perceived as (inferior) offshoots of conventional multi-asset processes.

Furthermore, in the early 2010s multi-asset portfolio managers struggled to find suitable investments within certain sub-asset classes critical to multi-asset portfolio construction. Later in this chapter, we include a full interview with Rick Lacaille, State Street's global head of ESG initiatives and former global chief investment officer (CIO) at State Street Global Advisors. Rick sheds light on the challenges faced by managers trying to build traditional multi-asset sustainable portfolios, stating that there were 'quite significant gaps from an asset class or sub-asset class perspective, where there simply isn't much being done'.

Not until 2018, for example, did the first exchange traded fund or mutual fund launch for multilateral development bank debt – a key substitute for US treasuries (UBS, 2022). In 2022, sustainable multi-asset investors finally got access to a scalable recycled gold investment product (HANetf, 2022), despite recycled gold providing 25 per cent of annual gold supply (World Gold Council, n.d.). It wasn't until 2021, as well, that dedicated corporate investment grade green bond funds were available in separate euro and US dollar sleeves, a standard requirement for asset allocators (DWS, 2021). With the availability of sustainable solutions skewed to equity strategies, it was difficult, historically, to build a credible sustainable multi-asset solution attractive to mainstream investors.

Scepticism over the return potential for sustainable investing also held investors and product creators back. According to a 2015 Morgan Stanley survey, just 19 per cent of retail investors described themselves as 'very interested' in sustainable investing with the majority of respondents seeing sustainability and investment returns as a 'trade off' (Morgan Stanley, 2017). This dampened the appeal of labelled sustainable multi-asset solutions as investors were likely to create their own core-satellite multi-asset solutions by purchasing a handful of sustainable solutions alongside a larger volume of conventional equity or debt funds.

It is hard to identify many major genuine sustainable multi-asset portfolios pre-2015. Until then portfolios were either provided by niche players and held limited assets or were sidelines to the much larger conventional businesses of traditional asset and wealth managers. In 2018, Swiss wealth manager UBS bucked the trend by launching its highly successful sustainable multi-asset portfolio, which, in 2020, was declared the company's 'preferred solution' amid inflows north of $20 billion (UBS, 2020).

Having reviewed the traditional approaches to sustainable multi-asset investing, we'll now examine the theory and reality in practice by asking and answering three important questions.

Traditional multi-asset sustainable portfolios: Do they add performance?

Short answer: No.

IN THEORY

Proponents of traditional multi-asset portfolios advance theories as to why they should improve investment performance. In 'Chapter 3 – Sustainable public equity markets' and 'Chapter 4 – Sustainable public debt markets', we highlighted that, in many cases, sustainable funds have outperformed their conventional peers. We constructively challenged the methodologies of some of the academic studies that found outperformance. Nonetheless, it empirically occurred, regardless of cause.

Given that individual building blocks for a traditional multi-asset sustainable portfolio had performed robustly, it is logical to infer that, by combining them, a multi-asset portfolio would show similarly favourable returns.

IN PRACTICE

Due to the challenges highlighted previously, traditional approaches to sustainable multi-asset portfolios were unable to reflect the strength of their single-asset-class cousins and add investment performance.

Why? Because the portfolios often lacked a large number of key building blocks, such as single currency investment grade funds, corporate emerging market bond funds and gold, each of which contributed critically to portfolio diversification. Their absence mechanically ensured that the standard approaches, whether based on screening, exclusions or core-satellite, sat below the efficient frontier generated by a full multi-asset universe (Markowitz, 1952).

In 'Chapter 3 – Sustainable public equity markets', we evidenced that a moderate number of exclusions, within an equity universe of several thousand companies, would not lead to underperformance of portfolios investing in the asset class (Evans and Archer, 1968; Fisher and Lorie, 1970; Statman, 1987; Campbell et al, 2002; Domian, Louton and Racine, 2007). A fully diversified equity portfolio could still be achieved using a relatively small subset of companies. This principle, however, does not hold true in a multi-asset context when a large minority of sub-asset classes are otherwise allocated to go missing from a traditional sustainable multi-asset portfolio.

Traditional multi-asset sustainable portfolios: Do they help people and the planet?

Short answer: No.

IN THEORY

Proponents of exclusion in public equities put forth theories as to why traditional multi-asset portfolios should help people and the planet. In 'Chapter 3 – Sustainable public equity markets' and 'Chapter 4 – Sustainable public debt markets', we outlined the thinking about how sustainable liquid investments could do so. Since traditional multi-asset sustainable portfolios merge various single-asset-class sustainable practices, their potential impact does not materially differ from the single-asset-class variant.

Broadly speaking, people and the planet can benefit, theoretically, via one of two channels. Either there is a change in the cost of capital for a company, making it easier or harder for it to raise capital or operate. Or there is a change in how its management behaves, for example, by pursuing more sustainable practices.

In the case of the first channel, the theory suggests that by refusing to purchase or by divesting securities, exclusionary-focused investors push down equity or bond prices, thus increasing the cost of capital (Rohleder, Wilkens and Zink, 2022). A higher cost of capital will make some projects economically unprofitable and thus unappealing to company management. If, say, a new oil pipeline is forecast to return 10 per cent in annual profits, but the cost to finance it is 12 per cent, then the pipeline almost certainly will not be built. Conversely, if the cost to finance it is 8 per cent, then the likelihood of a go-ahead is quite high.

As regards the second channel, the theoretical argument contends that investors can create public pressure on a company and affect its so-called 'social license to operate' (Impact Management Project, 2018). Or that the pressure applied can directly alter management behaviour through constructive dialogue and engagement (UNPRI, 2018; Hermes Investment, n.d.). If an investor identifies a sustainability deficiency within a target firm and the deficiency is then fixed, people and the planet benefit. A less aggressive interpretation suggests that the concerns raised by investors form part of a mosaic of information that may progressively push a topic up a corporate agenda and result in improvements.

IN PRACTICE

As with single-asset-class investing, the reality overwhelmingly points to public equity and debt markets being sufficiently liquid and asset demand elastic enough that exclusion doesn't work. The choices of an individual or even a sizeable group of investors about whether to buy or not buy publicly traded securities has little to no material impact on their price or on a company's cost of raising future capital (Berk and van Binsbergen, 2017).

An investor's ability to influence company behaviour, and thus have a positive impact, enjoys slightly greater empirical support, but the evidence is far from conclusive (Kölbel et al, 2020). Interestingly, studies show that social engagements tend to have a higher success rate than environmental ones (Dimson, Karakaş and Li, 2015). Attempting to explain this discrepancy, researchers have found that engagement succeeds most often when the cost to the corporation of changing its ways is lower (Barko, Cremers and Renneboog, 2017). The implication is that, in general, the influence extends only to minor elements of corporate strategy and so the impact is similarly limited.

In the case of traditional approaches to sustainable multi-asset portfolios, whether screening, exclusions or core-satellite, there is no proactive allocation to strategies that pursue sustainability improvement through active engagement. Therefore, without a deliberate emphasis on catalysing benefits for people and the planet through dialogue with corporate management, traditional sustainable multi-asset portfolios intend neither to trigger nor track such benefits.

How modern approaches to sustainable multi-asset portfolios operate

Value chain: From farm to table

In the culinary world a highly popular modern approach to the restaurant business is called 'from farm to table'. The concept re-engineers the value chain from farming practices through transportation to food preparation. The result is that food travels short distances and chefs showcase the best of local and seasonal produce. Farm-to-table concepts can be combined with other three-word hyphenated culinary movements such as nose-to-nail cooking, the art of using all of an animal's carcass without waste, to transform the entire value chain of food preparation. Sustainability is not an afterthought here but a concept present every step of the way.

When it comes to modern approaches to sustainable multi-asset portfolios, the investment value chain has, likewise, been fully re-engineered. It starts with the economic assumptions that underpin long-term asset class forecasts (commonly called capital market assumptions), proceeds through the choice of asset classes and asset class weightings and ultimately affects instrument selection and portfolio composition.

Unlike the traditional approaches to sustainable multi-asset portfolios, the modern approaches don't merely add sustainable screens or satellites. They embed sustainability into each investment step.

Sustainable variables are increasingly shaping macroeconomic outcomes. For example, on the environmental side, the shift from fossil to renewable energies can be inflationary if the transition is governed by politics rather than market forces alone. As a second-order effect, the transition could fundamentally alter the demand curves for commodities by, for instance, increasing demand for nickel and decreasing demand for coal.

These fundamental demand shifts will in turn affect a range of national gross domestic product growth expectations as well as other important factors such as unemployment rates (Schnabel, 2022). Social factors can also influence macroeconomic forecasts. For example, rising minimum wages can alter employment figures and productivity both, as well as labour participation rates.

Integrating sustainability into macroeconomic forecasting, however, is not without its difficulties. One significant challenge is Western bias in the perception of what good sustainability practices are. It leads Western researchers to favour their own economic and political practices, which generates a positive correlation between sustainability and a country's living standards. As a result, researchers are increasingly taking a more nuanced stance when incorporating sustainability into their economic forecasts (Dunga et al, 2019).

In practice, applying sustainability factors into capital market assumptions can take many forms. A key one is modelling economic forecasts for a range of climate scenarios. Large asset managers such as BlackRock (Hildebrand et al, 2021) and Wellington (Wattiau et al, 2022) have published some of their work. These forecasts can translate into allocations that favour technology over energy, that can exclude certain commodities and that can influence individual instrument selection (Gambera, Primmer and Finney, 2021). In summary, modern approaches to sustainable multi-asset portfolios increasingly seek to build in sustainable factors throughout the value chain rather than retrofit conventional processes.

Substitution: The rise of dedicated assets

The exteriors of electric cars closely resemble their combustion engine cousins. One sees four wheels, a windscreen and wing mirrors that wiggle at the touch of a button. It's under the bonnet where a number of crucial substitutions have taken place. The monstrously complex four- or six- or eight-cylinder engine is replaced by an electric motor. The fuel and exhaust system gives way to a battery pack. Alternators and starters also disappear in favour of converters and inverters. While elements of the electric car may be familiar, there are also wholesale innovations, substitutions and components that may be unfamiliar to enthusiasts of gas guzzlers.

With modern approaches to sustainable multi-asset portfolios, large parts of the asset allocation – particularly within public debt markets – can now be represented by dedicated assets. As discussed in 'Chapter 4 – Sustainable public debt markets', these assets differ from conventional ones in that they are designed with sustainability specifically in mind.

In contrast to the aforementioned traditional core-satellite approach, where instruments with sustainable characteristics are bolted on to the side of a conventional portfolio, the approach using dedicated assets replaces entire sub-asset classes within a multi-asset portfolio with sustainable instruments. It represents a wholesale restructuring of important sources of multi-asset portfolio return and requires a fundamental rethinking of multi-asset portfolio design.

An easy substitution for conventional investors to adopt is to replace high-quality developed-market government bonds with multilateral development bank bonds. The latter are issued by entities such as the World Bank and over a 70-year issuance history have never defaulted on their publicly traded debt. Multilateral development bank bonds boast AAA credit-ratings, exhibit a 0.99 correlation spread to US treasuries and trade at a typical credit spread of just 15 basis points (Perraudin, Powell and Yang, 2016). As of 2022, they comprised more than $400 billion of outstanding publicly traded debt, so all but the largest sustainable investors can mimic the maturity and duration of US dollar and euro sovereign curves within a multi asset portfolio (Spinoso, Purcell and Street, 2021).

Moving one step up the risk spectrum, investors can consider substitutions for corporate investment grade credit. The growth of the green bond market – where bond proceeds are ring-fenced solely for sustainable purposes – has been spectacular. A booming $500 billion issuance market was in place in 2021, making it possible to run the entirety of an investment grade credit allocation within the confines of the green bond universe (BloombergNEF, 2022).

Furthermore, the rise of the $200 billion per year sustainability-linked bond market, where the amount of interest payments partially depends on a company's performance on ESG metrics, adds further diversity and opportunity for investors who seek to build genuine sustainable public debt market allocations within a multi-asset portfolio (Mutua and Raimonde, 2021).

The use of green bonds to fully represent an entire sub-asset class can, increasingly, be applied to emerging market (EM) corporate bonds as well. Like their investment grade cousins, the EM green bond market has been expanding rapidly. Growth was catalysed by the 2017 partnership between the World Bank's International Finance Corporation and French asset manager Amundi, which sought to underpin all credible EM green bond issuance with a deep pool of capital (International Finance Corporation, 2017).

Amundi has since launched a liquid version of the EM strategy and has, as of 2022, gathered almost $500 million of assets in just two years. While the EM corporate green bond market is by no means as deep as the euro and US dollar developed markets, there is the potential for substitution in what is typically a niche sub-asset class within a multi-asset portfolio.

Replacing a conventional asset with a dedicated asset designed with sustainability in mind even stretches to the commodity complex, or at least to gold. Among commodities, gold processes a rare characteristic: it is infinitely recyclable with no degradation of quality. Consequently, it is well placed to be part of a circular economy and serve as a credible sustainable asset.

On average, recycled gold, whether in the form of jewellery or consumer electronics parts, generates just five per cent of the carbon emissions of its mined equivalent (Hinkel, 2021). It accounts for 25 per cent of annual gold supply (World Gold Council, n.d.) and the stock already above ground exceeds all known remaining mining reserves (Harper, 2020). In 2022, the UK's Royal Mint, which operates an investable $500 million exchange traded commodity, announced it would back at least 50 per cent of its investment product with recycled gold. This marked an important step for recycled gold as a standalone recycled asset (HANetf, 2022).

In summary, the rise of dedicated assets has enabled sustainable investors to go far beyond traditional techniques such as exclusion and integration. Entire sub-asset class allocations can consist of liquid investments that offer competitive returns and were designed explicitly with sustainability in mind.

Portfolio construction: Understanding strengths and weaknesses

In 2004, outsiders Greece won the 2004 UEFA European Football Championship at 150–1 odds, beating Portugal in the final. The Greek team didn't have the best players and just eight of their 23-man squad plied their club trade outside of their home country.

In the final, they faced the riches of a Portugal team that boasted 100-cap legend Luis Figo, AC Milan superstar Rui Costa and a youthful Cristiano Ronaldo (UEFA, n.d.). The Greek manager did not crudely impose off-the-rack tactics on their players but specifically created ones for them: their strengths were played to and their weaknesses were offset. A unique game plan was custom designed to fit the team's resources. This focus created a whole greater than the sum of its parts.

With modern approaches to sustainable multi-asset portfolios, sustainability is no longer viewed as a constraint, a suboptimal construction or a deliberate deviation from the efficient frontier. Instead, unique game plans are designed and factor exposures are both proactively sought and managed to achieve the desired risk premia, consistent with an investor's expected macroeconomic scenarios. The objective is to create a whole greater than the sum of its parts.

In 'Chapter 1 – What is sustainable investing?', we discussed how sustainability can mean different things to different people and how rational investors can interpret it in a number of ways. In subsequent chapters, particularly 'Chapter 3 – Sustainable public equity markets' and 'Chapter 4 – Sustainable public debt markets', we demonstrated how concepts could be applied to create a range of diverse investment strategies, each deploying sustainability differently.

In a multi-asset context, these different strategies produce factor tilts – portfolio exposures that will lead to outperformance or underperformance depending upon macroeconomic outcomes – that can be proactively pursued and managed to achieve the desired investment exposures.

For example, in 'Chapter 1 – What is sustainable investing?', we introduced the concept of differentiating between how a company *acts* and what a company *does*. We can think about how a company acts as how sustainable factors impact its value. Many forms of sustainable integration, for instance, look at the sustainability factors most material to the financial health of the company. These may include company policy and delivery, certain governance topics and how company actions interact with exogenous factors such as physical and transition climate risks.

In contrast, we can think about what a company does as how it impacts people and the planet. Many forms of sustainable thematic investing look at the products and services produced by a company and whether their net impact is positive or negative. In addition, investors will consider whether sustainability trends will lead to demand for the products and services rising or falling in the future.

As a result, investors focused on how a company acts can often purchase well-run companies with no clear connection to a sustainable economy (for example, large-scale consumer goods firms). Investors who buy shares in a company based on what it does, on the other hand, will often buy innovative, pioneering companies that may have sustainable deficiencies in areas such as governance or human resource management.

In a modern sustainable multi-asset portfolio, these different approaches can be purposefully combined to create desired factor exposures. Sustainable integration approaches that centre on how a company acts can lead to allocations that exhibit the so-called quality factor. This factor is often characterized by robust margins, steady (if unspectacular) revenue growth and efficient use of capital. Such companies tend to perform relatively well in times of market stress.

Sustainable thematic approaches that value what a company does can lead to allocations that exhibit the so-called growth factor. This factor is often characterized by rapid revenue growth and low (initial) profitability. Such companies tend to perform well in periods of low interest rates and/or limited economic growth. Thematic approaches may also favour smaller companies whose products and services are less mature (Bedel and Purcell, 2022).

Other elements from the sustainable repertoire can also be deliberately included in portfolio construction. Approaches that focus on engagement or sustainability improvement can create idiosyncratic sources of return as the improvements are company specific. Companies targeted for engagement may also be smaller than average, as the opportunity for improvement may arise because they have fewer resources to focus on sustainability.

Companies that need sustainability improvement may also exhibit a so-called value factor. This factor is often characterized by cheaper valuations than the market average. Such companies tend to perform well in periods of market enthusiasm (MSCI, 2021).

In summary, portfolio construction for a modern sustainable multi-asset portfolio places sustainability at the core of the process. It harnesses a set of risk exposures that can be explicitly modelled and combined in an octagonal manner in pursuit of superior investment returns. Sustainability factors are not viewed as an unwanted deviation from conventional indices – what the industry terms tracking error – but rather as a desirable set of heterogeneous exposures that can be curated and managed.

Having reviewed the modern approaches to sustainable multi-asset investing, we now examine it in theory and in practice by asking and answering three vital questions.

Modern multi-asset sustainable portfolios: How popular are they?

Short answer: Their popularity is growing.

IN THEORY

Proponents of modern multi-asset portfolios advance theories as to why such portfolios should be significantly more popular than their predecessors. Fiduciary duty requires those managing money on behalf of clients to seek the best possible risk-adjusted financial return.

Modern approaches to multi-asset sustainable portfolios are theoretically far more aligned with fiduciary duty than traditional ones were. Modern approaches seek to take advantage of the unique characteristics of sustainable assets, and informed managers see sustainability as an opportunity instead of a constraint. When viewed as a constraint, sustainability that must be retrofitted into a conventional framework is considered a deviation from the efficient frontier.

Positioned as a positive for the investment process, and assuming portfolio managers have adequate resources and knowledge, it follows that modern multi-asset sustainable portfolios should be markedly more popular than their traditional precursors.

IN PRACTICE

The reality is that the modern multi-asset sustainable industry still lags in popularity behind individual asset class funds.

Later in this chapter, we include an interview with Rick Lacaille, State Street's global head of ESG initiatives and former global chief investment officer (CIO) at State Street Global Advisors. Rick explains why this lag exists, stating that when 'you look at where people have got deep sustainability expertise, it tends to be in the narrow product area. It's not necessarily at the CIO or the asset allocator level'. In other words, the sustainable multi-asset portfolio industry is simply less mature than its equity or debt counterparts.

Modern multi-asset portfolios that incorporate all the elements discussed in this section remain uncommon. But they are growing in popularity. UBS Global Wealth Management launched a successful sustainable multi-asset portfolio in 2018 (UBS, 2019). While it doesn't fully reflect all the characteristics we have discussed, the resulting rapid inflows – in excess of $20 billion (UBS, 2020) – provide evidence that multi-asset portfolios which aggressively commit to sustainability can be commercially successful.

Luxembourg-headquartered Quintet Private Bank pledged in 2020 to make 'sustainability the default' investment proposition and has posted similar results. Its multi-asset portfolio comprises many of the previously discussed elements, and the bank reported that its sustainable assets doubled in calendar year 2021 as a result (Quintet, 2022).

In summary, while the popularity of modern multi-asset portfolios is rising, few investors as of 2022 have the resources and knowledge to execute on a fully sustainable value chain.

Modern multi-asset sustainable portfolios: Do they add performance?

Short answer: A little.

IN THEORY

Proponents of modern multi-asset portfolios put forward theories as to why such portfolios should boost investment performance. A modern approach to sustainable multi-asset portfolios, theoretically, should capture the risk premia available in the individual component asset classes. It should also proactively embrace the factor exposures present within sustainable assets and optimize them to create optimal risk-adjusted return, which, in turn, should lead to better investment performance than a traditional sustainable multi-asset approach.

On a wider view, however, theory also suggests that a sustainable-agnostic (i.e. conventional) investor can invest in any asset a sustainable investor might choose. A modern sustainable investor, by contrast, would not be able to select every asset available to a sustainable-agnostic investor: certain securities would be ruled out. Therefore, the multi-asset universe for a sustainable-agnostic investor is mechanically greater than that for a sustainable investor. All else equal, modern portfolio theory suggests that this would lead to superior risk-adjusted performance for the sustainable-agnostic investor.

IN PRACTICE

The modern approach to sustainable multi-asset portfolios fares much better than the traditional approach because the vast majority of desirable sub-asset class exposures can now be adequately represented via sustainable assets. By accessing the diverse risk premia across regions, sectors and credit segments, an investor can create a multi-asset portfolio far closer to the efficient frontier. As a result, modern approaches can capture any potential outperformance achieved by their single-asset-class components without suffering an offsetting drag from sub-optimal portfolio construction.

While sustainable-agnostic investors may theoretically be able to invest in every asset a sustainable investor can, in practice they often lack the necessary knowledge to fully exploit its sustainable characteristics. For example, if agnostic investors erroneously model climate transition and physical risk in their capital market assumptions, they will construct a sub-optimal multi-asset portfolio.

Alternately, agnostic investors may not be able to comprehensively model the use-of-proceeds and sustainability-linked bond markets, causing them to shun or misallocate to such asset classes. Therefore, while the theory suggests that agnostic investors have a greater multi-asset opportunity set than a sustainable investor, in practice the inverse can be true. This insight is supported by the demand among conventional investors for more sustainability expertise. In the years leading up to 2022, the hiring of sustainability professionals has been significant (Makower, 2021; Klasa and Masters, 2022). It suggests that incorporating sustainable practices into the investment value chain can enhance the investment process.

In summary, the practical examples and track record of modern multi-asset sustainable portfolios are too short to be rigorously decomposed and interrogated by academia. Yet there is a healthy indication that modern multi-asset sustainable portfolios need not be detrimental to investment performance and can, at least, capture the performance of their composite equity and debt components.

Modern multi-asset sustainable portfolios: Do they help people and the planet?

Short answer: Only as much as the underlying investments.

IN THEORY

Proponents of modern multi-asset portfolios advance theories as to why such portfolios should help people and the planet. Earlier in this chapter, we outlined how a multi-asset portfolio's impact would theoretically be neither greater nor less than that achieved by its composite single-asset-class holdings.

While the combination of individual assets into a multi-asset portfolio can, due to correlation, have a major positive or negative impact on risk-adjusted financial returns, the same is not true for the extent of the impact. The words of Nobel Prize-winning economist Harry Markowitz (Nobel Prize Organisation, 1990) that 'diversification is the only free lunch in finance' (Markowitz, 1952) thus only hold true for investment performance.

IN PRACTICE

The reality here mostly reflects the theory. Modern approaches to multi-asset sustainable portfolios do not achieve material impact beyond the sum of their composite parts. The one avenue through which such portfolios might do so is via signalling. But whether signalling does create additional, measurable real-world positive impact is contentious.

In 'Chapter 3 – Sustainable public equity markets', we first raised the concept. The idea of signalling is that by allocating capital an investor is making an explicit choice and raising awareness of what constitutes 'good' and 'bad' behaviour. In our analysis of equity signalling, we found little evidence to suggest that signalling caused company managements to alter their policies and actions. The conclusions in a multi-asset context, though, are less clear.

The waters are muddied by the largest institutional allocators of capital being multi-asset investors – namely, pension funds, insurance companies and sovereign wealth funds. These multi-asset investors have, to varying degrees, embraced sustainability and have contributed to the paradigm shift that has pushed sustainability up corporate and financial firm agendas (Shingler, 2021). The difficulty in validating or dismissing the impact of signalling arises from the need to disentangle correlation and causation. Has the steady embrace of sustainability by multi-asset investors triggered corporate change? Or did the prevailing zeitgeist migrate from the corporate to investment spheres?

In summary, despite signalling's potential value, it has not been rigorously tested as of 2022 by academics or in practical studies (Kölbel et al, 2020). On the balance of evidence, however, modern approaches to multi-asset sustainable portfolios do not appear to achieve a measurable and discernible impact beyond the sum of their composite parts.

In this interview, Simon sat down with Rick Lacaille to discuss sustainable investing with an emphasis upon multi-asset investing. Rick is executive vice president and global head of environmental, social and governance (ESG) initiatives at investment juggernaut State Street. Prior to this, Rick was the global chief investment officer (CIO) at State Street Global Advisors for more than a decade. He has thus witnessed first hand sustainable investing's growth as well as the challenges and opportunities that come with multi-asset investing.

Simon: Thanks for taking the time. Rick, you've worked in mainstream investing for several decades and now have a key sustainability role at one of the largest investment firms in the world. When it comes to sustainable investing's development, what has positively surprised you?

Rick: On the positive side, the sustainable investing landscape has become very granular in the way that the rest of investment already was. If you go back enough years, you could have, maybe, been a credit generalist. However, today that's rarely the case. Asset classes and investment expertise have evolved to the point where people have very narrow but deep areas of expertise in investments, analysis and research. I think it's the natural evolution of the investment practice to specialize more and more. On the positive side, that's becoming increasingly true of sustainable investing as well. There are deep areas of expertise that are beginning to connect with each other. So there's a maturing in the industry. Sustainable investing is not a static concept. People are looking for new opportunities to have an impact and they're exploring, increasingly, new areas. And I think that's a positive thing because when you look at it from an end result perspective, the more expertise that you can throw at something, the more specialized you can get, the more effective and efficient any enterprise becomes.

Simon: What about on the negative side?

Rick: The downside of that is, as in mainstream investing, ultimately you need to be able to put the picture back together again. If you are CIO you need to achieve some long-run investment outcome for a client and think holistically. People don't necessarily buy niches. They may value the expertise in a niche, but in the end, you need someone to put the kaleidoscope together in a way that achieves the overall objective that you really want. What's important is the ability to understand the component parts well and combine them in a way that makes sense for end investors in numerous different ways.

Simon: How do you see the approaches to sustainable investing?

Rick: I think impact investing is in a sense at one end of the spectrum, non-sustainable investing is the other, but one of the more interesting areas to explore is the area in the middle where you are integrating and actively trading off different aspects of the investment process. I'd offer a caveat as there is a degree of sophistication required, in the sense that there may not always be easy tradeoffs. You may need to invest with things that have challenges because you've got some other attribute that you value highly.

Simon: How does this come together in a multi-asset portfolio?

Rick: There are two challenges I would highlight. One is lack of product, in the sense that if you want a genuinely multi-asset portfolio consistent with your beliefs around sustainability, then there's probably quite significant gaps from an asset class or sub asset class perspective, where there simply isn't much being done. So that would be one of the observations. The other is that those who are putting the portfolios together may not be so mature in this area. So, if you look at where people have got deep sustainability expertise, it tends to be in the narrow product area. It's not necessarily at the CIO or the asset allocator level.

Simon: What's your view on some of the big sustainable debates – for example, exclusion versus engagement?

Rick: Firstly, so many are signed up to net zero alliances of various sorts. And that's great, they're expressing a strong viewpoint that they need to be part of the change process. However, I think that the tide is turning on divestment and even those who've advocated it previously seem to be altering their position a little. I think the reason they're doing that is not because engagement is obviously always going to work. We know that ultimately it may not. They are changing because divestment as a tool to change the real economy is coming under increasing challenge. I think for good reasons. And people are looking at different ways of approaching the problem. They're looking at some of the more difficult areas, such as coal. Divesting from, for example, coal might be an obvious way to avoid risk, but there are many countries in an emerging world that depend on coal for power generation, for electricity. If they can't turn the electricity on then we've got a problem. We need to be responsible when we decommission. We need to responsibly wind those [old coal-burning stations] down as we also invest in renewable electricity. I think that's one of the things that's changing. People are facing up to the fact that we may need to have capital invested in things that don't look very sustainable for a while in order to execute a good transition. So I think that's a change that's underway. There's still an enormous interest in high-impact investing as well. So I think they're on parallel tracks. You've got investors who will finance the brown decommissioning. You've got others who say, well, that's not me, I don't understand it or don't like it. I'm going to focus on high-impact renewables or nature-based solutions that will have more visible impact that's positive. But the reality is we need both.

Simon: For a multi-asset portfolio, where do see the best equity investment opportunities?

Rick: I don't want to become too short term on this subject. I think by best, I'm going to talk about best as in prospective, long-run returns. I think the best long-run returns will be almost certainly related to technology and hard science. And the reason I say that is we need not only to get to the net zero economy, but also to address the depletion of natural capital. The leverage points around technology are very, very valuable. So, if you take the example of electricity, we will be much more dependent on electricity, electricity generation distribution and related technologies in the future than we ever have been. If you look at the value added to the efficiency of that process – even fractionally – it's enormous. So, technology that will have incremental positive effects – let alone breakthrough changes – will be a really great place to be invested. I think what might be less interesting, although high volume, will be the basic infrastructure that we all need to get from 'A' to 'B'. Sure, there is going to be growth. There's going to be enormous capital expenditure and infrastructure needed to build a sustainable economy, but it may not be a very high return option. It may have many great sustainable and portfolio characteristics but it may not be a very high-return investment opportunity.

Simon: Within the multi-asset portfolio, public debt market (fixed income) solutions often stand out. What are your thoughts?

Rick: If we are to successfully achieve a low-carbon shift I think a lot of the capital will be fixed income. I also think that a lot of the money will be supported by other forms of capital or either philanthropic or through blended finance structure. There will be big opportunities for fixed income investors in emerging countries. Now there's a proviso. We need to make sure that some of the risks – risks that many investors are not well equipped to take – are absorbed either by multinational banks or some other new institutions. Some of the political and currency-related risks up front are quite challenging. If you look at it through the other end of the telescope, there will be a price to pay because there's so much capital required. And that means that fixed income investors will earn a reasonable spread on those investments. I think it's a little bit, it's analogous to the late 19th century, where you had this enormous buildout infrastructure around the world. Turning to green bonds specifically, it's a 2 trillion market now. We were involved at the very, very early stages and it was frustrating because there was a lack of liquidity. So, it's gone through the growth phase and now it's got liquidity, we've got good frameworks and good verification. That said, I think it's going to become a more complex area, again. If you think about the comments I made about brown assets, we have to ask whether there's a role for, if not a green bond, a light brown bond? Once the concept of use-of-proceeds has been established there's quite a significant potential for further specialization. Again, it comes back to this point at the beginning. You start with a sort of general idea and then as it becomes more sophisticated, you become a more granular specialist.

Simon: What role can private market investment play?

Rick: Private market investments have enormous potential because they have very clear lines of control over what happens in the business. So that's the beautiful thing about governance and impact within private markets. The snag they have at the moment is a lack of disclosure. However, I think there are many who are working on that. I think the underexplored area from a private market thematic perspective is nature-based capital. We need to find ways of channelling financial capital given the need to restore natural capital. There are some great businesses out there doing it, but they're not large. And I think the industry has struggled to think through what the value proposition is. How can I turn what's obviously a human need into a financial need and then a financial story? But I think that's a great untapped area. And I think the announcement on deforestation at COP 26 should get everyone in our business thinking, how can I participate? How can I assist this very important step that those nation states are taking to stop deforestation and to start afforestation?

Simon: Thank you, Rick.

The potential opportunities and how we might get there

Multi-asset class sustainable portfolios possess significant potential as they can represent the entirety of an individual's liquid financial wealth. Furthermore, large institutional investors such as pension funds, insurance companies and sovereign wealth funds predominantly operate in a multi-asset context.

Despite their potential though, holistic multi-asset sustainable approaches have been slower to develop than their single-asset-class counterparts. Traditional approaches to multi-asset investing were typically crude combinations of sustainable assets or the poorer cousins of conventional multi-asset approaches. While this situation has improved thanks to more modern approaches to sustainable multi-asset investing, significant challenges and therefore opportunities remain.

We focus on three potential opportunities by suggesting how we might get there. The first one calls for new sub-asset class solutions to enhance the investment opportunity set, typically, utilizing what we term 'dedicated assets'. The second suggests methods for incorporating alternatives into multi-asset portfolios for those investors lacking the wealth or the regulatory-defined sophistication to make large-scale alternative investments. And the third urges personalization. As the bench of sub-asset class solutions grows, so does the opportunity to tailor sustainable multi-asset portfolios to an individual's preferences.

New sub-asset classes

Use-of-proceeds bonds are well established and sustainability-linked bonds are growing rapidly in popularity and availability. It is time, in our view, to launch the next wave of dedicated assets that can populate multi-asset portfolios. We are greatly encouraged by the World Bank International Finance Corporation's (IFC) and Amundi's work to develop an emerging market green bond ecosystem (International Finance Corporation, 2017). Our outlook is also buoyed by the UK's Her Majesty's Royal Mint's efforts to create an investment product backed by recycled gold (HANetf, 2022). These are examples of industry players who seek to be catalytic and to further the investable universe for sustainable investors. However, we believe that the sustainable investment industry can go even further.

As discussed in 'Chapter 4 – Sustainable public debt markets', the use-of-proceeds model can evolve to target inefficiency and waste. Waste is a multi-trillion dollars a year issue and is present within every supply chain. While some sustainability-inclined corporate issuers have been struggling to match their operations to the existing green bond frameworks (De Santis et al, 2018), an explicit expansion of the frameworks to address waste would broaden the scope of the use-of-proceeds model and encourage participation from additional sectors. This concept finds support from State Street's Lacaille, who stated in our interview, 'You start with a sort of general idea and then, as it becomes more sophisticated, you become a more granular specialist.'

We also see the potential for the use-of-proceeds and green bond markets to expand into different sub-asset classes. The growth thus far, which encompasses the UK government's first green bond (HM Treasury, 2021), has been encouraging, but we believe the market can expand faster. Potential sub-sectors yet to benefit from this model include emerging market sovereign debt, both hard and local currency and inflation-linked bonds such as US TIPS (Treasury Inflation-Protected Securities).

In a sustainable multi-asset context, these sub-asset classes remain difficult to allocate to. They require investors either to resort to screens and integration or to use imperfect proxies. Given the rise of sustainability-linked bonds, there may be scope to combine the use-of-proceeds and sustainability-linked methodologies to create innovative solutions in these underrepresented sub-asset classes.

OPPORTUNITIES

Accelerate the growth of new sustainable sub-asset classes for sustainable multi-asset portfolios. Top of our list are waste reduction bonds to further expand the use-of-proceeds market. Underpinning innovation via public-private partnerships, such as the World Bank IFC and Amundi's sponsorship of the emerging market corporate green bond market, will likely turbo-charge growth.

Alternatives

In 'Chapter 5 – Sustainable private markets', we discussed a range of impact private market offerings issued by tier one conventional players such as TPG Rise, KKR and Apollo. For many individuals, however, access to private markets in a multi-asset context is restricted both by regulation (which ironically seeks to protect 'retail' investors) and by minimum ticket sizes that are prohibitively large.

In addition, within alternatives, a range of semi-liquid solutions, such as Microcredit (addressed in 'Chapter 4 – Sustainable public debt markets'), exists. Semi-liquid solutions can provide a degree of uncorrelated investment returns and, to some extent, have a positive impact. For institutional and retail investors alike, the sustainable multi-asset portfolio of the future would optimally include both illiquid and semi-liquid alternatives.

Regulation that governs investors' access to alternatives differs around the world. Even within the EU, regulatory regimes are not homogenous. Consequently, increasing the availability of alternatives within a sustainable multi-asset portfolio is a complex problem that requires a number of challenges to be resolved.

For example, within the EU, the wonderfully named Undertakings for the Collective Investment in Transferable Securities (UCITS) governs which investments can be sold to retail investors. In 2020, a ruling denied retail investors access to funds whose investment strategy is to grant loans from UCITS-eligibility (Ogier, 2020). The ruling effectively barred retail investors, as well as the multi-asset sustainable funds sold to them, from investing in microcredit, a sustainable semi-liquid debt alternative.

In the case of microcredit, certain workarounds can be found. For example, in the Netherlands an Alternative Investment Fund (AIF) can be used to own a microcredit, while in several jurisdictions a retail-specific microcredit share class can be combined with a segregated mandate. Such approaches are complex, however, and subject to legal opinion. This situation retards development of sustainable alternatives, particularly semi-liquid alternatives, from microcredit to agricultural finance and microinsurance.

OPPORTUNITIES

Simplify and harmonize the regulatory landscape to enable retail investors and sustainable multi-asset portfolios to invest responsibly in semi-liquid alternatives, such as microcredit.

Personalization

In 'Chapter 1 – What is sustainable investing?', we introduced the idea that what sustainability means can be highly personal. In fact, two rational individuals may disagree on what constitutes or does not constitute a sustainable company or investment.

As the sustainable multi-asset space matures, it is becoming increasingly possible to build multi-asset portfolios that emphasize different aspects of sustainability. For example, German asset manager DWS demonstrated in a 2022 research paper how a multi-asset portfolio can be conditioned to achieve a range of quantitative sustainable criteria, such as lower carbon emissions, waste volumes or water usage (Friede, G et al, 2022). Other leading investors such as JP Morgan and Credit Suisse have proposed low-carbon or decarbonization portfolios that target a specific niche or theme within sustainable investing (Hodges et al, 2022; Gifford, Stettler and Drew, 2021).

Personalization could be combined with our recommendations in 'Chapter 2 – Sustainable data and ESG ratings', where we argued for the need to develop a small pool of consistently reported corporate sustainability metrics. With consistent data, sustainable multi-asset portfolios could then be tailored to a range of investor preferences.

OPPORTUNITIES

Agree on a small number of sustainability metrics, reported consistency by all companies, to enable mass customization of end investors' multi-asset portfolios. This would increase retail investor engagement and accelerate adoption of sustainable investing.

References

Akgun, O T, Mudge, T J and Townsend, B (2021) How company size bias in ESG scores impacts the small cap investor, *The Journal of Impact and ESG Investing*, 1(4), pp 31–44, doi.org/10.3905/jesg.2021.1.022 (archived at https://perma.cc/64MF-T9M6)

Barko, T, Cremers, M and Renneboog, L (2017) Shareholder Engagement on Environmental, Social, and Governance Performance, SSRN Scholarly Paper 2977219, doi.org/10.2139/ssrn.2977219 (archived at https://perma.cc/2XLH-VBT4)

BBC Food (no date) How do supermarkets tempt you to spend more money? www.bbc.co.uk/food/articles/how_supermarkets_tempt (archived at https://perma.cc/SS6U-9XJS)

Bedel, E and Purcell, J (2022) Should private client portfolios be sustainable by default? Professional Wealth Management, www.pwmnet.com/Comment/Great-Debate/Should-private-client-portfolios-be-sustainable-by-default (archived at https://perma.cc/8C2K-58YA)

Berk, J B and van Binsbergen, J H (2017) Regulation of Charlatans in High-Skill Professions, Working Paper 23696, National Bureau of Economic Research, doi.org/10.3386/w23696 (archived at https://perma.cc/FVY5-L7Q7)

BloombergNEF (2022) Sustainable debt issuance breezed past $1.6 trillion in 2021, 12 January, about.bnef.com/blog/sustainable-debt-issuance-breezed-past-1-6-trillion-in-2021/ (archived at https://perma.cc/7F6H-9WE9)

Campbell, J Y et al (2002) Have individual stocks become more volatile? An empirical exploration of idiosyncratic risk, *The Journal of Finance*, 56(1), pp 1–43, doi.org/10.1111/0022-1082.00318 (archived at https://perma.cc/HXP8-5TNK)

Conde-Herman, P C (2014) UBS launches dedicated 'values-based' investment team in APAC, SRP, structuredretailproducts.com/News/Details?id=19832 (archived at https://perma.cc/R3P8-JQJL)

De Santis, R A et al (2018) Purchases of green bonds under the Eurosystem's asset purchase programme, ECB Economic Bulletin, (7/2018), www.ecb.europa.eu/pub/economic-bulletin/focus/2018/html/ecb.ebbox201807_01.en.html (archived at https://perma.cc/5GUA-6HJC)

Deese, B et al (2019) Sustainability: The bond that endures, BlackRock Investment Institute, www.blackrock.com/us/individual/literature/whitepaper/bii-sustainable-investing-bonds-november-2019.pdf (archived at https://perma.cc/6E4D-YYT5)

Dimson, E, Karakaş, O and Li, X (2015) Active ownership, *Review of Financial Studies*, 28(12), pp 3225–68, doi.org/10.1093/rfs/hhv044 (archived at https://perma.cc/6HB9-J8MA)

Domian, D L, Louton, D A and Racine, M D (2007) Diversification in portfolios of individual stocks: 100 stocks are not enough, Financial Review, 42(4), pp 557–70, doi.org/10.1111/j.1540-6288.2007.00183.x (archived at https://perma.cc/4J5Z-F3FN)

Dunga, Y et al (2019) Social capitalism: Incorporating sustainability factors into macroeconomic analysis, VoxEU, 25 March, voxeu.org/article/incorporating-sustainability-factors-macroeconomic-analysis (archived at https://perma.cc/P4A2-SQHW)

DWS (2021) DWS launches euro and US dollar Xtrackers corporate green bond ETFs, DWS, etf.dws.com/en-gb/about-us/press-releases/dws-launches-euro-and-us-dollar-xtrackers-corporate-green-bond-etfs/ (archived at https://perma.cc/DT3Q-9XNS)

Evans, J L and Archer, S H (1968) Diversification and the reduction of dispersion: An empirical analysis, *The Journal of Finance*, 23(5), pp 761–67, doi.org/10.1111/j.1540-6261.1968.tb00315.x (archived at https://perma.cc/AMN6-8HVD)

Fisher, L and Lorie, J H (1970) Some studies of variability of returns on investments in common stocks, *The Journal of Business*, 43(2), pp 99–134.

Friede, G et al (2022) ESG in strategic asset allocation: The 2022 update, DWS, www.dws.com/insights/global-research-institute/esg-in-strategic-asset-allocation-the-2022-update/ (archived at https://perma.cc/6KEZ-XJJC)

Gambera, M, Primmer, R and Finney, L (2021) Asset allocation for an ESG world, UBS, www.ubs.com/global/en/assetmanagement/insights/thematic-viewpoints/sustainable-impact-investing/articles/asset-allocation-for-an-esg-world.html (archived at https://perma.cc/PD3W-B6KU)

Gifford, J, Stettler, A and Drew, M (2021) The decarbonizing portfolio, Credit Suisse

HANetf (2022) The Royal Mint partners with Quintet Private Bank to introduce the use of recycled gold in an exchange-traded commodity, www.hanetf.com/article/1162/the-royal-mint-partners-with-quintet-private-bank-to-introduce-the-use-of-recycled-gold-in-an-exchange-traded-commodity (archived at https://perma.cc/S454-79C6)

Harper, J (2020) How much gold is there left to mine in the world? BBC News, 23 September, www.bbc.com/news/business-54230737 (archived at https://perma.cc/7S9J-DVTE)

Hermes Investment (no date), Hermes responsible ownership principles, www.hermes-investment.com/ukw/wp-content/uploads/sites/80/2018/03/final-responsible-ownership-principles-2018.pdf (archived at https://perma.cc/3RVW-DFL9)

Hildebrand, P et al (2021) Launching climate-aware class return expectations, BlackRock Investment Institute, www.blackrock.com/corporate/insights/

blackrock-investment-institute/publications/investing-in-climate-awareness (archived at https://perma.cc/V9JR-DPZA)

Hinkel, A (2021) From gold recycling to urban mining, Xetra-Gold, www.xetra-gold.com/en/gold-news/from-gold-recycling-to-urban-mining/ (archived at https://perma.cc/5TV6-8PZL)

HM Treasury (2021) Second UK Green Gilt raises further £6 billion for green projects, GOV.UK, www.gov.uk/government/news/second-uk-green-gilt-raises-further-6-billion-for-green-projects (archived at https://perma.cc/8EF8-VCM5)

Hodges, P et al (2022) Net-zero investing for multi-asset portfolios seeking to satisfy Paris-aligned benchmark requirements with climate alpha signals, *The Journal of Portfolio Management*, 48(4), pp 33–58, doi.org/10.3905/jpm.2022.1.334 (archived at https://perma.cc/X37U-Q3QL)

Impact Management Project (2018) Guide to classifying the impact of investments, impactmanagementproject.com/investor/new-guide-to-mapping-the-impact-of-investments/ (archived at https://perma.cc/V2UC-KNJW)

International Finance Corporation (2017) IFC, Amundi to create world's largest green-bond fund dedicated to emerging markets, pressroom.ifc.org/all/pages/PressDetail.aspx?ID=24624 (archived at https://perma.cc/SXM7-H58U)

Klasa, M and Masters, B (2022) Sustainable investing boom prompts fierce fight for talent, *Financial Times*, 21 March, www.ft.com/content/fe5853a4-ba3e-434a-abe0-1b43c094ae85 (archived at https://perma.cc/ZG85-9BYH)

Kölbel, J F et al (2020) Can sustainable investing Save the world? Reviewing the mechanisms of investor impact, *Organization & Environment*, 33(4), pp 554–74, doi.org/10.1177/1086026620919202 (archived at https://perma.cc/Y3GQ-GXYF)

Makower, J (2021) Inside the war for ESG talent [Blog] Greenbiz, www.greenbiz.com/article/inside-war-esg-talent (archived at https://perma.cc/BWJ2-UJQT)

Markowitz, H (1952) Portfolio selection, *The Journal of Finance*, 7(1), p 77, doi.org/10.2307/2975974 (archived at https://perma.cc/JBL9-8LE4)

McDonald's rolling out green logo in Europe (2009) NBC News, www.nbcnews.com/id/wbna34111784 (archived at https://perma.cc/P2UC-N3YS)

McGachey, K (2019) M&G rolls out sustainable multi-asset fund, ESG Clarity, 26 February, esgclarity.com/mg-rolls-out-sustainable-multi-asset-fund/ (archived at https://perma.cc/VAS8-CACX)

Morgan Stanley (2017) Sustainable signals: New data from individual investor, www.morganstanley.com/pub/content/dam/msdotcom/ideas/sustainable-signals/pdf/Sustainable_Signals_Whitepaper.pdf (archived at https://perma.cc/FNK7-QDJP)

Morningstar (2022) Global sustainable fund flows report, www.morningstar.com/lp/global-esg-flows (archived at https://perma.cc/5P5C-VJBE)

MSCI (2021) Factor focus: Value, www.msci.com/documents/1296102/8473352/Value-brochure.pdf (archived at https://perma.cc/7BUT-74WN)

Mutua, D C and Raimonde, O (2021) Runaway ESG debt issuance poised for fresh boost from junk sales, Bloomberg, 23 December, www.bloomberg.com/news/articles/2021-12-23/runaway-esg-debt-issuance-to-see-junk-bump-as-scrutiny-rises (archived at https://perma.cc/9AJU-8X7W)

Nobel Prize Organisation (1990) The Sveriges Riksbank Prize in Economic Sciences in memory of Alfred Nobel 1990 [Blog] NobelPrize.org, www.nobelprize.org/prizes/economic-sciences/1990/press-release/ (archived at https://perma.cc/R8E8-ARQW)

Ogier (2020) CSSF prohibition of loan investments for UCITS [Blog] Ogier, 27 August, www.ogier.com/publications/cssf-prohibition-of-loan-investments-for-ucits (archived at https://perma.cc/XSZ2-N5Q2)

Patton, L (2013) McDonald's pushing meat as salads fail to lure diners, Bloomberg, 29 May, www.bloomberg.com/news/articles/2013-05-29/mcdonald-s-pushing-meat-as-salads-fail-to-lure-diners (archived at https://perma.cc/BJM6-ZPYX)

Perraudin, W, Powell, A and Yang, P (2016) Multilateral Development Bank Ratings and Preferred Creditor Status, IDB Working Paper Series IDB-WP-697, publications.iadb.org/publications/english/document/Multilateral-Development-Bank-Ratings-and-Preferred-Creditor-Status.pdf (archived at https://perma.cc/QY8Q-WM2M)

Quintet (2022) 2021 Annual Report, www.quintet.com/getmedia/51a62c9c-387c-4948-a395-2aa62848f618/2021-annual-report-quintet-private-bank.pdf (archived at https://perma.cc/A68M-8GMW)

Rohleder, M, Wilkens, M and Zink, J (2022) The effects of mutual fund decarbonization on stock prices and carbon emissions, *Journal of Banking & Finance*, 134(C), ideas.repec.org/a/eee/jbfina/v134y2022ics0378426621003034.html (archived at https://perma.cc/XN24-5MTX)

Rooks, M (2022) How many products are in a typical grocery store? ICSID, 16 February, www.icsid.org/uncategorized/how-many-products-are-in-a-typical-grocery-store/ (archived at https://perma.cc/2GWS-M72H)

Schnabel, I (2022) A new age of energy inflation: climateflation, fossilflation and greenflation, European Central Bank, www.ecb.europa.eu/press/key/date/2022/html/ecb.sp220317_2~dbb3582f0a.en.html (archived at https://perma.cc/88CQ-4VYN)

Shingler, T (2021) Callan survey finds nearly 50 per cent of respondents incorporate ESG, Highest level ever, Callan, www.callan.com/blog-archive/2021-esg-survey/ (archived at https://perma.cc/26Q9-UB84)

Spinoso, M, Purcell, J and Street, B (2021) Strategy primer: Sustainable dedicated assets, Quintet Private Bank, www.quintet.com/en-gb/articles/strategy-primer-sustainable-dedicated-assets (archived at https://perma.cc/6ZFW-8P3G)

Statman, M (1987) How many stocks make a diversified portfolio, *The Journal of Financial and Quantitative Analysis*, 22(3), pp 353–63, doi.org/10.2307/2330969 (archived at https://perma.cc/E44K-Q339)

Taylor, K (2020) McDonald's hasn't served a single salad in almost nine months, and it's part of a strategy helping the chain cash in during the pandemic, *Business Insider*, 3 December, www.businessinsider.com/mcdonalds-salads-disappeared-from-menu-april-2020-2020-12 (archived at https://perma.cc/3ZTN-KC4Q)

UBS (2019) Invest for good, www.ubs.com/content/dam/assets/wma/us/shared/documents/Sustainable_Investing_Brochure.pdf? (archived at https://perma.cc/BEU9-6F6F)

UBS (2020) UBS makes sustainable investments the preferred recommendation for clients of its US $ 2.6 trillion global wealth management business, UBS, www.ubs.com/global/en/media/display-page-ndp/en-20200910-gwm-si.html (archived at https://perma.cc/ZX9R-VHBL)

UBS (2022) UBS ETF (LU) Sustainable development bank bonds UCITS ETF (USD) A-dis | LU1852212965 | UBS Netherlands, UBS, www.ubs.com/nl/en/asset-management/etf-private/etf-products/etf-product-detail.html (archived at https://perma.cc/7F6Q-YJC3)

UEFA (no date) Euro 2004: History, UEFA.com, www.uefa.com/uefaeuro/history/seasons/2004/ (archived at https://perma.cc/H3VA-XJYH)

UNPR1 (2018) How ESG engagement creates value for investors and companies, Principles for Responsible Investment, www.unpri.org/research/how-esg-engagement-creates-value-for-investors-and-companies/3054.article (archived at https://perma.cc/U4LA-5LLA)

Walsh, S W (1986) McDonald's tosses up a salad, *Washington Post*, 10 April, www.washingtonpost.com/archive/business/1986/04/10/mcdonalds-tosses-up-a-salad/4a37a920-d7c2-43b0-a2e5-dd6c1042db84/ (archived at https://perma.cc/S2TN-WGB8)

Wattiau, P et al (2022) Capital markets and climate change, Wellington Management, www.wellington.com/en/insights/climate-change-capital-market-assumptions-us/ (archived at https://perma.cc/B2NM-KQJG)

World Gold Council (no date) Gold supply, www.gold.org/gold-supply (archived at https://perma.cc/6XJL-L7PY)

Conclusion

Introduction

All good things must come to an end. Whether it's Tony Montana going out in a blaze of machine-gun glory in 1983's *Scarface* or Joe Montana completing 16 sensational NFL seasons with the San Francisco 49ers and Kansas City Chiefs, ultimately, you've got to finish your huckleberries and honey (the state of Montana's most famous food products, for the uninitiated) and call it day.

And so we reach the end of *Sustainable Investing in Practice: ESG challenges and opportunities*. In this final chapter, we aim to tie together various threads in the following three sections.

The first, 'How we might get there', consolidates the multiple opportunities we've highlighted throughout the book into three aggregated observations. Bundling common themes and our repeated asks, we call for *simplification, personalization* and *impact*. These three actions, if adopted, can help us to reach a place where sustainable investing's popularity booms, its resilience rises and its outcomes are achieved for the betterment of people and the planet.

The second section, 'Opportunities', goes deeper and brings together, in sequential order, all our recommendations in one ambitious place. We hope that this section inspires our readers: students, finance professionals, regulators, development practitioners, activists and anyone else waist deep in the subject. While time will undoubtedly prove some of our suggestions impractical or outright wrong, we expect that the combined brainpower of our readers will borrow, adapt and iterate some of these concepts and ideas into power programmes that drive positive change.

The third and final section, 'In practice', is the closest we come to offering advice. Unlike the previous sections that focus on ideas for the industry, we share here three learnings from our practical experience. We think that they have relevance beyond our own careers and can nudge readers into pushing for both greater commercial success and the greater good – even if their ideas and identified opportunities differ from ours. Our first learning, 'What people say and what they do are different', dives into the folly of sustainability-focused surveys and discusses how to adjust your tactics and responses accordingly. The second, 'The importance of the mass middle', cautions against designing solutions that appeal solely to 'true believers' or those otherwise enthusiastic about sustainable investing. In the final observation, 'Creating win-wins', we remind readers about the power of incentives for producing commercial yet credible outcomes.

How we might get there

We've ended each of the last seven chapters with a section entitled 'The potential opportunities and how we might get there'. These sections took the challenges identified earlier in each chapter and sought to pinpoint practical opportunities that have the potential to bring about meaningful positive impact.

We sought to avoid hubris, acknowledged our fallibility and drew on our experience as industry practitioners. In most cases, the opportunities we spotlighted already had their first promising shoots poking into view and we tried to find solutions that aligned stakeholder incentives and avoided impractical ivory tower ideas.

Across these 21 opportunities, we wrote about three common topics that, to our mind, signpost the way towards achieving the realistic goals we spelt out. The three topics are *Simplification, Personalization* and *Impact.*

Simplification

This book is filled with observations about the myriad terms, standards and approaches that proliferate in the sustainable investing community. We argue that, while a degree of ambiguity pervades financial markets, sustainable investing stands alone as a discipline characterized and defined by it.

Disappointingly, attempts to address this situation often muddy the waters further, as the temptation arises, in trying to make yourself understood, to (re)define what *you* mean when using certain sustainability phrases. We lament how uncertainty results as readily from too much terminology as from no shared vocabulary at all. It also follows that the incentive to misbehave, such as by inflating one's sustainable asset figures, intensifies when uncertainty is greatest. Put plainly, in the absence of clear rules, the likelihood of misrepresentation increases.

The problem of non-standardized definitions and methodologies is, unfortunately, not likely to vanish anytime soon as it is perpetuated by what psychologists term 'additive bias' (*The Economist*, 2021). Humans, when confronted with a challenge, typically seek to resolve it by 'adding' rather than 'subtracting'. This bias manifests itself in everything from domestic do-it-yourself projects (add just one more screw to that sagging shelving unit) to initiatives at work that limp along when another steering committee is formed.

In our attempts to avoid becoming another victim of this bias, many opportunities we identify in this book already have precedents in the market. Achieving more optimal outcomes, we believe, will require individuals, corporates and regulators to put their egos aside and back horses already in the race rather than seek to enter new ones in it.

This is easier said than done. But aiming for minimum standards rather than common ones seems to us a useful start. The quest for perfection is often the enemy of the good and can lead to regulations and taxonomies whose excessive detail is certain to provoke opposition, splinter coalitions and stall progress. There is nothing preventing a willing stakeholder from exceeding minimum standards, disclosing additional information or developing a more complex process. Plenty, we know from experience, stops a stakeholder from signing on to a complicated or burdensome set of rules.

Several motifs and comparisons occur across the opportunities we write about, none more often or vividly than nutritional information. Food packaging labels are wonderful. They offer a (sorry) digestible amount of data that is measured consistently and presented clearly. A consumer can make quick, informed decisions based on it. The body-builder, for instance, might focus on the protein and carbohydrate content of a product while the traditional dieter will count calories.

By adopting similar practices, the sustainable investing ecosystem will get closer to where it needs to be, we believe. Clear, consistent, simple frameworks and regulations create a common base and vocabulary that encourage market participants to participate and innovate. This innovation, in turn, will stimulate greater real-world impact and enable providers to personalize their offerings and meet the needs of clients who may hold a diversity of views.

HOW WE MIGHT GET THERE

Collectively, we need to overcome additive bias and seek simplification. Developing more frameworks, standards and principles only complicates things further. Sustainable practitioners who employ complex vocabulary to prolong debate and tease out endless nuances rather than pursue solutions can hinder real-world change just as much as those who refute sustainable investing.

Personalization

In what may be a controversial opinion in these politically polarized times, we contend that two rational individuals are entitled to form considered opinions and disagree with each other. Sustainability is rarely binary, coloured as it is by shades of green. Some broad trends are identifiable, of course: controversial weapons are normally seen as 'bad' and renewable energy production is typically regarded as 'good'. But personal preferences differ and diversity has an essential role to play.

Some individuals, for instance, will express a strong aversion to investing in tobacco stocks. Others will not. Some may consider nuclear power a key technology for a low-carbon future. Others may fear reactors melting like ice lollies in the sun.

Preference-based investing can also reflect cultural or religious beliefs. Alcohol is forbidden in some Islamic countries but forms an integral part of social culture in most of Europe. What seems normal to one individual may appal another. With values there is rarely any objective right or wrong.

It's with this in mind that most of the opportunities we present highlight the potential for, and the value of, personalization. If sustainable investing is to achieve true scale and deliver an outsized positive impact for people and the planet, a one-size-fits-all model is unlikely to work. Homogeneity often fails to generate the desired client engagement and can lead to clients discovering that the sustainable investment they purchased does not appear, to them, sustainable.

Our call for personalization might evoke thoughts of higher costs, greater complexity and a subsequent lack of commerciality. The opposite is true, we argue. The desirable commercial attributes generated by sustainable investing, namely, faster growth, increased retention and superior price realization, only manifest if end-clients have an emotional stake in their investments. Because clients have different views, personalization becomes essential to creating a connection and elevating an investment from a mere transaction to a value-added service. By contrast, sustainability in name only is unlikely to generate much enthusiasm or commercial success.

HOW WE MIGHT GET THERE

The path to scale, commercial success and benefits for people and the planet originates in personalization, in our view. Personalization generates emotive reactions and emotive reactions stir action and investment. To advance sustainable goals in a real way, personalization needs to be informed by our previous recommendation – simplification. Technical jargon acts as a barrier to widespread adoption.

Impact

As practitioners and proponents of sustainable investing we work to catalyse real-world impact for the benefit of all.

We are well aware that global temperatures go on rising, that many millions of people still live in poverty, and that a range of social justice causes remain, sadly, unfulfilled. These challenges continue to exist despite a rapid increase in sustainable investing's popularity and an explosion of sustainable-themed government and corporate policy, commitments and marketing communications.

As a result, many of our opportunities centre on increasing positive real-world impact. The growth of sustainable investing, as we have illustrated, has not been particularly impact-intensive, and changing this unfortunate fact requires, we contend, an honest assessment of real-world impact. Broadly speaking, impact stems from altering either a company's behaviour or its capital structure to facilitate sustainable growth.

In public markets, our identified opportunities include investors fully leveraging their power and authority by engaging with public companies and adopting a more activist tone. This increased activism can be combined with scalable public market investments that marry liquidity with real-world effects. In 'Chapter 3 – Sustainable public equity markets', we use the example of climate funds that measure their portfolio's carbon footprint and simultaneously plant trees to sequester an equivalent amount of carbon dioxide. We also see potential in embracing current and future dedicated assets, such as waste-reduction bonds.

We regard private markets as having the greatest potential to do good. Many private market strategies enable investors to purchase a controlling interest in a company and repurpose and retool it to create powerful effective change. We argue for incorporating private market investments into multi-asset portfolios to increase their adoption. We also see the potential to expand impact investing within private markets beyond its growth equity heartland to areas such as venture capital and private debt.

HOW WE MIGHT GET THERE

Sustainable investing has not been particularly impact-intensive and changing this unfortunate fact requires, we contend, an honest assessment of real-world impact. To channel capital to activities that truly have a real-world impact necessitates both simplification and personalization. Greater transparency and simplification will give end-investors more clarity about whether their investments are having a material impact. With increased personalization comes deeper engagement, which leads to larger sums being invested in a more impactful fashion.

Opportunities

This section is for readers who scream, 'Give me solutions, not problems!' We've extracted (and shortened) all the opportunities identified in the previous chapters from the recurring sections entitled 'The potential opportunities and how we might get there'.

Chapter 1 – What is Sustainable Investing?

'Chapter 1 – What is Sustainable Investing?' highlighted numerous challenges. They included the lack of standard definitions and the large discrepancy in market size estimates. There are also myriad ways that sustainable investors construct their strategies, a heterogeneity that creates 'horizontal hostility' – conflict among practitioners – within the sustainable investing community and often leaves end-investors baffled and reluctant to invest. We identified three key stakeholders – retail investors, institutional investors and regulators – who need to work in concert to seize the opportunities we enumerated.

RETAIL INVESTORS

Making information more transparent would aid retail investors, enabling them to reach their own informed decisions. Nutritional information labels found on food packaging – a consistent, straightforward listing of fat, protein and salt content – is the analogue here. For financial products, we envisage a set of simple, understandable disclosures on popular sustainable topics such as climate, diversity and waste, issued in a consistent format across companies and funds. The principle would expand on standard retail investor practices that currently make use of a limited number of financial metrics, such as price-to-earnings ratios, dividend yields and return on equity.

Steps are already being taken in this direction. The groundwork for disclosures about how companies *act* is being laid by the Sustainability Accounting Standards Board (SASB) in its merger into the International Financial Reporting Standards Foundation (IFRS). Meanwhile, the EU's sustainable legislative package includes the Taxonomy for Sustainable Activities. This classification system publishes lists and thresholds for environmentally sustainable economic activities, essentially defining sustainability for what companies *do*.

An optimal playing field for retail investors will require further regulatory support as well as significant simplification to ensure commerciality.

> OPPORTUNITIES
>
> Seek a limited number of sustainable disclosures applicable to companies and investment products to help investors understand exactly what they are purchasing and enable them to choose the instruments appropriately.

INSTITUTIONAL INVESTORS

The crux of the problem for institutional investors, who shift huge sums of capital and have considerable expertise, is the lack of clear definitions and measurement metrics.

The solution we envision relies on incentivizing institutional investors by showcasing the value of their processes and expertise, the very things that justify their fees. Institutional investors need shared definitions of sustainable investing strategies so that customers can compare like with like and be impressed (or not) with a given institution's approach.

The exact definitions themselves are of secondary importance to their establishment. We do see potential avenues for progress. They could draw on nascent frameworks such as what was proposed by the IIF in 2019 (IIF, 2019) or be derived from the work of regulators, such as the EU's Sustainable Finance Disclosure Regulation.

Once armed with a consistent set of definitions, institutional investors can spend less time clarifying what they are talking about and more time showcasing their capabilities. This will better align client needs with institutional investor delivery and is likely to facilitate greater innovation and real-world impact.

OPPORTUNITIES

Align to a single set of clear definitions to describe different sustainable investing strategies.

REGULATORS

Regulators set the 'rules of the game' and can have considerable real-world impact through the incentives they create. Given that the sustainable investing industry has failed to self-regulate, the answer to the fundamental question 'What is sustainable investing?' unfortunately falls to regulators to mediate and resolve.

Faced with sustainability's heterogeneity, regulators have the opportunity to draw up minimum standards based on principles rather than all-encompassing, rules-based taxonomies.

Any regulatory program also necessitates strict, able enforcement. Financial regulators can take inspiration from the increasingly tough line that the EU has adopted with so-called 'Big Tech'. For example, in 2018, Google was hit with a $5 billion fine for allegedly forcing smartphone manufacturers using its Android operating system to pre-install its search and browser apps on devices (Newell, 2019).

OPPORTUNITIES

Write a handful of definitions for what is expected from a given sustainable approach. Mandate a limited number of corporate disclosures supported by strong enforcement.

Chapter 2 – Sustainable data and ESG ratings

In 'Chapter 2 – Sustainable data and ESG ratings', we outlined problems with unaudited, self-originated data and with companies either not reporting necessary information or doing so using non-standardized measurement units and units with a unique scope. We also underlined the dangers of simplifying complex issues by reducing them to a single rating or number and showed how ratings diverge due to (often non-transparent) methodological differences. Again, we identified three key stakeholders – retail investors, institutional investors and corporations – who could benefit from the opportunities we put forth.

RETAIL INVESTORS

The average person doesn't require hundreds of data points to make a decision. A half-dozen is usually enough. Developing a small number of consistent indicators applicable to all companies, regardless of materiality, would improve the general population's understanding of, and engagement with, sustainable investing.

Exactly which indicators should be selected is of secondary importance to establishing them. Armed with key sustainability information similar to the way in which dieters, reading labels, can count the calories of the products they consume, one retail investor could focus their investments on water while another could emphasize diversity.

Small practical moves have already been made. A 2020 World Economic Forum (WEF) report identified 'A set of 21 more-established or critically important metrics and disclosures' for all companies (World Economic Forum, 2020).

A set of consistent metrics would enable wealth managers to pursue mass customization of retail portfolios that focus on investors' specific values and preferences. Each metric could also be weighted to create a single overall personalized score. Variants of this approach have already been tested in the market.

> OPPORTUNITIES
>
> Agree on a small number of sustainability metrics, reported consistently by all companies, to enable mass customization of retail investors' portfolios and boost retail investor engagement and adoption.

INSTITUTIONAL INVESTORS

In the institutional sphere, a limited number of consistent sustainable data points provides a good base, but the analysis undertaken by these more sophisticated investors requires that greater sector-specific information be reported and presented in a consistent manner.

Institutional investors could wait for regulators to decide what data they will receive, but we urge them to actively shape the future by backing a proverbial horse. Our favoured thoroughbred is the integrated ISSB, formed by the coming together of SASB and IFRS. The ISSB combines what is arguably the most preferred corporate reporting framework with a broader, more established accounting standard.

To get there and seize this opportunity, institutional investors will have to make their voices heard by lobbying corporates and regulators alike to align to a common set of standards. Larry Fink, CEO at BlackRock, has publicly led the way in this regard.

> OPPORTUNITIES
>
> Actively shape the future by pressing for consistent, sector-specific disclosure regulations that enable sustainability factors to be fully integrated into the investment process.

CORPORATIONS

Of all stakeholders, corporations are in the toughest position. They are constantly pulled in multiple directions as regulators, stock exchanges, data aggregators and accolade givers all clamour for information. It's no wonder that 58 per cent of executives want a single sustainability reporting standard and 66 per cent are prepared to support mandatory, legally binding issuance of sustainability reports (Bernow et al, 2019).

Like their institutional investor counterparts, they can take an active role in shaping the future by supporting the SASB and IFRS combination. They can also accelerate real-world impact by adopting integrated reporting, which involves including sustainability information into pre-existing financial reports with the same rigour as audits do. In addition, they can back impact-focused initiatives such as the Harvard-designed product, impact-weighted accounts.

> OPPORTUNITIES
>
> Align to a single reporting framework, further integrate sustainability information into financial accounts and focus on real-world impacts, both positive and negative.

Chapter 3 – Sustainable public equity markets

In 'Chapter 3 – Sustainable public equity markets', we reviewed the processes of exclusion, integration and engagement and highlighted a host of challenges. Exclusion suffers due to imperfect data and differing cultural norms. Integration is challenged by its nebulous nature and is consequently difficult to assess. Engagement, meanwhile, faces difficulties due to a lack of accountability and clear cause and effect. The equity asset class, as a whole, is often criticized for its lack of real-world positive impact. The opportunities we identify focus on standardization (for exclusion and integration), a more authoritative stance (engagement) and addressing public equities' historical lack of impact.

EXCLUSION AND INTEGRATION

Heterogeneous industry processes and standards and the effort of communicating how sustainable investment processes operate can be improved by using standardized sustainability data. If public equity products disclosed consistent metrics for all their holdings on such popular topics as water and waste, a clear picture with a central thread running through it would emerge throughout the sustainable investing industry. This consistent approach to data would start with a presence in corporate reporting, form part of public equity product disclosure and enable retail investors to act on their preferences in an informed way.

Seizing this opportunity would not preclude institutional investors from adopting additional, more complex exclusionary or integration approaches. Our proposal would merely create a tangible entry point for retail investors to demonstrate their preferences and understand the holdings within their portfolio, as well as the activities of the companies in which they invest.

OPPORTUNITIES

Define a small number of sustainability metrics and ensure that all public equity products report them consistently. This would promote mass customization of retail investors' portfolios and increase the adoption of sustainable investing practices.

ENGAGEMENT

Engagement can be made more effective, we think, by adopting and acting from a more authoritative position. Practitioners of sustainable engagement can take inspiration from activist shareholders and seek to reorient corporate business models toward a more sustainable and profitable future. Such an opportunity, we acknowledge, may require an infusion of traditional activist talent.

A less ambitious opportunity is to further the rights and reach of shareholders by expanding shareholder resolutions at annual general meetings (AGMs). Institutional investors can step up their activity further and retail investors can pool their efforts through organizations such as As You Sow, which attempt to 'seed' change and rally retail shareholders. This type of approach has the potential to be far reaching, as countless companies, regardless of sector or economic activities, can be subject to shareholder resolutions.

Importantly, to get there, further regulatory support is needed. For example, in the US, a public company can petition the US Securities Exchange Commission (SEC) to strike would-be shareholder proposals off its AGM agenda (Johnson and Kerber, 2021). In various jurisdictions, shareholder rights may need to be reviewed and strengthened.

> OPPORTUNITIES
>
> Institutional investors could carry out engagement in increasingly activist terms. They could fight to increase the number of shareholder proposals at AGMs and, in jurisdictions where it's necessary, alter legislation to ensure that well-thought-out proposals make it onto the ballot.

IMPACTING PEOPLE AND THE PLANET

Public equities suffer from a lack of real-world impact. Buying and selling securities in a liquid secondary market has limited to no effect on a company's cost of capital, so allocation decisions have little effect on people and the planet.

A sizeable opportunity beckons. A public equity product that makes a tangible real-world difference needs to be defined and brought to market, all while maintaining the investment's risk-adjusted return and liquidity profile (typically, daily or intraday), which is a prerequisite for retail investor participation.

A rudimentary offering might involve donating part of the management fees from a public equity product to charity (Perron, 2020; Kennedy, 2022). In this model, the greater the assets in the fund, the greater the charitable donation, which could demonstrably benefit the world. However, retail investors could legitimately wonder why the management fee isn't simply lower to begin with, which would allow them to choose which charity, if any, they'd like to support.

A more advanced approach linked to fund assets has been pioneered by Belgium asset manager Candriam (Schroeder, 2019) and the Luxembourg bank Quintet (Quintet Private Bank, n.d.). In both cases, the managers operate thematic climate funds. They measure the carbon footprint of their investments, acknowledging responsibility for their ownership share of each investee company's emissions.

Using this figure, they offset or sequester the same amount of CO_2 through concrete actions, such as reforestation. The real-world benefits are directly linked to their funds' holdings and investment process. If the fund manager invests in carbon-intensive public equities, then the cost of offsetting increases, thereby lowering the firm's profits.

OPPORTUNITIES

Develop public equity financial products that deliver tangible, evidence-based, real-world impact. They may include climate funds that deploy exclusion, integration and engagement, along with a commitment to climate neutrality pursued by counterbalancing activities such as reforestation projects.

Chapter 4 – Sustainable public debt markets

The challenges identified in 'Chapter 4 – Sustainable public debt markets' are numerous. We argued that the traditional approaches of exclusion, integration and engagement are either more difficult to apply within public debt markets than equities or have less investment value. We also assessed dedicated assets – debt investments that contain features unique to sustainability. While excited by them, we enumerated obstacles that hinder standardization, scale and market accessibility. To address these challenges, we highlight opportunities for investors, regulators and issuers of debt. These three stakeholders, when working in concert, have the potential to transform sustainable public debt markets.

INVESTORS

Multilateral development bank debt, we contend, should become mainstream and take its overdue place within most conventional investor portfolios. With their 70-year issuance history, 0.99 correlation to traditional risk-free asset (US treasuries) and a half-trillion dollars of debt outstanding, these bonds are perhaps the most under-appreciated and underutilized financial asset by average investors.

In 2018, the Swiss-domiciled bank UBS created the world's first exchange-traded fund for multilateral development bank debt. It enables investors, retail and institutional alike, to access a diversified pool of US $ denominated bonds (UBS, 2022). In 2020, BlackRock, the world's largest asset manager, launched a competing product (UBS, 2020).

> **OPPORTUNITIES**
>
> Mainstream investors should adopt multilateral development bank debt as a mainstay allocation within their multi-asset investment portfolios.

REGULATORS

Stronger, more consistent regulation across dedicated assets such as green bonds and sustainability-linked bonds is essential for further asset growth and high-quality issuance. It would boost investor confidence and accelerate dedicated asset adoption and development.

With EU, Chinese and industry (ICMA) leaders unable to agree on a consistent green bond framework (MSCI, 2019), a considerable degree of uncertainty clouds use-of-proceeds bonds.

Resolving these ambiguities is likely to go a long way towards increasing investor and issuer adoption alike. Improving the per-dollar impact of use-of-proceeds and sustainability-linked issuance would constitute a happy bonus. By tightening the rules that govern bonds used to refinance pre-existing activity, regulators can nudge the dedicated asset market toward issuance that genuinely creates incremental, positive change. Stricter disclosure requirements would enable investors to seek greater evidence of the additionality generated by the bonds, making issuer greenwashing more difficult and leading to better real-world outcomes.

> OPPORTUNITIES
>
> Establish globally consistent regulations and tighten the requirement for additionality across use-of-proceeds and sustainability-linked issuance.

ISSUERS

We advocate for expanding the use-of-proceed models to target waste, a multi-trillion US $ annual global problem that affects the vast majority of companies, sectors and governments. Waste-reduction bonds could target it and eloquently align profit with people and planet.

As 80 per cent of corporate green bond issuance originates from only two sectors, financials and utilities (Wacker, Bolliger and Seimen, 2020), a large number of potential sustainability-inclined corporate issuers struggle to match their operations to the use-of-proceeds model.

Waste in all forms is a natural fit for it. Collectively, despite 10 per cent of the global population going hungry, we throw away around 30 per cent of all food produced around the world, at a cost of $1 trillion per year. The volume of plastic packaging, a scourge of our beaches, could more than quadruple by 2050, and 95 per cent of the value of plastic is lost after a single use, at a cost of up to $120 billion annually. If our consumption habits don't change, plastics in the sea could outweigh fish by 2050 (Haefele et al, 2020). Yet the Climate Bond Initiative's review of 2021 green bond issuance estimates that just 5 per cent of the bonds fund projects related to waste (Harrison, MacGeoch and Michetti, 2022).

This needn't be the case. Waste is inherently measurable. Corporate sustainability reports frequently cite the tons of paper, food and solid waste that wind up in landfills, as well as the KWh of electricity needlessly consumed. Waste is also emotive and easily understood by retail investors, employees and the general population.

OPPORTUNITIES

Formalize a taxonomy for waste reduction bonds within an existing use-of-proceeds framework – to expand the market to underrepresented economic sectors and increase the positive contribution to people and the planet.

Chapter 5 – Sustainable private markets

'Chapter 5 – Sustainable private markets' identified inadequacies of efficiency and scale with 'old world' sustainable private market investors. While these shortcomings were largely solved when mainstream private market firms entered the fray, the enthusiasm of these firms for sustainable investing created new challenges. Many lacked the skill sets to perform meaningful ESG integration.

Among the asset classes considered in this book, private markets, in our view, have the greatest potential to do good for people and the planet. Many private market strategies enable investors to purchase a controlling interest in a company and repurpose and retool it to create powerful effective change.

The three opportunities we identify in this chapter grow progressively more ambitious. We see scope to adopt prosperous public market practices. We also observe an opportunity to build on a bright spot and align behind World Bank-led initiatives. And, finally, we call for innovation and a broadening of impact investing within private markets beyond growth stocks to areas such as venture capital and private debt.

PUBLIC MARKET PRACTICES

The heterogeneous world of private markets can take inspiration from their public cousins. Public market investors have gone to great lengths to seek (relatively) consistent data from the corporations they invest in. They have gone to even greater lengths to categorize and assess that data according to the principles of financial materiality.

Private companies are not routinely subject to the same regulatory-enforced mandatory disclosures as public ones are. But private market investors can exert their considerable influence and demand similar transparency to better inform their investment decisions. These fundamental processes and actions long practised in public markets would materially enhance sustainable private market investment.

> OPPORTUNITIES
>
> Adopt SASB's sector-specific disclosure frameworks to increase data availability and standardization. Use the information to integrate ESG factors into the investment process and corporate strategy in proportion to their financial materiality.

BRIGHT SPOTS

Among the multiple heterogeneous investor bodies that seek to govern, score and rank sustainable private markets, the World Bank stands out as the most credible participant seeking market alignment. We believe that the opportunity for sustainable private markets requires the industry to align behind the world's leading multilateral development bank.

The World Bank convened the Operating Principles for Impact Management which, since being launched in 2019, has acquired over 150 high-profile signatories (Operating Principles for Impact Management, n.d.). This framework is fast becoming the dominant holistic methodology for impact investing and distinguishes itself by demanding third-party verification of signatories' disclosures and reports.

The World Bank also acts as a convener of common measurement metrics. Its Joint Impact Indicators seek to harmonize the popular private sector IRIS+ framework with the multilateral development bank-favoured HIPSO framework (International Finance Corporation, 2021).

In an environment of fragmented standards and limited regulation, the World Bank occupies a unique industry position of credibility and impartiality. This eminent position empowers the nearly 80-year-old organization to establish market norms and drive convergence as well as real-world impact.

OPPORTUNITIES

The sustainable private market industry needs to rally behind the World Bank's attempts to standardize sustainable private markets. Investor disclosure should align with the Operating Principles of Impact Management and measurement should draw on the Joint Impact Indicators.

INNOVATION

Taking a cue from public debt markets' creation of dedicated assets, private markets could expand impact investing beyond growth equity to areas such as venture capital and private debt. Given the breadth of strategies available, ample opportunity exists to create instruments and sub-asset class strategies that place people and the planet at the heart of the investment strategy.

History has shown that 'old world' approaches have struggled to scale up. Adopting innovative ones widely is likely to rely on a subset of mainstream multi-disciplinary private market investors who have already embraced impact investing in part of their business. In many cases, this will mean firms with strong growth private equity franchises deploying their skills and learnings across a wider set of sub-asset classes.

> OPPORTUNITIES
>
> Knowledge transfers within multi-disciplinary private market firms can expand private market impact investing beyond its growth-stage private equity heartland. Impact-focused venture capital, which can fund the innovative technologies and services needed to transform the world, is the most logical candidate.

Chapter 6 – Themes and the United Nations Sustainable Development Goals

In 'Chapter 6 – Themes and the United Nations Sustainable Development Goals', we identified a number of hurdles that sustainable thematic investing has to overcome. Historically, its investment performance has been poor, its real-world impacts have been limited and the SDGs have more frequently been used as a set of promotional stickers than as a genuine investment framework. In response, we suggest three concrete actions, one for each key stakeholder: retail investors, institutional investors and corporations.

RETAIL INVESTORS

We argued that thematic investing results in limited incremental impact, as publicly traded shares are merely exchanged among investors without consequences for the underlying company. Thus, investment action must be accompanied by other practical, even more systematic efforts in the fight against climate change and other ESG issues.

Our view runs counter to a common narrative of investment firms, several of which were either sanctioned or heavily criticized in the early 2020s for implying that liquid investments would lower carbon emissions or have other 'real world' impacts (Verney, 2021; Mair, 2021).

OPPORTUNITIES

Retail investors may find it tempting to invest thematically and ease their conscience. Unfortunately, there is no substitute for personal action. Sustainable investing must go hand in hand with reducing the number of one's airline flights, lessening the amount of meat one consumes and lending one's voice to stimulate political change.

INSTITUTIONAL INVESTORS

Investing in private markets, we contend, holds the greatest promise for doing good for people and the planet. Many market participants have the wherewithal to purchase a controlling interest in a company, repurposing and retooling it to advance powerful effective change. As a result, we argue that sustainability-conscious institutional investors should, to the extent possible, concentrate their thematic investing efforts on the private sector and fund the sustainable products and services of the future.

While some of the world's largest private market investors such as TPG and KKR operate sustainable thematic funds, or at least general impact funds, the majority of the largest private market players are yet to meaningfully enter the fray (New Private Markets, 2021; Private Equity International, n.d.). Furthermore, the largest public market thematic investment houses, such as Ark, Pictet and Robeco, have limited to no exposure to private markets (Morningstar, 2022a).

Consequently, the path to getting there may involve public market thematic firms combining with their private market counterparts.

OPPORTUNITIES

Increasing thematic exposure to the most impactful sub-asset class – private markets – can generate the greatest positive impact. Opportunities may arise by facilitating a knowledge transfer between leading public market thematic investors and private market managers.

CORPORATIONS

Research has shown that corporations tend to align their reporting to the SDGs without markedly altering their behaviour in a way likely to advance them (Kramer, Agarwal and Srinivas, 2019). Stakeholder incentives must be better matched, we believe, to resolve this situation. Catalysing business models via changes that advance the SDGs will necessitate opportunities that also support corporate profitability.

We focused on a topic with sizeable real-world impact well suited to the corporate environment. That topic is waste.

Waste is specifically referred to throughout the official indicators used to track the SDGs. It's there in 6.3.1 'Proportion of wastewater successfully treated'; in 11.6.1 'Proportion of urban solid waste regularly collected'; and in 12.3.1 'Global food loss index'. Reducing waste can also help to achieve dozens of other indicators, even those where waste is not explicitly mentioned. For example, 2.1.1 'Prevalence of undernourishment' and 7.1.1 'Proportion of population with access to electricity' would both be furthered by waste reduction (UN General Assembly, 2017).

Corporations serious about generating an incremental and material benefit to the SDGs should consider a deep dive into the waste they generate, we contend. Cutting back on it is inherently profit-enhancing, as inefficiencies in operations and supply chains result in additional costs that would otherwise be profit. This creates a natural alignment between corporations and the UN SDGs.

OPPORTUNITIES

Corporations seeking SDG action and contribution rather than mere alignment should take action on waste – an annual multi-trillion US dollar global problem/opportunity and a key enabler of the UN SDGs.

Chapter 7 – Sustainable multi-asset portfolios

In 'Chapter 7 – Sustainable multi-asset portfolios', we considered some shortcomings of traditional sustainable portfolio construction techniques and the challenges that remain for modern construction approaches. The latter included integrating sustainability into capital market assumptions and blending different approaches to sustainability to capture the desired risk premia. The opportunities that we identify seek to continue the positive momentum of multi-asset solutions. Our suggested opportunities look to new sub-asset classes, a greater use of alternatives and the potential for personalization.

NEW SUB-ASSET CLASSES

Use-of-proceeds bonds are well established and sustainability-linked bonds are growing rapidly in popularity and availability. In our view, it is time to launch the next wave of dedicated assets that can populate multi-asset portfolios.

As discussed in 'Chapter 4 – Sustainable public debt markets', the use-of-proceeds model can evolve to target inefficiency and waste. We also see the potential for it and for the green bond market to expand into different sub-asset classes. Potential sub-sectors yet to benefit from this model include emerging market sovereign debt, both hard and local currency and inflation-linked bonds such as US TIPS.

In a sustainable multi-asset context, these sub-asset classes remain difficult to allocate to. They require investors either to resort to screens and integration or to use imperfect proxies. Given the rise of sustainability-linked bonds, there may be scope to combine the use-of-proceeds and sustainability-linked methodologies to create innovative solutions in these underrepresented sub-asset classes.

OPPORTUNITIES

Accelerate the growth of new sustainable sub-asset classes for sustainable multi-asset portfolios. Topping our list are waste-reduction bonds that can expand the use-of-proceeds markets. Underpinning innovation via public-private partnerships, such as the World Bank IFC and Amundi's sponsorship of the emerging market corporate green bond market, is likely to turbocharge growth.

ALTERNATIVES

For many individuals, access to private markets in a multi-asset context is restricted both by regulation (which ironically seeks to protect 'retail' investors) and by minimum ticket sizes that are prohibitively large.

However, within alternatives, a range of semi-liquid solutions, such as microcredit (addressed in 'Chapter 4 – Sustainable public debt markets'), exists. Semi-liquid solutions can provide a degree of uncorrelated investment returns and, to some extent, produce a positive impact. For institutional and retail investors alike, the sustainable multi-asset portfolio of the future would optimally include both illiquid and semi-liquid alternatives.

Regulation that governs investors' access to alternatives differs around the world. Even within the EU, regulatory regimes are not homogenous. Consequently, increasing the availability of alternatives within a sustainable multi-asset portfolio is a complex problem that requires regulators to work together to seize the opportunity.

> **OPPORTUNITIES**
>
> Simplify and harmonize the regulatory landscape to enable retail investors and sustainable multi-asset portfolios to invest responsibly in semi-liquid alternatives, such as microcredit.

PERSONALIZATION

In 'Chapter 1 – What is sustainable investing?', we introduced the idea that the topic of sustainability can be a highly personal one. In fact, two rational individuals may disagree about what constitutes or does not constitute a sustainable company or investment.

As the sustainable multi-asset space matures, it is becoming increasingly possible to build multi-asset portfolios that emphasize different aspects of sustainability. Personalization could be combined with our recommendations in 'Chapter 3 – Data and ratings', where we argued for the need to develop a small pool of consistently reported corporate sustainability metrics. With consistent data, sustainable multi-asset portfolios could then be tailored to a range of investor preferences.

OPPORTUNITIES

Agree on a small number of sustainability metrics, reported consistently by all companies, to enable mass customization of end investors' multi-asset portfolios. This would amplify retail investor engagement and accelerate adoption of sustainable investing.

In practice

A key learning we've taken from our careers is that sustainable investing differs greatly in practice and in theory. When we sit with fellow members of the community, we may discuss hypothetical questions such as how to balance 'single', 'double' and 'dynamic' materiality. We sometimes passionately defend the need for 'impact investing' to demonstrate 'additionality' and bang the table when someone falsely portrays 'alignment' as contributing to the good of people and the planet. While these debates can be fun (obviously our dinner parties make the Burning Man festival look tame) they are detached from the interests and concerns of the vast majority of individual investors, corporate CEOs and fellow financial decision makers.

Time and time again we've seen intelligent, well-meaning sustainability experts miss the mark by failing to take their target audience into account. Their influence and impact are limited because they prove unable to persuade their stakeholders into supporting their desired course of action. Bluntly speaking, few 'Heads of Investment' want to read your 50-page governance document detailing how you compiled your 'materiality matrix', developed a proprietary methodology for blending third-party data-sets and reviewed dozens of academic papers to define the optimal approach to handling missing data.

This is not to say that the practice of sustainable investing should be dumbed down and made superficial for public consumption. Far from it. What is required is a 'commercial yet credible' approach. A wonderful example comes from the consumer electronics industry. The specialists marketing the first iPod didn't wax lyrical about its five-gigabyte hard drive and firewire connectivity that enabled simultaneous charging and high-speed music synchronization. All that pioneering technology was there under the hood, but the message to the target audience, an example of commercial simplicity at its finest, emphasized the user benefit. 'A thousands songs in your pocket' trumpeted the tagline, which was accompanied by an iconic dancing silhouette (Anand, 2021).

We hope that the three following learnings we've gleaned from our successes – and failures – will prove useful to those seeking to put sustainable investing into practice, whether they are career starters, seasoned investors or regulators. We think these observations remain relevant beyond our own spheres and careers and can nudge our readers to push for greater commercial success that has a larger positive impact on people and the planet, even if the ideas our readers champion differ from our own.

What people say and what they do are different

Whether it's the popular clique at school that invited you to a beach party and then never showed up, or the manager at the office who congratulated you on your work mere days before making half of your team redundant, what people say and what they do are two different things.

In terms of sustainable investing, there is a chasm between what retail investors say they want and how they act. A typical survey will suggest an overwhelming desire for sustainable investing products. In 2021, for instance, a Morgan Stanley sampling found that 79 per cent of the general public is 'very' or 'somewhat' interested in sustainable investing; among millennials this figure rose to 99 per cent (Morgan Stanley, 2021). But, as we've discussed previously, self-identification tends to lead to over-identification. So a gap often opens between intention and action. A credible measure of sustainable assets, such as Morningstar's, indicates that they represent just a few percentage points of all professionally managed assets (Morningstar, 2022b). Meanwhile, academic studies find that, when it comes to making sustainable choices, the gap between those who 'say' and those who 'do' can be as large as three times (White, Hardisty and Habib, 2019).

This dispiriting truth has many implications for the practice of sustainable investing. First, it acts as a cautionary tale for those who use such datasets to gauge public appetite when securing external investment or seeking to win internal management endorsement for their latest sustainable product or service. Relying on what people say means you risk overpromising and overestimating demand.

Second, it underlines the danger of confirmation bias, that human tendency to search for, interpret and recall information in a way that confirms our prior beliefs (Nickerson, 1998). Because we as practitioners want sustainable investing to be successful, we can fall prey to blindly accepting positive news without thinking critically. This can result in overlooking the components essential to ensuring success, such as aligning incentives, and can lead to a misdiagnosis of a product's or service's true chances in the marketplace.

Another difficulty that arises when interpreting what people say is a function of linear bias (discussed in a different context in 'Chapter 6 – Themes and the United Nations Sustainable Development Goals'). Consider a classic client preference scale, numbered 1 to 5, with five representing a high affinity for sustainable investing and one a low favourability ranking. A linear interpretation of client preferences assumes that 'fours' are more inclined to invest sustainably than 'threes', who in turn are more likely to act than 'twos'.

In fact, research shows that, while people may use a linear scale to indicate their preferences, what they do is anything but linear. Writing in the *Harvard Business Review*, researchers note that the actions of 'twos', 'threes' and 'fours' don't show linear progression. They are, in fact, nearly identical. However, the difference in consumer behaviour jumps substantially when one compares 'fours' with 'fives' (de Langhe, Puntoni and Larrick, 2017).

These insights have consequences when investing sustainably. In the aforementioned 2021 Morgan Stanley survey that concluded 99 per cent of millennials were interested in sustainable investing, just 57 per cent of them opted for the highest affinity choice – 'very'. The rest said that they were 'somewhat' interested (Morgan Stanley, 2021). Misinterpreting their affinity could lead to product misspecification, as the desired features voiced by the very interested will be overrepresented. A product or service can then become trapped within a niche sustainable investing echo chamber and fail to scale.

> PRACTICAL LEARNING
>
> People say and do different things. Practitioners of sustainable investing must overcome multiple heuristics such as confirmation and linear bias to understand the true demand for their product or service. Successfully scaling any sustainable investment requires self-awareness, objectivity and critical thinking.

The importance of the mass middle

There are numerous impressive ideas that charmed a niche of true believers but failed to win over the mass middle and reach widespread popularity. The Segway, introduced in 2002, generated an avid cult following but has failed to transform urban transportation. More recently, Google Glass momentarily brought science fiction from the big screen to two very small screens before finding its niche as an accessory best suited to filming clandestine videos in coffee shops.

In our careers of implementing sustainable investing we've found that it's difficult to overestimate the importance of what we call the 'mass middle'. What we mean by this term is the proportion of the population that has neither a strong preference for nor a strong aversion to something. These individuals don't proactively seek to invest sustainably but are willing to do so if the narrative is made to sound compelling, the fees are appropriate and the prospective investment returns are competitive. The mass middle comprises everyone who buys free-range eggs on occasion, thinks racism is wrong but doesn't attend marches denouncing it and recycles their plastic when the collection bin is within easy walking distance.

Gauging the size of the mass middle is more art than science. Based on the data sets we've seen and our experience, we estimate that those with a strong affinity or a strong aversion each make up 10–20 per cent of the population. That leaves the mass middle representing something in the range of 60–80 per cent of all persons.

To be commercially successful – and this may seem obvious – one needs to target the mass middle. Yet many practitioners of sustainable investing, with their strong affinity for the topic, too often neglect to do so. They wind up creating the product that they – and sometimes they alone – want to invest in. Service providers ranging from innovative data companies to first-time funds with complex and high-quality methodologies have stumbled as soon as we asked them, 'And who is going to buy this?' The failure of many parts of the sustainable investing ecosystem to reach scale, including the 'old world' of sustainable private market investments discussed in 'Chapter 5 – Sustainable private markets', can be laid at the doorstep of this fundamental oversight.

'Horizontal hostility' can also play a role in hindering wider adoption. It occurs between groups one would expect to share allegiances, such as the old Russian Bolsheviks and Mensheviks (Martocci, 2017). As we detailed in 'Chapter 1 – What is sustainable investing?', the sustainable investing practitioner community has a habit of passionately debating nuances of methodology and approach. This infighting makes selling to high affinity individuals, who can hold heterogeneous views and be very opinionated, difficult. While the mass middle may become enthused by a limited number of compelling proof points, those with high affinity may demand much more information, which can cause them to reject a product or service on a technicality.

The mass middle, we believe, is the best avenue for delivering the greatest benefits to people and the planet, the ultimate motivation and objective of the sustainable investment community. Our former boss Mark Haefele, the Chief Investment Officer at UBS Global

Wealth Management, often told us that the formula for impact was intensity multiplied by scale. Directing many billions of dollars into investments with a medium impact intensity will produce superior results than distributing a high-impact product on a small scale. These dynamics are discussed in 'Chapter 5 – Sustainable private markets', where we lament how many well-intentioned 'old world' solutions failed to gain traction. It took until the long-established conventional private market firms entered sustainable private markets before sizeable impact ensued.

PRACTICAL LEARNING

We've found that many sustainable practitioners fail because their products and services reflect their own world views rather than their prospective clients'. We believe that the 'mass middle', a larger addressable market, is easier to serve than the more specialized, high-affinity market. Commercial yet credible solutions that combine investment performance and compelling narratives have the greatest potential to scale. This scale, in turn, will ultimately create the greatest benefit for people and the planet.

Creating win-wins

How many times have you asked someone what they hoped to achieve and their answer was word-for-word identical to yours? Or their reply was, 'My objectives are to do whatever you want?' Not often, right?

In our experience, few people enquire of others what their goals are. Instead, they list their own priorities, projects and objectives. Unsurprisingly, this is not an optimal strategy, yet people keep doing it. Stakeholders are far more likely to collaborate with you – and in the process help you achieve what you set out to do – if you proactively work with them to achieve their goals. They are far less likely to want to assist you if you are asking them to simply do as they are told.

We have found that creating win-wins and enlarging the pie, rather than competing over it, is the secret to successful sustainable investing. Instead of telling the 'Head of Investments' that you would like to launch a new sustainable portfolio, try asking them about the challenges they currently face. Typical answers to your enquiry might include difficult investment performance, poor client retention or sluggish sales, all of which can be mitigated to some extent by embracing sustainable investing.

Our (occasionally painful) experiences have taught us that seeking win-wins beats pursuing more confrontational approaches. We've also learnt that, when discussing the potential of sustainable investing, using the stakeholder's preferred terminology and referring to their incentives are much more effective than making abstract appeals in the name of people and the planet.

Again, the majority of people you encounter in your professional life will not have a high affinity for sustainable investing. But they are likely to be open to adopting it if your reasoning is compelling and the commercial benefit is clear. With certain business stakeholders, we recommend discussing sustainable investing by mentioning growth, retention and pricing, while other stakeholders may respond best when sustainability is framed as a risk-mitigating technique or as part of a regulatory program.

Regardless of your chosen line of argumentation, it needs to be rooted in data and fact. To illustrate let's first take the growth argument.

Sustainable investing is, mechanically, a pathway to superior growth. Customer spending data and numerous surveys (such as the aforementioned one by Morgan Stanley) find that younger people favour sustainable investing more than older generations do. That's unsurprising given that the younger generations will have to deal with the societal and planetary consequences of our current choices.

Younger people, in aggregate, grow their wealth faster than older generations do thanks to entrepreneurship, inheritance and good-old salaried labour. Even without taking market share, a business exposed to fast-growing end markets will expand faster than a business operating in slower-growth segments.

Growth is not the only commercial benefit that sustainable investing offers. It can also facilitate better retention and price realization. When providers offer greater product quality or better service, they receive more in return. Consider how Apple's all-encompassing ecosystem created customer loyalty while Motorola's hardware-driven model did not; or how, at the supermarket, six-ply toilet paper costs more than its two-ply cousin.

Because sustainability is emotive, customer loyalty can be enhanced. Research has shown that in periods of market turbulence clients with sustainable investments are more loyal to their investment product providers (Renneboog, Ter Horst and Zhang, 2011). The value-added provided by sustainable strategies can also, in some circumstances, command a price premium (Renneboog, Ter Horst and Zhang, 2007).

PRACTICAL LEARNING

When seeking to scale sustainable investing, we believe it is essential to seek 'win-wins' and to view the challenges and opportunities through the eyes of your stakeholders. Designing incentives and considering individual motivations – from money to status to purpose – is likelier to create a coalition of supporters than pursuing confrontational approaches and grandstanding about sustainable investing being 'the right thing to do'.

And just like that, it was over. Thank you for reading,
James and Simon

References

Anand, V (2021) iPod – a thousand songs in your pocket, Medium, 2 August, medium.com/@onlykutts/ipod-a-thousand-songs-in-your-pocket-c307931d626a (archived at https://perma.cc/4NS2-S7QD)

Bernow, S et al (2019) More than values: The value-based sustainability reporting that investors want, McKinsey Sustainability, www.mckinsey.com/business-functions/sustainability/our-insights/more-than-values-the-value-based-sustainability-reporting-that-investors-want (archived at https://perma.cc/KSP6-GWS6)

de Langhe, B, Puntoni, S and Larrick, R (2017) Linear thinking in a nonlinear world, *Harvard Business Review*, 1 May, hbr.org/2017/05/linear-thinking-in-a-nonlinear-world (archived at https://perma.cc/2UHL-LFSA)

Haefele, M et al (2020) Future of waste: Finding opportunities in waste reduction, UBS, Available from: https://doi.org/10.1596/978-1-4648-1329-0 (archived at https://perma.cc/3P2G-SR4X)

Harrison, C, MacGeoch, M and Michetti, C (2022) Sustainable debt global state of the market 2021, Climate bonds initiative, www.climatebonds.net/files/reports/cbi_global_sotm_2021_02f.pdf (archived at https://perma.cc/P3H9-NYP3)

IIF (2019) The case for simplifying sustainable investment terminology, Institute of International Finance, www.iif.com/Portals/0/Files/content/IIF%20SFWG%20-%20Growing%20Sustainable%20Finance.pdf (archived at https://perma.cc/V25K-EF97)

International Finance Corporation (2021) Leading impact investors make progress toward harmonized impact measurement with release of joint indicators, pressroom.ifc.org/all/pages/PressDetail.aspx?ID=26260 (archived at https://perma.cc/M63N-D375)

Johnson, K and Kerber, R (2021) Top US financial regulator reverses stance on social issues, Reuters, 3 November, www.reuters.com/business/us-sec-staff-outlines-how-companies-might-exclude-shareholder-proposal-corporate-2021-11-03/ (archived at https://perma.cc/9SH4-9JVY)

Kennedy, E (2022) Double your ESG impact with funds tied to charities, Kiplinger, www.kiplinger.com/investing/esg/604114/double-your-esg-impact-with-funds-tied-to-charities (archived at https://perma.cc/7KPE-NQZF)

Kramer, M R, Agarwal, R and Srinivas, A (2019) Business as usual will not save the planet, *Harvard Business Review*, 12 June, hbr.org/2019/06/business-as-usual-will-not-save-the-planet (archived at https://perma.cc/FQW4-WMEZ)

Mair, V (2021) UK green pensions campaign branded 'misleading' and 'unethical', Responsible Investor, 13 July, www.responsible-investor.com/uk-green-pensions-campaign-branded-misleading-and-unethical/ (archived at https://perma.cc/6QVW-H3XZ)

Martocci, L (2017) What are 'Horizontal Hostilities?', *Psychology Today*, www.psychologytoday.com/us/blog/you-can-t-sit-us/201704/what-are-horizontal-hostilities (archived at https://perma.cc/U2D9-W95Z)

Morgan Stanley (2021) Sustainable signals: Individual investors and the COVID-19 Pandemic, www.morganstanley.com/assets/pdfs/2021-Sustainable_Signals_Individual_Investor.pdf (archived at https://perma.cc/Q9RP-YLV4)

Morningstar (2022a) Morningstar global thematic funds landscape 2022, www.morningstar.com/lp/global-thematic-fund-landscape (archived at https://perma.cc/V2KY-TUFN)

Morningstar (2022b) 'Global sustainable fund flows report', www.morningstar.com/lp/global-esg-flows (archived at https://perma.cc/5P5C-VJBE)

MSCI (2019) Bloomberg Barclays MSCI Green Bond Index Consultation, www.msci.com/documents/1296102/12275477/Bloomberg+Barclays+MSCI+Green+Bond+Index+Consultation.pdf/e887b067-1513-c94d-4441-e18b39f6170d?t=1561734332189 (archived at https://perma.cc/424L-WZE9)

New Private Markets (2021) Impact 20: Ranking the largest private markets impact managers, 29 June, www.newprivatemarkets.com/impact-20-ranking-the-largest-private-markets-impact-managers/ (archived at https://perma.cc/23FF-3WCP)

Newell, M (2019) Top 5 largest fines levied on tech companies by the European Commission, TNE, 18 February, www.theneweconomy.com/business/top-5-largest-fines-levied-on-tech-companies-by-the-european-commission (archived at https://perma.cc/Q38J-TBPD)

Nickerson, R S (1998) Confirmation bias: A ubiquitous phenomenon in many guises, *Review of General Psychology*, 2(2), pp 175–220, doi.org/10.1037/1089-2680.2.2.175 (archived at https://perma.cc/YMH5-BFB5)

Operating Principles for Impact Management (no date) Signatories & reporting, www.impactprinciples.org/signatories-reporting (archived at https://perma.cc/M4GU-TG3S)

Perron, V B (2020) AXA IM to donate 5 per cent of management fees on impact fund range to charity, CityWire Selector, citywireselector.com/news/axa-im-to-donate-5-of-management-fees-on-impact-fund-range-to-charity/a1354053 (archived at https://perma.cc/C3ER-C598)

Private Equity International (no date) PEI 300 2022 full ranking, www.privateequityinternational.com/pei-300-2022-ranking/ (archived at https://perma.cc/KX55-NB46)

Quintet Private Bank (no date) The Quintet Earth Fund, www.quintet.com/en-gb/quintet-earth-fund (archived at https://perma.cc/2XEV-34KX)

Renneboog, L, Ter Horst, J and Zhang, C (2007) Socially responsible investments: Methodology, risk and performance, CentER Discussion Paper, 2007–31, research.tilburguniversity.edu/en/publications/socially-responsible-investments-methodology-risk-and-performance (archived at https://perma.cc/49CB-WJ49)

Renneboog, L, Ter Horst, J and Zhang, C (2011) Is ethical money financially smart? Nonfinancial attributes and money flows of socially responsible investment funds, *Journal of Financial Intermediation*, 20(4), pp 562–88, doi.org/10.1016/j.jfi.2010.12.003 (archived at https://perma.cc/4JVY-4FT4)

Schroeder, J (2019) Candriam launches its first carbon-neutral investment fund, South Pole, www.southpole.com/news/candriam-launches-its-first-carbon-neutral-investment-fund (archived at https://perma.cc/U3PV-5WSA)

The Economist (2021) Why people forget that less is often more, 16 April, www.economist.com/science-and-technology/2021/04/14/why-people-forget-that-less-is-often-more (archived at https://perma.cc/GLN9-NCDT)

UBS (2020) UBS and BlackRock partner on new development bank debt ETF, www.ubs.com/global/en/media/display-page-ndp/en-20200218-ubs-blackrock.html (archived at https://perma.cc/J39Q-ZKTF)

UBS (2022) UBS ETF (LU) Sustainable development bank bonds UCITS ETF (USD) A-dis, www.ubs.com/nl/en/asset-management/etf-private/etf-products/etf-product-detail.html (archived at https://perma.cc/7F6Q-YJC3)

Verney, P (2021) DekaBank drops impact calculator for sustainability funds to avoid lawsuit over greenwashing claims, *Responsible Investor*, 19 April, www.responsible-investor.com/dekabank-drops-impact-calculator-for-sustainability-funds-to-avoid-lawsuit-over-greenwashing-claims/ (archived at https://perma.cc/M4GH-4PKF)

Wacker, T, Bolliger, M and Seimen, M (2020) Green bond slide pack: Introduction and issuer profiles, UBS

White, K, Hardisty, D J and Habib, R (2019) The elusive green consumer, *Harvard Business Review*, 1 July, hbr.org/2019/07/the-elusive-green-consumer (archived at https://perma.cc/YC8Y-DLM8)

World Economic Forum (2020) Measuring stakeholder capitalism: Towards common metrics and consistent reporting of sustainable value creation, www.weforum.org/reports/measuring-stakeholder-capitalism-towards-common-metrics-and-consistent-reporting-of-sustainable-value-creation/ (archived at https://perma.cc/LQP6-YZTC)

INDEX

Note: Page numbers in *italics* refer to tables or figures

Printed in the USA
CPSIA information can be obtained
at www.ICGtesting.com
LVHW062212111023
760883LV00049B/1479

9 781398 607903